Faithfulness in FELLOWSHIP

REFLECTIONS ON HOMOSEXUALITY AND THE CHURCH

Papers from the Doctrine Panel of the Anglican Church of Australia

John Garratt Publishing

Published in Australia
by John Garratt Publishing
32 Glenvale Crescent
Mulgrave Vic 3170

First published 2001
Edited by Catherine Hammond Editorial Services
Typesetting by Bloomfield Advertising
Cover design by Katrina Blundell
Printed in Australia by Aristoc Offset

The National Library of Australia
Cataloguing-in-Publication Data:
Faithfulness in fellowship : reflections on homosexuality and the church.

Bibliography.
ISBN 1 875938 47 8.

1. Christian ethics. 2. Sexual ethics. 3. Homosexuality -
Religious aspects — Christianity. 4. Homosexuality -
Relgious aspects — Anglican Church of Australia. 5.
Homosexuality in the Bible. I. Anglican Church of
Australia. Doctine Panel.

241.66

CONTENTS

PREFACE

At the General Synod of the Anglican Church of Australia, meeting in Adelaide in 1998, it was proposed that a statement, known as the *Kuala Lumpur Statement*, should be adopted and endorsed. This statement originated from a meeting of delegates from Anglican Provinces of the Developing World at the Second Anglican Encounter in the South, held in Kuala Lumpur, Malaysia in 1997. Its particular concern was to respond to moves in some Provinces of the Anglican Communion to look favourably on 'the ordination of practising homosexuals and the blessing of same-sex unions'. The *Kuala Lumpur Statement* reaffirmed what was referred to as 'the long-held traditional Anglican teaching on human sexuality'.

However, after consideration of the proposal, the General Synod decided that, rather than simply adopt the *Kuala Lumpur Statement*, a task force should be appointed to study the matter with a view to producing this Church's own statement on the subject. Subsequently, the Standing Committee of General Synod requested its Doctrine Panel to do this work. (The *Kuala Lumpur Statement* may be found appended to this Report as Appendix 1; the Resolution of General Synod asking for an Australian statement may be found as Appendix 2.)

At the Lambeth Conference of 1998, the same *Kuala Lumpur Statement* was introduced, with the request that it be endorsed by the Conference. However, the matter of human sexuality had already been the subject of a detailed resolution of the Conference, and this proposal relating to the *Kuala Lumpur Statement* was resisted. The relevant successful Lambeth Resolution (1998/Resolution 1. 10) is appended to this Report as Appendix 3. This Resolution was passed with an overwhelming majority (526 votes for; 70 votes against; with 45 abstentions).

There can be no disputing the fact that this Resolution of the 1998 Lambeth Conference met with a mixed reception. Though it had been adopted by the Conference with a significantly large majority, very strong expressions of dissent were registered to it in some sections of the Anglican Communion. Indeed, in some places the lack of authority of a Lambeth Conference to legislate for member Churches was cited as reason for receiving the Resolution as nothing more than advice, while at the same time the autonomy and independent legislative power of member Churches was re-affirmed. Unfortunately, in some places Resolution 1:10 was not handled with the respect due to a sincerely made determination of such a large majority of Church leaders. Indeed, disagreement was sometimes registered with a hostile sense of acrimony. In the period immediately after the Lambeth Conference, Resolution 1:10 certainly generated a good deal of controversial debate and angst. There is evidence that homosexual people were distressed by it.

It is to be noted, however, that the Lambeth Resolution, while affirming that 'abstinence is right for those not called to marriage' and that it therefore could not 'advise the legitimising or blessing of same-sex unions nor ordaining those involved in same-gender unions', nevertheless itself called for the monitoring of continuing work on human sexuality in the Communion and requested that member Churches of the Communion 'share statements and resources'. The Anglican Church of Australia had already appointed its Doctrine Panel to enquire into the matter. Accordingly, this collection of essays is offered to this Church and to other member Churches of the Anglican Communion as a contribution to corporate thinking as we seek to discern the truth in love and to come to unity of heart and mind on the matter.

It may be noted, too, that the *Kuala Lumpur Statement*, perhaps unwittingly, signalled the need for further study. The *Statement* correctly affirms the biblical teaching against promiscuity. Promiscuous behaviour falls short of the ideal of loyalty and fidelity in interpersonal relationships that is reflective of the faithfulness of God. Apart from the moral questionableness of the potential of promiscuous behaviour to foster the individual's exploitation of others for his/her own selfish sexual gratification, it is also patently clear that promiscuity is a very serious health hazard in the contemporary world. The Church rightly and with confidence counsels against promiscuous behaviour. Furthermore, this is a teaching that can be unequivocally affirmed in an even-handed way in relation to both homosexual and heterosexual people. The *Kuala Lumpur Statement* thus affirms that 'the Holy Scriptures are clear in teaching that all sexual promiscuity is sin'.

However, we have to concede that this very statement begs a crucial question, which happens also to be the question that currently faces the Church almost at every turn in contemporary society: is sexual behaviour between people of the same gender in long-term committed and faithful relationships rightly categorised as 'promiscuity'? Do long-term and committed, faithful relationships between people of the same gender fall within the biblical condemnation of promiscuity? Would the *Kuala Lumpur Statement* have done better to have spoken of 'fornication' rather than 'promiscuity'? Clearly, it is at this point that the Church is challenged to do some very careful and critical thinking. All this bears directly on the question of whether the Church should somehow recognise as tolerable or even acceptable – and confer its blessing upon – the commitment of homosexual people to long-term and faithful relationships. The answer to these questions also bears upon the question of whether people in long-term committed relationships may be ordained.

The question of whether the category of 'promiscuity' and the clear biblical and moral teaching of the Church against promiscuity can be rightly brought to bear in the case of people of the same sex in long-term committed and faithful relationships is made even more difficult because of our contemporary awareness that homosexual orientation was only defined, named and thus conceptualised and known as a condition, from the middle of the nineteenth century onwards. Prior to this time sexual behaviour between people of the same sex could be more simply understood as morally deviant behaviour, because all human people were understood to be by nature (as we would say today) heterosexual. This is clearly presupposed in some of the biblical texts relating to the matter (e.g. Genesis 19:8 and Romans 1:26-27). It is also implicit in the Church's long-established view that the main purpose of sexual activity is the procreation of children. Given the unquestioning assumption of a monochrome and undifferentiated (in today's terms, heterosexual) human nature, so far as sexual identity and orientation is concerned, any sexual behaviour between people of the same sex could therefore be clearly condemned as deviant or promiscuous.

However, the discernment of what we speak of today as homosexual orientation and identity from the middle of the nineteenth century onwards clearly poses a new challenge: what is the exact application today of biblical teaching fashioned in a period when such distinctions were unknown? This question impels us to an examination of the current medical and scientific understanding of the causes of homosexuality, and of the justifying grounds for speaking of a recognisable sub-category – homosexual identity – as something ontologically distinct. Or are those we refer to, in a manner of speaking, as 'homosexual people' really 'heterosexual people' who behave in a particular kind of way which they could modify as a matter of will? Clearly, we are already entering very deep and complex waters.

These fundamental questions have driven the members of the General Synod Doctrine Panel back to a more detailed study of the relevant biblical and historical material. The membership of the Panel may be found appended to this Report – see Biographies. The Panel met on seven occasions as follows:

17-19 September 1998	Melbourne
22-2 June 1999	Melbourne
9-11 November 1999	Sydney
1-2 February 2000	Sydney
21 August 2000	Teleconference
18 October 2000	Teleconference
1 Nov 2000	Teleconference

The meeting in Sydney in November 1999 was devoted to hearings from a wide variety of perspectives so as to ground the Panel's deliberations in medical advice and in the actual experiences of homosexual people, including those living in 'long-term committed relationships', those who had made the choice to leave a homosexual lifestyle in order to pursue a heterosexual one and those who had chosen to lead a celibate lifestyle. The views of those with first hand experience in specialist pastoral ministry with homosexual people were also sought.

Members of the Doctrine Panel feel that they have learned an enormous amount in the course of pursuing this study. We have become acutely aware of the complexities of the issues relating to human sexuality, including the fact that the interpretation of the biblical material is not nearly as straightforward as many of us imagined. We have also become acutely aware of the social tragedy of homophobic reactions to homosexual people in the community, and of the difficulties they experience in managing their sexuality. No less intractable are difficulties experienced by those charged with the handling of such sensitive matters when the lives of other human persons are involved. One cannot study such a subject without becoming aware of the burden of one's own misapprehensions and unchallenged prejudice.

We are also all too aware that, even after two years of study, we have made only the first tentative steps towards achieving greater clarification and understanding of the issues. We do not, therefore, wish to advocate any changes to this Church's traditional disciplines; instead we offer these essays as study material, with the recommendation that the General Synod at Brisbane in July 2001 should commend them as a basis for a more widespread study in the Church at large.

Faithfulness in Fellowship

CHAPTER ONE

Introduction

In the course of this study, members of the Doctrine Panel have become aware that there are a number of quite fundamental matters that condition the current approach to the understanding of homosexuality. For example, in the first essay Muriel Porter has examined the Church's so-called 'traditional approach' to matters relating to human sexuality, only to find that the perceived morality of sexual relations has, in fact, changed enormously over time. Talk of 'the Church's traditional teaching' is in many respects a figment. The decision to allow clergy to marry at the time of the Reformation is one decisive change. Amongst the most significant of recent changes is that embedded in the resolution of the 1958 Lambeth Conference, which authoritatively expressed the view that the procreation of children is not the only purpose of sexual activity within marriage. This opened the way for the Church's endorsement of artificial methods of birth control, and for the development of a new appreciation of the re-creative role of sexual activity within a loving and faithful relationship of 'mutual society, help and comfort'. But the re-creative role of non-reproductive sexual activity in marriage inevitably leads logically to the consideration of the place of sexual activity outside of marriage relationships, and particularly in the lives of couples of the same sex for whom marriage is not currently a desirable possibility.

Fundamental attitudes about the nature and purpose of sexual activity have clearly shifted in the last fifty years in the secular environment around us as well. We all, therefore, need to be aware of the subtle historical forces that may be playing upon us, almost unknowingly, in the changed intellectual environment we inhabit in the Church, particularly since Lambeth 1958. To some extent these changes explain why it is that a question relating to the appropriateness of sexual relations within long-term committed relationships between people of the same gender is now on our agenda; it is a part of the air we breathe.

In the second, third and fourth chapters, our biblical scholars examine the biblical texts that in the past have been cited as relevant to a consideration of same-gender sexual relationships. The rest of us on the Doctrine Panel have learned a great deal from this aspect of the study, and are very grateful to John Dunnill and Glenn Davies. It has become clear to us that, in the past, the Church has assumed that the interpretation of this biblical tradition was rather more straightforward than it actually is. For example, there is a question as to whether the teaching of Genesis 19 refers to the treatment of strangers with hospitality and respect, rather than issues relating to sexuality as such. On the other hand, in some cases where the word 'homosexual' has been used in English translations of the biblical texts, the original Greek sometimes conveys a more narrow meaning. In 1 Corinthians 6:9, for example, Paul includes the word *malakoi* to describe those who will be excluded from the kingdom of God. While it is clear that Paul has a certain type of behaviour in view (rather than a disposition), it must be borne in mind that the root meaning of the word *malakos* is 'soft'. The word was used pejoratively of those who were soft or effeminate, but it would need a clear indication from the context of the passage before determining whether or not it designated an effeminate cross-dresser or the passive partner of homosexual intercourse. A careful examination of the text of the New Testament is, therefore, required before resolving this issue. Nonetheless, the New Testament provides no justification for singling out homosexual persons as objects of derision, as has been evidenced in the rise of homophobia. All men and women are made in the image of God and, therefore, should be accorded the appropriate dignity that belongs to bearers of the divine image.

Don Edwards and Cathy Thomson have worked together on the question of natural law, and the meaning and validity of the judgment that homosexual relationships are 'not natural' and therefore 'not good'. They suggest that such a judgment stems from context rather than universal absolutes. Still, they find that consideration of natural law continues to be of significance in dealing with issues in contemporary moral theology, including those concerning human sexuality. For instance, it can provide a point of contact between Christians and non-Christians who seek to address such issues. It can also identify a moral imperative in the human person (including a prohibition on 'using' other people for our own gratification) that becomes effective in concrete situations. So, while an examination of natural law in itself does not result in a definitive Christian view of homosexuality, it can complement engagement with Scripture and tradition in the quest of a Christian understanding of, and attitude to, homosexual persons.

Sean Mullen, who has acted as a research assistant to the Panel, has also helped the Panel by writing up a review of scientific and medical assessments relating to the question of the origin and nature of homosexual orientation. The Panel has been much helped by this essay, which fills what would otherwise be a gap in its work, and is pleased to include it in this published outcome. Once again, the ambiguity and mystery remaining because of the ultimately unresolved nature of contemporary knowledge on the subject prevent us from coming to a final determination of the questions.

Peter Carnley explores the outcomes of re-framing the Christian understanding of homosexual relationships within a discussion of the biblical theme of friendship, as against the contemporary secular tendency to employ the category of the marriage union to understand long-term and faithful same-gender relationships. It is suggested that this may be a more helpful and appropriate way to approach a Christian understanding of such relationships than 'marriage', which more properly applies to heterosexual unions. In terms of sexual activity, friendship is a more neutral concept, which then allows for an exploration of the 'limits of touch' within a friendship.

Scott Cowdell then moves the discussion to the question of how we make moral judgments in the Church. He looks at the Anglican moral compass points of Scripture, tradition and reason, arguing that gay and lesbian marriage may be a valid development of doctrine. He then goes on to explore whether, in fact, other unacknowledged items of our mental agenda, such as a particular understanding of biblical authority, might condition the debate on the specific issue of human sexuality. What appears to be a discussion about the rightness or otherwise of sexual activity between people of the same sex may, in fact, be a debate about different hermeneutical approaches to the interpretation of Scripture and different assessments of the precise nature of the authority of the biblical texts – reflecting, in turn, inherited divisions in our Church.

In focussing on the question of the possible ordination of practising homosexual people in long-term, committed relationships, Peter Jensen has provided a defence of the Church's traditional stance. Regrettably because Dr Jensen's paper was available only at the last minute, the rest of the panel has not had the opportunity to offer a response, nor to reflect together on the material presented.

Graeme Garrett then gives a personal reflection on his own struggle in reaching moral conclusions with regard to the question of homosexuality. The experience of his own niece's 'coming out' led him to question not only his own attitudes but the typically theoretical approach to the question. He allows that personal relationships do, and perhaps should, affect the ways we reach an understanding of the many issues we have considered. And he suggests that a theology of the Spirit challenges us to consider that God is again leading the Church to new pathways.

It will already be clear that, while the Doctrine Panel has learned a great deal, we do not feel that we have come anywhere near the end of the story. More careful reflection needs to be done. On some issues we continue to hold differing views of the possible outcomes. Meanwhile, the members of the Panel are glad to offer the following brief essays as an invitation to members of the Church at large to enter with a little more information than they might otherwise have into what remains an essentially deep and difficult conversation. Only on the basis of a more mature and reflective assessment of the evidence, will it be possible for our Church as a whole to work together towards a consensus viewpoint.

CHAPTER TWO

Homosexuality in the Christian Tradition

Muriel Porter

Christian tradition has always treated homosexual practices – though not always homosexual love – as sinful. However, the degree of sinfulness it has accorded homosexuality has varied, creating a tradition that can best be regarded as ambivalent. For considerable periods in Western Christian history, homosexual activity has been regarded as no more sinful than gluttony; at other times, it has been regarded as the grossest of abominations, punishable by death.

It is worth noting that the condemnation of homosexuality has waxed and waned according to the secular environment. This condemnation has been strongest in periods when heterosexual activity was most stringently controlled, such as during the campaign against clerical marriage in the eleventh and twelfth centuries, or during the Victorian era, when heterosexual practice was subject to a rigid conformity. The traditional teaching on homosexuality needs always to be understood alongside traditional mainstream Christian teachings on heterosexual activities, which include teachings now generally abandoned by the Church, such as the condemnation of pleasure in intercourse even within marriage, or – in the Protestant, Anglican and Orthodox churches – artificial contraception.

The basis for the most persistent and influential Christian teaching against homosexuality has not been biblical exegesis on its own, or even pre-eminently, but rather claims that it was 'against nature', which drew as much on continuing pre-Christian Western philosophies as on Scripture.

Traditionally, the Jewish Scriptures have been interpreted as explicitly forbidding homosexual practices *per se*. Precisely what understanding of homosexual activity they condemn is the subject of modern debate among Scripture scholars: is it the modern concept of a monogamous loving relationship between consenting adults of homosexual orientation, or is it ritualistic, coercive, or abusive same-sex practice that is condemned? This debate is engaged elsewhere in this report. It should simply be recorded here that male homosexual activity is forbidden in Leviticus 18:22 and 20:13. Judges 19:16-30 and Genesis 19:1-8 have traditionally been seen as providing evidence of God's judgement on homosexuality, though these texts have been the subject of significant reinterpretation in recent times.

The key New Testament text is Romans 1:26, 27, with other references in 2 Peter 2:6-7, Jude 7, 1 Corinthians 6:9,10 and 1 Timothy 1:10. Again, the same question of interpretation is brought to these texts by modern scholars.

Nevertheless, there can be no doubt that the early Church believed it was building on the testimony of the Bible when it developed its opposition to homosexuality. This was not, however, the only reason for its opposition, or even the major one. It was strong in its opposition to homosexual activity of all kinds, at least in part because of the culture in which it came to birth. The early Church Fathers were in reaction to the Graeco-Roman world, which was the context within which they developed their system of Christian ethics. High Greek culture, in the golden age of the fifth century before Christ, had regarded homosexual practices as entirely acceptable. Homosexual relationships were seen as normal and valuable, an important part of male intellectual and emotional friendship. At a time when female company was purely for purposes of procreation and domestic and dynastic arrangements, strong male bondings were sought and celebrated. Physical homosexual relationships between older men and younger boys, particularly teachers and students, or masters and apprentices, were believed to 'enhance the learning process', though such relationships were only acceptable where the older man was the active partner.[1] Commercial exploitation and abusive relationships were condemned.

Greek philosophers in general preached an ethic of moderation, in sexual activity as in other aspects of life. They gave high importance to a doctrine of asceticism. But although Plato in his final work, Laws, insisted that sex must be restricted to married people and always potentially procreative to 'avoid the frenzied madness of love', thereby condemning homosexual activity, this was regarded as a highly idiosyncratic view. The philosophers did not generally distinguish between heterosexual or homosexual acts, so long as moderation was sought. The writings in this vein of Philo, a Jewish neo-platonist of late first-century Alexandria, were especially influential on early Christian thinking.[2]

The period that covered the composition of the major books of the New Testament and beyond was, according to numerous contemporary writers, a time when several of the Roman emperors were renowned for their sexual licence and cruelty. Both adultery and homosexual licentiousness seemed to be common in certain aristocratic circles. Modern scholars question the 'Roman orgy' cliché, claiming that literary evidence of high-level sexual corruption is possibly more a metaphor for the political corruption and disintegration of the time, than a factual historical record. Whatever the real situation, though, the ideology of sexual corruption was clearly a powerful one. It is noteworthy that this ideology coincided with the early Christian persecutions, and so understandably had a powerful influence on the thinking of the early Christian theologians. Likewise, the scattered Jewish communities around the Mediterranean, where Christianity began its missionary outreach, were uncompromising in their rejection of the supposed sexual lifestyle of the Greeks and Romans around them.

In the Jewish tradition, in any case, homosexual practices were regarded as a very serious matter. The prohibitions against them in the book of Leviticus were treated seriously. Homosexual activity was at least as grave as intercourse with a menstruating woman. As historian David Greenberg points out, though to modern minds the latter 'offence' seems utterly archaic and trivial, it needs to be accepted as a 'marker' of the seriousness with which ancient Palestine viewed homosexual activity. The menstrual taboo was an important one in primitive societies.[3]

Surrounded, and indeed nurtured, by such powerful influences, it is not surprising that the first Christian theologians developed a moral code that was harsh on all aspects of human sexuality, even sexual intercourse within marriage. Bodily pleasure was to be resisted in the name of a rigid asceticism that exalted a dualistic concept of human nature. Homosexual practice, because it had not even the excuse of procreation, the only acceptable reason for heterosexual activity – let alone the biblical sanction for marriage – was unambiguously sinful.

In particular, the competition from dualist Gnostic and Manichaean sects, which taught the sinfulness of sex and pleasure, and indeed the evil of procreation, provided a powerful additional impetus for the development of a strict Christian code of sexual conduct. Formulated by St Augustine of Hippo, once himself a Manichaean, this code has dominated traditional Christian teaching on sexuality.[4]

In part, this code was built on many pre-Christian ideas about 'nature' and natural law, ideas that were based on Platonic and Aristotelian concepts, and Stoic versions of 'natural morality'. St Paul adopted them formally into Christian teaching in the first chapter of Romans. A three-pronged analogy with nature was developed: First, sexual processes were compared to the sowing of a field; second, sexual behaviour in animals was compared to that of humans; third, there was an attempt to determine the natural functional structure of the sex organ.[5] Vern Bullough, an historian with a special interest in the history of Christian attitudes to sexuality, has written:

> In effect, the appeal to nature was a teaching device used to reinforce theoretical assumptions. It was not really based upon observations of what took place in nature since any thing contrary to the preconceived notions was ignored. Procreation was the chief criterion for judging whether sexual activity was natural or unnatural, and anything that did not lead to procreation was regarded as unnatural. [6]

These principles became the fundamental 'rule of thumb' for judging everything connected with human sexual activity. So artificial contraception was condemned as 'against nature', marital relations that were not explicitly procreative were 'against nature', and homosexual practices were 'against nature'.

Homosexuality was condemned as unnatural and depraved by St John Chrysostom and St Augustine of Hippo, both writing in the early fifth century. John Chrysostom was particularly harsh, and believed male homosexuals deserved to be driven from the church and stoned. At least part of Chrysostom's horror of homosexuality seemed to be linked to disgust with a male taking the passive role of a woman, and therefore ceasing to be male. In Graeco-Roman society, the only males expected to accept the passive role in homosexual intercourse were youths, slaves or other lesser males, as it was regarded beneath the dignity of full citizens to 'play the woman'.[7] In Christian society, this violation of customary gender expectations may have been one factor in the history of attitudes to homosexuality. Traditional Church teaching on heterosexual relations always insisted on what is facetiously known as the 'missionary position'. Any other position, particularly those where the female might have been 'on top', was categorically forbidden.[8] Is this a subliminal reason why the Christian Church has been so concerned about male homosexuality and rarely about lesbianism, though lesbianism was well known in the Hellenic world?

In general, though, the hostility of Christianity's first theologians was 'directed to all sexual experiences not intended to lead to procreation within marriage – homosexual or heterosexual'. While some theologians, notably Tertullian, were more hostile to homosexuality, adultery was, for Gregory of Nyssa, as serious as homosexual intercourse.[9]

The first significant legislation against homosexuality was enacted by the Emperor Justinian in the sixth century.[10] The development of anti-homosexual legislation in the later Roman Empire was probably as much based on a growing antipathy to sexual pleasure among non-Christian Romans as among Christians. What is important to note in Justinian's legislation, however, is his condemnation of homosexuality on the basis that this crime threatened not just the individual, but the whole community: 'because of such crimes, there are famines, earthquakes and pestilences'. This rationale initiated a long tradition of making forbidden forms of sexuality the scapegoat for society's ills, suggesting that God sent plagues, earthquakes and, in recent times, AIDS, as a punishment. This accords with the teaching of Leviticus, that defilements such as these would cause the people to be 'vomited out of the land'.[11] By the same legislation of Justinian, swearing and blaspheming were forbidden, and adultery was made a capital offence.[12]

So far we have used the word 'homosexuality' in the modern sense, that is, as pertaining to specifically male-to-male sexual acts. However, the word 'homosexual' is relatively modern. It was first used in 1869.[13] The concept of homosexuality as an innate sexual identity, affecting a certain proportion of the male population, is also a modern concept, a development from the nineteenth century medicalisation of the subject.[14]

The terms most commonly used in history were 'sodomy' and 'sodomite', derived from the biblical story of the destruction of the city of Sodom. (The sin for which Sodom was destroyed has, in the past, been interpreted as homosexuality.) However, numerous historians have pointed out that the term 'sodomy' was not historically used to imply homosexual activity exclusively. In medieval usage, sodomy was sin against nature, the worst category under the general heading of the deadly sin of lust. Sin against nature had itself three subdivisions: 'by reason of species' (with animals); 'by reason of sex' (with a person of the same gender); and 'by reason of manner' (with a person of the opposite sex, even a legal spouse, but in a manner that excluded procreation).[15] This last subdivision included heterosexual anal or oral sex – in other words, sex using the 'wrong orifice'. Some theologians classified 'coitus interruptus' and masturbation as sodomy, because both prevented procreation.[16] Homosexuality *per se* was not the 'primary category for distinguishing acceptable sex from unacceptable', writes Greenberg; the principal distinction was the potential for conception.[17] In Christian tradition, then, the sin of sodomy has been condemned, but in recent times the definition of that 'sin' has changed markedly. Much that once came under that vague umbrella term, including masturbation and varied marital sexual relations, is no longer condemned.

Johansson has pointed out that another layer of meaning grew around the term 'sodomy' in the Middle Ages. It came to be associated with the mythical archetype of the satyr, which embodied the concept of rampant, uninhibited sexual appetite. It had demonic overtones. It also came to be connected with blasphemy. (Sexual intercourse between Christians and Jews, or Christians and Saracens, was classified as sodomy.)[18]

The connection with heresy was also long-standing. The terms 'bugger' and 'buggery' for sodomites/sodomy are a direct link with heresy, as they are derived from names used for those who adhered to the Albigensian heresy, introduced into France in the thirteenth century by Bulgarians.[19] It is interesting to note that 'bugger' was a term also used for usurers, a class of people more consistently and rigorously condemned on the basis of Scripture by the Church until the seventeenth century than homosexuals.[20]

The heresy link, in fact, increased the repression of homosexual activity, because of growing antipathy to Muslims (who were believed to practice homosexual sex freely) in the wake of the Crusades. From the thirteenth century on, stiff new secular penalties were introduced against homosexuality in Europe. The 'sodomite', like the heretic, was someone who had to be destroyed.[21] Inevitably, as sodomy came to be defined more narrowly as homosexual activity, it carried with it the emotive connotations of its earlier definitions.

Further, though there were occasional suggestions that some men were more inclined towards sex with other men than with women, the general assumption throughout Christian history has been that all men were capable of being tempted to homosexual sex. It was no different to temptation to commit adultery or fornication or 'unnatural' sex with a woman. Homosexual sex was a form of sexual vice, not an identity.[22]

Other factors in the Church had contributed to the development of a stricter attitude to homosexual practice. In particular, increasing pressure on clerical marriage had a marked and, in some ways, unexpected impact. The campaign to outlaw clerical marriage began during the eleventh century, with a series of decrees that ordered the laity not to attend masses conducted by priests known to be in intimate relationships with their wives. (The theoretical situation at the time was that clergy were permitted to remain married after ordination, so long as they did not continue sexual relations with their wives.) Peter Damian, the eleventh-century Benedictine and Doctor of the Church renowned for his uncompromising teachings on personal austerity and mortification, was harsh in his condemnation of married clergy. He it was who elaborated the 'cultic purity' argument for clerical celibacy in its most extreme form:

> If, therefore, our Redeemer so loved the bloom of perfect chastity that he was not only born of a virgin womb, but also fondly handled by a virgin foster-father, and this while he was still an infant crying in the cradle, by whom, I ask, does he wish his Body to be handled, now that he is reigning in all his immensity in heaven? [23]

This same theologian, not surprisingly, was supremely harsh in his condemnation of homosexuality. He insisted that monks and clergy must be removed from their orders for any form of homosexual expression, but this met with considerable resistance. After much unsuccessful lobbying of the Papacy, Pope Leo IX finally decreed that the penalty was only for those who persisted in practising sodomy.

The Church was far less amenable when it came to tolerance for heterosexual relations between clergy and their lawful wives. There is some suggestion that the anti-clerical-marriage campaign, which culminated in the Second Lateran Council decree of 1139 forbidding clerical marriage, represented in some ways a struggle between homosexual and heterosexual clergy. Certainly, the Church's actions in condemning and outlawing clergy marriage were far more severe than its actions against homosexuality, and came forty years before a council would condemn homosexuality.[25] When the Third Lateran Council of 1179 became the first ecumenical council of the Church to rule on homosexual acts (clerics were to be deposed from office, and laymen excommunicated), it treated homosexuality as comparable in gravity to clerical marriage.[26] The same council also imposed sanctions on usurers, heretics, Jews, Muslims and mercenaries, and presaged a period obsessed by a quest for 'intellectual and institutional uniformity' in Europe.[27] During this period, there was a steep rise in popular hostility towards minority groups, including Jews and heretics.

The late Middle Ages saw the development of a fear and loathing of homosexuality that at times became quite hysterical and irrational. Greenberg has suggested that the growing pre-occupation with homosexuality at this time was an 'indirect and unanticipated consequence of the efforts of church reformers to establish sacerdotal celibacy'. The elimination of heterosexual outlets for the clergy could only have fostered homoerotic feelings, as often happens among men deprived of female company on ships, in prisons and in monasteries. (The eleventh and twelfth centuries witnessed the growth of a literary subculture celebrating homoerotic love, much of it emanating from the cloister. The writings of St Aelred of Rievaulx are an important example.) The need for emotional and physical intimacy can override sexual orientation in such circumstances, Greenberg writes.[28]

It was against this background that the rediscovery of classical writings, including those of the Stoics, gave an impetus to a reinvigoration of the concept of 'nature' as the standard by which sexual activity should be judged.[29] In the last decades of the thirteenth century, St Thomas Aquinas gave detailed consideration to homosexuality in his Summa Theologica. He argued that homosexuality was not only contrary to reason, but also contrary to the natural order. There were four divisions in the 'sin against nature' for Aquinas: masturbation; bestiality; same-sex activity; and deviation from the natural manner of coitus (which was restricted to face-to-face contact, with the woman on her back). Of these, bestiality was the most grievous, followed by homosexual sex, then intercourse in an 'unnatural' position, with masturbation the least serious. In each case, the possibility of procreation was once more the key to deciding whether acts were natural or not.[30] These sins against nature were more serious, he argued, than adultery, seduction, or rape, even though these involved injury to others and were also contrary to charity.

Aquinas held that as the order of nature was derived from God, its 'contravention was always an injury done to God, whether or not any offence was at the same time committed against one's neighbours'.[31] This offence to God was the more serious form of injury. It may be significant that Aquinas wrote the Summa from 1265, as civil law codes in Europe were increasingly legislating against homosexual practices. The death penalty was often prescribed, even for a single proven act.[32]

It is noteworthy that Aquinas' main line of argument was derived from the natural law theory, rather than from the Bible directly.[33] Though controversial in his own time and not established as the key

Catholic moral authority until the sixteenth-century Counter Reformation, Aquinas's writings, nevertheless, have permanently established the 'natural' as the touchstone of Roman Catholic sexual ethics and, by derivation, Protestant ethics as well. 'Since the teaching of Aquinas has remained in many respects the dominant influence in the theology of the Western Catholic Church', his writing has 'proved to be the definitive ground for all subsequent rejection of homosexual behaviour by the Catholic Church'[34] Vatican declarations on homosexuality up to the present continue to reflect Thomistic thinking.

The sixteenth-century Protestant reformers, though they came slowly to a higher view of women and marriage than their predecessors, made no concession to homosexual behaviour. It continued to be, for them, one of the many manifestations of the sinfulness of fallen human nature. Between 1555 and 1678 in Geneva, there were 62 prosecutions (resulting in 30 executions) for sodomy.[35]

In England, sodomy cases, though rare, were heard in the ecclesiastical courts until the sixteenth century. They were always treated leniently. The first English secular law to deal with sodomy was an Act of 1533, instituted by Henry VIII in the aftermath of the formal break with Rome. In that Act, 'the abominable vice of buggery' was made a capital offence. The vice was defined as carnal knowledge 'by mankind with mankind or with brute beast or by womankind with brute beast'. It was harsh, but so was all Tudor criminal legislation. For instance, under Tudor law, vagabonds who refused to work on three occasions could be hanged.[36]

Re-enacted by Elizabeth I in 1563, this Act was only rarely enforced over the centuries that it remained on the law books. It was at first invoked only in connection with religious or political prosecutions. Walter Lord Hungerford was beheaded in 1540 for sodomising his servants over a period of years, but he was also convicted of harbouring a traitor.[37] Though the Act was more rhetoric than reality, its symbolic power was significant. The death penalty was finally removed in England in 1861. The result of the 1861 Act was that 'homosexuals who kept their physical activities private among themselves were left tolerably free from legal prosecution'.[38]

But that freedom was to be short-lived. In 1885, an infamous last-minute additional clause to the Criminal Law Amendment Act opened the gates to the prosecution of homosexual activities between consenting adult males. The Act itself was designed, among other things, to protect women and girls against sexual assault. The Labouchere amendment was supposedly designed to protect men and boys as well, given the large number of male prostitutes, and the high level of pederasty, in London at the time. But it was ill-considered and poorly worded, particularly in allowing the interpretation that private homosexual acts, as well as public assaults, were misdemeanours. The clause instantly became a 'blackmailer's charter'. It was under the provisions of this clause that Oscar Wilde and other high-profile victims were prosecuted. Given the high level of heterosexual immorality in London at the time, to which Parliament and society in general turned a convenient blind eye, the prosecution of homosexual men was gross hypocrisy.

What of lesbianism? It had been almost totally ignored in the Christian tradition, perhaps because male theologians and canonists were largely ignorant of, and uninterested in, female sexuality. Nor could it offend male concerns about passive and active roles. In 1921, there was an attempt in the British Parliament to legislate against 'acts of indecency by females'. The promoter, a Scottish Conservative lawyer, claimed 'lesbianism was sapping the highest and best in civilisation now as it had previously to a large extent caused the destruction of the early Grecian civilization and was still more the cause of the downfall of the Roman Empire'.[39] Another speaker claimed lunatic asylums were packed with nymphomaniacs, many women were having nervous breakdowns after being tampered with by members of their own sex, and the decline of the British race was imminent because lesbians were refusing to have children. Despite these extraordinary claims, the clause was passed by a large majority of votes. But some sanity entered the debate when the Bill reached the House of Lords. The clause was abandoned, and the House of Commons did not seek to reintroduce it.[40]

The issue of the prosecution of consenting adult male homosexuals finally came up for scrutiny in Britain in the 1950s. The trigger was the exorbitant increase in the number of 'offences' known to police.

Between 1931 and 1955 the annual number had grown from 622 to 6,644, with between a third and a half actually making it to the courts. The main reason for this jump was a change in police policy at the highest level, which encouraged police officers to step up the number of arrests in a crusade against 'male vice'. Another reason was the defection of Guy Burgess and Donald Maclean to the Soviet Union in 1951. Both men were believed to be homosexuals and, given the cold war paranoia about security, homosexuals were readily assumed to be prone to blackmail, thus endangering Western freedom. The final goad to reform was a series of trials of prominent men accused of homosexual activity, to all of whom harsh sentences were meted out.[41]

A vigorous public debate ensued. On the one hand, defenders of public morality saw the level of prosecution as a sure sign of post-war malaise and corruption in society, but on the other, more thoughtful people, including some church people, began to agitate for homosexual law reform. In the debate in the British Parliament calling for a royal commission, an important clause from a report by the Church of England Moral Welfare Council was read. That clause stated: 'In no other department of life does the State hold itself competent to interfere with the private actions of consenting adults. A man and a woman may commit the grave sin of fornication with legal impunity, but a corresponding act between man and man is liable to life imprisonment, and not infrequently is punished by very long prison sentences.'[42] In a nutshell, this was the main argument of most of those, including some prominent Church leaders, who fought for the decriminalisation of homosexuality at that time. While the Church of England still regarded homosexual behaviour as sinful, for instance, officially it no longer believed it should be treated as criminal.

Bishop F. R. Barry, the Bishop of Southwell, a noted churchman who spoke for the Bench of Bishops, called on the House of Lords to 'disinfect' itself of the idea that the state of being a homosexual was necessarily 'in itself, something morally reprehensible'. It happened to a man 'like colour-blindness or paralysis'. It demanded sympathy, he said. However, he still adhered to the natural law argument formulated by Thomas Aquinas 700 years earlier: 'These forms of unnatural association are, of course, morally evil and sinful in the highest degree, because they are a violation of natural law', he insisted.[43]

Commentators have noted that Church spokesmen in the British Parliament at this time were instrumental in disturbing the moral complacency among parliamentarians and opening the way for reform. Records of the crucial speeches indicate that the Church of England had departed from the notion that homosexuality was of a different order of sexual sin from that practised by heterosexuals.[44]

The upshot of the parliamentary debate was the formation of the Wolfenden Committee, which deliberated for three years before producing its report in 1957. Its chief recommendation was the abolition of the law relating to private homosexual acts between consenting adults. It was not proper for the law to concern itself with what a man does in private, it said, unless 'it can be shown to be so contrary to the public good that the law ought to intervene in its function as the guardian of that public good'.[45]

It took ten years of intense public debate and repeated Parliamentary attempts before the Wolfenden recommendation was finally enshrined in law in 1967. (Australian states would follow suit in the following decades, with Tasmania finally falling into line only in 1997.[46]) During those years, the reform was strongly supported by the Archbishops of Canterbury and York, as well as the General Assembly of the Church of England, the Roman Catholic Advisory Committee, the Methodist Conference, and the Quakers.

In more recent times in Britain, a 1995 General Synod working party report recommended that gay and lesbian families should 'find a ready welcome within the whole family of God'.[47] This was in line with the more cautious welcome extended by the earlier (1991) influential report by the Church of England's House of Bishops, *Issues in Human Sexuality.* While not able to commend same-sex partnerships, the bishops called on congregations to welcome gay people as members. The language is supremely cautious, but nevertheless surprisingly generous.[48]

The bishops' report, however, revealed that they were still responding to an understanding of human sexuality based on 'natural law' and specifically, procreative purpose. Heterosexual activity served 'the purposes of procreation', they wrote:

> Furthermore, since it is the interaction of the male and female genital organs which makes procreation possible,

> that too must be part of God's purpose... In short, the biological evidence is at least compatible with a theological view that heterosexual physical union is divinely intended to be the norm.[49]

Heterosexual unions, in every way, reflected 'their essential place in God's providential order'. They were, therefore, truly 'natural' in a way that homosexual unions never could be.[50]

However, as early as 1958, a Lambeth Conference had decided that procreative purpose was not the sole key to what was acceptable for sexual behaviour. The 1958 Conference passed the following resolution on contraception:

> The Conference believes that the responsibility for deciding upon the number and frequency of children has been laid by God upon the consciences of parents everywhere: that this planning, in such ways as are mutually acceptable to husband and wife in Christian conscience, is a right and important factor in Christian family life and should be the result of positive choice before God. Such responsible parenthood, built on obedience to all the duties of marriage, requires a wise stewardship of the resources and abilities of the family as well as a thoughtful consideration of the varying population needs and problems of society and the claims of future generations.[50]

That the Lambeth reaffirmation of contraception came a decade before the Church of Rome would prohibit artificial contraception in *Humanae Vitae* is surely telling. However, the Anglican Church fathers were still uncomfortable with real sexual freedom in marriage. In Resolutions 112 and 113, they condemned 'sins of self-indulgence and sensuality' in marriage, and commended 'self-discipline and restraint'. The ancient primacy of asceticism was still alive, if no longer as strong as it once had been.

The committee that had prepared these resolutions had produced a thoughtful report that examined carefully the arguments about the purposes of marriage. While it acknowledged the purpose of procreation, it gave equal weight to sexual union for relational reasons:

> Husbands and wives owe to each other and to the depth and stability of their families the duty to express, in sexual intercourse, the love which they bear and mean to bear to each other. Sexual intercourse is not by any means the only language of earthly love, but it is, in its full and right use, the most intimate and the most revealing; it has the depth of communication signified by the Biblical word so often used for it, 'knowledge'; it is a giving and receiving in the unity of two free spirits which is in itself good (within the marriage bond) and mediates good to those who share it. Therefore it is utterly wrong to urge that, unless children are specifically desired, sexual intercourse is of the nature of sin. It is also wrong to say that such intercourse ought not to be engaged in except with the willing intention to procreate children.[52]

This paragraph represents perhaps the most radical reversal in all the long centuries of Christian teaching on sexuality. It overturns not only the concept of procreation as primary cause, but also notions of marital sex as remedy for sin. At long last, it allows that sex is not only a valid expression of marital love, but actually the pre-eminent one. The implications of this historically novel attitude for sexual relationships in general, and homosexual relationships in particular, so far remain unexplored in official Anglican teaching.

In Australia, in the debate over decriminalisation of homosexuality activity, the Anglican Church revealed deep divisions. The Diocese of Melbourne followed the line taken by the Church of England. In 1971 — a decade before the state law was changed — Melbourne Diocese's Social Questions Committee recommended the decriminalisation of homosexual acts between consenting adults in private; Melbourne Synod endorsed the recommendation in 1972. It was one of the first Australian Churches to take such a stance. However, the Diocese of Sydney's committee, reporting two years later, called for a continuation of criminal sanctions against homosexuality.[53] Sydney Synod passed resolutions opposing government moves to decriminalise homosexual activity, or legislate to protect homosexual people from discrimination. In 1985 — a year after the NSW law was changed — a sub-committee of the Diocese's Standing Committee, in a report on homosexuality and ministry, claimed that homosexual people who engaged in homosexual acts could not occupy any office or perform any ministry in a parish.[54]

The present situation

The mainstream Christian churches had, by the second half of the twentieth century, decided that they could no longer support the criminalisation of homosexual practices. The *sinfulness* of these practices remains a major theological issue. Nevertheless the Western Church has significantly changed its stance. Most mainstream Churches are now agreed that homosexuality as an orientation is not evil *per se*, a considerable change from their earlier understanding. Most Churches, likewise, have agreed that homosexual practice between consenting adult males in private should not be pursued as a criminal matter; this, too, is a significant change from their earlier collaboration with secular authorities.[55] All the Churches, however, still officially regard homosexual practice as sinful to a greater or lesser degree.

What has brought about even this limited change? From the evidence examined, it is reasonable to argue that the change has been a response to a changing understanding of homosexuality in the wider community. From the mid-nineteenth century on, homosexuality has come to be seen first as an involuntary condition (often as a form of illness) and then as an identity. Homosexual behaviour, then, could no longer be seen as a form of criminal sexual vice, much as it might, in official Church circles, still be regarded as sinful. (Similarly, as we have seen, the harsh communal attitudes towards homosexuality in the late Middle Ages provided the cultural context in which the Church developed a stricter theological condemnation of it.)

It is important to note that this changed understanding has prompted renewed examination of the scriptural references to homosexuality, and not vice versa. It is rarely a fresh understanding of Scripture that initiates changes to doctrine; rather, it offers a justification for changes already in process. The origin of these changes usually lies outside the institutional Church. Similarly, the changing social understanding of homosexuality has prompted fresh interpretations of natural law theology, and particularly the arguments from natural law that have been traditionally used to ascribe sinfulness to homosexual practice.[56]

Many long-held theological teachings on human sexuality have changed down the centuries, at least in theory. The Church no longer publicly declares women to be a lesser creation than men, though that was official teaching until the twentieth century. Celibacy is no longer officially promoted in the Catholic Church on the grounds that it is a holier lifestyle than marriage, though that was the main reason proffered in Christian tradition until very recently. The Anglican Church permits artificial contraception, at least within marriage, though the long tradition of the Church had held that it was murder. Sexual pleasure within the marital relationship is affirmed in modern Christian teaching, though it was condemned universally by theologians until recent centuries. In most parts of the Anglican Communion, there is now recognition that marriages can and do die, and that new marriages can bring healing and grace. Theologians have recognised that their predecessors often misinterpreted or ignored Scripture, or at least misunderstood its meaning because of their mistaken understanding of human biology. This substantial revision of traditional teaching on human sexuality has largely been possible because the experience and insights of married clergy and more recently, female theologians, have been taken seriously.

The present debate on homosexuality is a logical development from these radical changes that have occurred in the Church's teachings on women, marriage, sexuality, contraception and divorce. When the Church viewed the human body with distaste, and all sexual expression, even within marriage, with suspicion, it was not surprising that the Church condemned homosexual activity outright. When the Church taught that heterosexual activity was only permissible for the express purpose of procreation within marriage, and condemned all other forms of heterosexual expression, let alone sexual pleasure, then logically homosexual expression had to be similarly forbidden. Only in recent times, as the Church has come falteringly to understand that sexual expression is just as important for human relationship as it is for procreation, and has come to understand something of the complexity inherent in long-term sexual relationships, has it been possible for a fresh reassessment of homosexuality to develop.

Endnotes

[1] David F. Greenberg, *The Construction of Homosexuality* (University of Chicago Press, Chicago and London, 1988), 204-205.

[2] *Ibid.* Various writers have pointed out their influence on St Paul, particularly in the key passage in Romans 1:19f. James Barr, *Biblical Faith and Natural Theology: the Gifford Lectures for 1991* (Clarendon Press, Oxford, 1993), 51-57 points out that Paul's terminology and thought-framework here is 'unmistakably Hellenic' in the pattern of both Plato and the Jewish writer Josephus, who taught that sexual intercourse was only lawful between men and women, and then only for the begetting of children. See also Brendan Byrne, *Romans* (Liturgical Press, Collegeville, Minnesota, 1996), 92-93.

[3] Greenberg, *Op.cit.*, 195-196.

[4] See Vern L. Bullough, 'Introduction: The Christian Inheritance', *Sexual Practices and the Medieval Church*, Vern L. Bullough and James Brundage, eds. (Prometheus Books, Buffalo, New York, 1982), 1-12 for a useful discussion of the Gnostic/Manichaean influence on Christianity.

[5] Vern L. Bullough, 'The Sin against nature and homosexuality', *Sexual Practices and the Medieval Church, Op. Cit.*, 56.

[6] *Ibid*, 57.

[7] See Warren Johansson and William A. Percy, 'Homosexuality', *Handbook of Medieval Sexuality*, Vern L. Bullough and James A. Brundage, eds. (Garland Publishing, New York, 1996), 158-159.

[8] See Pierre J. Payer, 'Confession and the study of sex in the Middle Ages', *Handbook of Medieval Sexuality*, 3-17, for a full discussion of marital sexual sins identified in the Medieval penitentials.

[9] Greenberg, *Op.cit.*,227.

[10] *Ibid*, 230.

[11] *Ibid*, 232-235; Johansson and Perry, Op.cit., 161.

[12] Greenberg, *Op.cit.*, 238-239.

[13] Johansson and Perry, *Op.cit.*,156.

[14] Greenberg, Op.cit.,14; Robert Shephard, 'Sexual rumours in English politics: the cases of Elizabeth I and James I', *Desire and Discipline:Sex and Sexuality in the Pre-modern West*, Jacqueline Murray and Konrad Eisenbichler, eds. (University of Toronto Press, Toronto, 1996), 114.

[15] *Ibid.*

[16] Greenberg, *Op.cit.*, 275-276.

[17] *Ibid*, 265.

[18] Johansson and Percy, *Op.cit.*, 157-158.

[19] *Ibid*, 158; Greenberg, *Op.cit.*, 20.

[20] Johansson and Percy, *Op.cit.*, 158.

[21] Greenberg, *Op.cit.*, 276.

[22] *Ibid*, 328f.

[23] Quoted in Bernard Verkamp, 'Cultic Purity and the law of celibacy', *Review for Religious*, 30, 1971, 199-217. This reference: 217.

[24] Bullough, 'The sin against nature and homosexuality', *Op.cit.*, 61.

[25] For a description of this struggle, see Muriel Porter, *Sex, Marriage and the Church, Patterns of Change* (Dove, Melbourne, 1996), 29-34

[26] Greenberg, *Op.cit.*, 288.

[27] *Ibid*, 269ff.

[28] *Ibid*, 280-283.

[29] *Ibid*, 275.

[30] Bullough, 'The sin against nature and homosexuality', *Op.cit.*, 65.

[31] *Ibid.*

[32] John Boswell, *Christianity, Social Tolerance and Homosexuality: Gay People in Western Europe from the Beginning of the Christian Era to the Fourteenth Century* (University of Chicago Press, Chicago, 1980), 293.

[33] However, the key scriptural text cited against homosexuality is Romans 1:26-27, where Paul contrasts natural and unnatural intercourse. Brendan Byrne, *Romans* (Liturgical Press, Collegeville, Minnesota, 1996), pp.92-93, claims this reference to natural law demonstrates Paul's dependence on Philo and Stoic concepts of natural law. Paul, Byrne writes, reflects the conventional Stoic sense of 'nature' as the established order of things. 'Central to that established order was the dominance of the male over female as far as gender relationship was concerned' (p.69).

[34] Peter Coleman, *Christian Attitudes to Homosexuality* (SPCK, London, 1980), p.132.

[35] Greenberg, *Op.cit.*,

[36] *Ibid*, 303.

[37] *Ibid*, 323.

[38] Coleman, *Op.cit.*,140.

[39] *Ibid*, 159.

[40] *Ibid,* 159-160.

[41] *Ibid,* 161ff.

[42] *Ibid,* 164.

[43] *Ibid,* 166-167.

[44] *Ibid.*

[45] *Ibid,* 168.

[46] Homosexual acts between consenting male adults in private were decriminalised in South Australia in 1972 and 1975; the ACT in 1976; Victoria in 1981; NSW and the Northern Territory in 1984; Queensland and Western Australia in 1990; and Tasmania in 1997.

[47] *Something to Celebrate, Valuing Families in Church and Society* (Church House Publishing, London, 1995), 118.

[48] *Issues in Human Sexuality, A Statement by the House of Bishops...,* (Church House Publishing, London, 1991), 41.

[49] *Ibid,* 36

[50] *Ibid.*

[51] Resolution 115, *The Lambeth Conference 1958* (SPCK, London, 1958).

[52] *Ibid,* 147.

[53] *Report on Homosexuality,* Diocese of Melbourne Social Questions Committee 1971; *Report on Homosexuality,* Diocese of Sydney Ethics and Social Questions Committee, Sydney, 1973.

[54] See *Year Book of the Diocese of Sydney,* 1978, 249, and 1986, 245-6, 309-13. For these references, I am indebted to David Hilliard, 'Gender Roles, Homosexuality, and the Anglican Church in Sydney', *Gender and Christian Religion,* Studies in Church History, vol. 34 (Ecclesiastical History Society, Suffolk, 1998), 509-523.

[55] The Anglican Diocese of Sydney was still calling for the continuation of criminal sanctions against homosexuality in 1977: *Year Book of the Diocese of Sydney* 1978, 249.

[56] See Don Edwards, 'Natural Law and Homosexuality', *General Synod Doctrine Panel Report on Homosexuality* (work in progress), unpublished paper, June 1999.

Bibliography

Books and articles

Barr, James. *Biblical Faith and Natural Theology: the Gifford Lectures for 1991.* Oxford: Clarendon Press, 1993

Boswell, John. *Christianity, Social Tolerance and Homosexuality: Gay People in Western Europe from the Beginning of the Christian Era to the Fourteenth Century.*
Chicago: University of Chicago Press, 1980

Brundage, James A. *Law, Sex and Christian Society in Medieval Europe.* Chicago: University of Chicago Press, 1987

Bullough, Vern L. 'Introduction: The Christian Inheritance', in Vern. L. Bullough and James Brundage, eds, *Sexual practices and the Medieval Church.* Buffalo, New York: Prometheus Books, 1982

—— 'The Sin against Nature and Homosexuality', in Vern. L. Bullough and James Brundage, eds, *Sexual practices and the Medieval Church.* Buffalo, New York: Prometheus Books, 1982

Byrne, Brendan. *Romans.*
Collegeville, Minnesota: Liturgical Press, 1996

Coleman, Peter. *Christian Attitudes to Homosexuality.*
London: SPCK, 1980

Greenberg, David F. *The Construction of Homosexuality.*
Chicago and London: University of Chicago Press, 1988

Hilliard, David. 'Gender Roles, Homosexuality, and the Anglican Church in Sydney', *Gender and Christian Religion,* Studies in Church History, vol. 34. Suffolk: Ecclesiastical History Society, 1998, 509-523

Johansson, Warren and Percy, William A. 'Homosexuality', *Handbook of Medieval Sexuality,* Vern L. Bullough and James A. Brundage, eds. New York: Garland Publishing, 1996

Payer, Pierre J. 'Confession and the Study of Sex in the Middle Ages', *Handbook of Medieval sexuality.* Vern L. Bullough and James A. Brundage, eds. New York: Garland Publishing, 1996

Porter, Muriel. *Sex, Marriage and the Church: Patterns of Change.* Melbourne: Dove, 1996

Shepard, Robert. Sexual Rumours in English Politics: the Cases of Elizabeth I and James I,' *Desire and Discipline: Sex and Sexuality in the Pre-modern West.* Jacqueline Murray and Konrad Eisenbichler, eds. Toronto: University of Toronto Press, 1996

Verkamp, Bernard. 'Cultic Purity and the Law of Celibacy', *Review for Religious,* 30, 1971, 199-217

Year Book of the Diocese of Melbourne, 1972

Year Book of the Diocese of Sydney, 1978

Unpublished materials

Edwards, Don. 'Natural Law and Homosexuality', *General Synod Doctrine Panel Report on Homosexuality* (work in progress). June 1999

CHAPTER THREE

Human Sexuality and its Purpose from a Biblical and Theological Perspective

John Dunnill

In the modern world it sometimes seems that sex is everywhere, and this can be unsettling for those accustomed to think of sex as one obviously important, but essentially private and self-contained area of human experience. The Bible does not present sex everywhere, but it certainly depicts it as a pervasive and many-sided phenomenon which, if we are to understand it, must be approached in several different ways and on a number of levels.

This chapter looks at the Bible's understanding as a whole, largely bypassing for a moment the specific issue of homosexuality, in order to place that issue in the widest context. It tries to describe what the Bible has to say about the place of marriage and sexuality in human life, and to interpret what it means for a Christian understanding of these matters. The Bible's view turns out to be richer and more complex than is sometimes supposed, and more challenging in what it says about God and about human nature.

Marriage in Ancient Israel

The Old Testament is extremely rich in its presentation of human sexual relations, especially in the picture of marriage that emerges in the patriarchal and historical narratives.

The institution of marriage encompasses the patriarchal household (the *beth 'ab*, 'house of the father') as a subsection of the clan or tribe, an enlarged family consisting typically of the household chief with his wife or wives and concubines, with adult sons and their wives and children (until in due time the sons leave to establish their own 'house'). It exists as a procreative community, in which 'honour' attaches to the number of progeny (and by extension, the number of cattle and slaves) as a means of giving continuity to the 'name' of the patriarch. Wealth expresses itself not only in the multiplying of cattle and slaves, but also in the multiplying of wives and concubines (e.g.Abraham, Job, Solomon).

The importance of procreation and the continuance of the kinship group overrides relational factors, as when Abraham secures descendants for himself by means of his concubines, actively encouraged by his wife Sarah (Gen 16:1-4). Conversely, the practice of levirate marriage (Deut 25:5-10) allows a man to 'beget children' after his death through the coupling of his brother with his widow. The purpose of this practice is explicitly to maintain the procreative community 'so that his name may not be blotted out of Israel' (Deut 25:6).

The institution of marriage is focused on the leading male, whose honour it serves to establish. The capable wife is a blessing to her husband, bringing him honour as he sits among the elders (Prov 31:10-31). Divorce, permitted according to Deuteronomy 24:1-4, depends only on the husband's perception of some undefined 'fault' in the wife. Women who are unable to contribute to the procreative project are regarded as figures of shame (1 Sam 1). Adultery is transgressing the male's property rights in relation to his wives or concubines (Lev 19:20-22; Deut 22:30). Virginity, in this context, is a necessary attribute of a bride to ensure that the honour of her father or any potential husband has not been tarnished (Deut 22:13-21). When a woman is raped, this is treated chiefly as an act likely to cast dishonour upon her males (husband, master, brothers), not as an act of personal violation or a traumatic experience (Gen 34; Judg 19:25-8).

Along with these dishonouring actions, it is consistent with the procreational emphasis that certain kinds of non-procreative sexual activity are prohibited in the Priestly legislation. These include intercourse between males (Lev 18:22), or with animals (Lev 20:15f), incestuous relating (Lev 20:19-21), the spilling of male seed (Gen 38:6-10; Lev 15:16f) and sacrificing children to Molech (Lev 8:21, 20:1-5). So also consorting with prostitutes is criticised as wasteful of 'strength' (i.e. wealth or semen?) (Prov 31:3).

In the Priestly legislation the marital bond is placed directly under the purposes of God. Here the prohibited actions are treated not only as dishonouring to males, but also as 'defiling', and therefore offensive to God. It is consistent with this that, although the shame of adultery and prostitution is generally regarded as falling on the woman (Ezek 16:37f), the legal penalty for adultery, where both are judged equally responsible, is death for both parties (Lev 20:10; Deut 22:22-24).

The early patriarchal narratives assume the existence of polygamy as a normal practice, and there is no legislation prohibiting a man from having a plurality of wives and concubines. However, it is a symbol of conspicuous wealth and power, and it is unlikely that it was practised very widely outside the households of tribal leaders and kings. In the historical period of the monarchy, monogamy seems to be the invariant practice, at least among ordinary people. Alongside marriage there flourished the institution of prostitution, which is regarded by some texts as inadvisable activity for men, but is not prohibited. In the prophetic and wisdom literature, women are depicted as temptresses inciting to adultery, such as the 'strange woman' of Proverbs (Prov 5:2-5). This theme of sexual danger must be evidence of social tensions, but may also reflect the attraction of goddess worship among the population and perhaps the practice of cultic prostitution. In the prophets, adultery becomes a sign of idolatry (e.g. Isaiah, Hosea) as a covenant ideology emerges regarding Yahweh as Israel's lord or husband (Is 62).

Creation

The theological valuations placed on marriage and sexuality in this material are chiefly implicit. By contrast, Genesis 1-3 attempts an explicit and very different kind of reflection on the nature of humanity as what Lear calls a 'forked animal'.[2] It is characteristic of humans that they are beings in whom sexuality, with all it entails, has both anatomically and socially a central place. Being biologically sexual, humanity subsists in duality and in the union of two into one.

The interdependence of male and female is a leading theme in these early chapters of Genesis. In 1:27, the Priestly writer says:

> So God created humankind (*'adam*) in his image, in the image of God he created him, male and female he created them.

Here humanity is described, firstly, as being made 'in the image of God' and exercising God's dominion over all the rest of creation. The status of humanity is uniquely close to the Creator. Secondly, humanity is described as biologically differentiated ('male and female') in preparation for the command to 'be fruitful and multiply', so that procreation is the means by which God's dominion is exercised.

This rather scientific account is completely different from the social narrative of chapters 2-3. It has been argued[3] that underlying the narrative of Genesis 2 is a conception of an androgynous humanity (*'adam*), both male and female at once, a single whole that is, like the egg-shaped ancestor described in Plato's myth,[4] split into two incomplete (i.e., sexually differentiated) parts, as *'ish* and *'ishshah* (man and woman). While this is possible, the canonical text, by continuing to use the term *'adam* after the emergence of the woman, and by describing the woman's unequal origin from the rib of the *'adam*, depicts a state much closer to the unequal sexual status embodied in known marriage customs. The male is regarded as essential human being, for whom the woman has the singular status of 'helpmeet': derived from the male and therefore both superior to the animals and mysteriously related to the male as 'bone of my bone and flesh of my flesh' (*basar*) (2:23). The text celebrates the mysterious power of sexuality that both differentiates and unites.

This originating mystery is related to the mystery of marriage in 2:24:

> Therefore a man (*'ish*) leaves his father and mother and clings/cleaves to his wife (*be'ishto*), and they become one flesh (*basar*).

The subject, however, is not sexual intercourse, but marital union. *Basar* can be used to refer to sexual activity, but nearly always refers (as in Gen 2:23: 'flesh of my flesh') to the bond of kinship (compare Gen 29:14, 37:27; Lev 18:6; 2 Sam 5:1; Is 58:7).[5] Despite a long tradition of seeing here a euphemistic reference to what Iago more coarsely calls 'the beast with two backs',[6] this is not the meaning of the passage. Compare 1 Corinthians 6:16, where Paul recoils at the idea that a fleeting connection with a prostitute could constitute the mysterious 'one flesh' of marriage, let alone the union of the Christian with Christ. The mention of leaving father and mother does not accurately describe preparations for marriage (since in all known Israelite practices, it would be the wife who would leave the parental home to enter that of the husband[7]) and it is irrelevant to sexual activity as such. The mystery here is the creation, through the marriage bond, of a new kinship, a new united 'flesh', subsisting in the social identity of the man and the woman and their descendants. Here lies the mystery of all human sociality.[8]

But beside the celebration is the shame, and although the act of the *'ish* and the *'ishshah* leading to their expulsion from the garden can be understood as their rebellion against the commandment of God, readers find an inescapable sexual reference in the couple's shame at their nakedness (3:7), and in the woman's punishment through the pain of childbirth and subservience to her husband (3:16). If the 'knowledge of good and evil' means, in one aspect, sexual knowledge (compare 2 Sam 19:35; Deut 1:39; Num 14:29-31),[9] what is forbidden is the dangerous delight of sexuality which gives to humanity power 'like gods' to make life. But it is a power that can control (note how Paul sums up the whole Law in Rom 7:7 as 'you shall not desire'), and there is an inescapable connection (as Gen 1:28, 4:11 show) between procreation, dominance, rivalry and death. Is it also a reflection on the fact that sexual generation entails (and is entailed by) the processes of ageing and death unknown to other, less complex, species?

In the conflated texts of Genesis 1-3, sexuality is not a product of a 'fall', but essential to human beings at every level: biological, social and spiritual. It is a quality tinged with wonder, as it confers on human beings the status of being 'like gods'(3:5), 'made in the image of God' (1:27), but which also names the tragic destiny of those who must 'labour' painfully to bring forth children from their bodies and bread from the earth, before returning at last to the dust from which they came (3:16-19).

The idea of a 'fall', in the sense of a penal transformation of human beings, derives from later speculation (4 Ezra 7:118; Sirach 25:24; Rom 5:12) that Adam and Eve were immortal until this event.[10] This is based on the divine warning in Genesis 2:17 ('in the day you eat of it you shall die') and an understanding of their mortality as punishment ('you are dust, and to dust you shall return', (Gen 3:19)). But the threatened punishment is not delivered, at least as stated, while 3:22 implies that they are already mortal, seeking immortality ('and now he might reach out his hand and take also from the tree of life, and eat, and live forever'), so that their punishment takes the form, not of death, but of expulsion from the garden and a life of pain (3:23, 16-19). That this created existence might have been lived in closer communion with God and with each other is the tragic meaning of the text, and gives rise in Israel's reflection to a great hope.

Covenant

At the heart of Israel's understanding of itself as a nation is the idea that it lives in covenant relationship with God. In the prophets and psalms, but equally in the sources of the Pentateuch, is expressed the belief that at Sinai/Horeb — or further back, with Abraham or Noah — Yahweh chose this people and committed himself to them. No doubt, in this Israel was borrowing an idea of the relation of a people to its god common among ancient Near Eastern peoples, an idea which owes much to trade contracts and suzerainty treaties. All these imply the establishment of mutual (though not necessarily equal) rights and obligations. But what is distinctive is the way this motif is developed in the prophetic writings into a theology of fully personal relating, a theology that implicitly — and, in some key passages, explicitly — employs the metaphor of marriage to express who Yahweh and Israel are for each other.

Foundational to the covenant is a choosing exercised by Yahweh in the distant past, a choosing not based on any virtue in Israel, but simply in Yahweh's choice (Deut 4:37, 7:7f; Is 43:4; Am 3:2). Yahweh's choice is exclusive and excluding, so that Israel is called to respond by putting aside their desire for other gods and choosing Yahweh with a similarly exclusive commitment. The relationship, with its ups and downs, is dramatised in the richly anthropomorphic language of a yearning heart, of compassion, of lovers who 'know' each other in a fully personal sense, long and tenderly (Is 63:15; Jer 31:20; Hos 4:6, 6:6, 11:9, 13:4). Over against Israel's rebellious and fickle promiscuity, ever 'whoring after strange gods', the prophets extol God's faithfulness and loving-kindness, his endless fixed determination to go on loving.

The expression of this in terms of marriage springs naturally out of the personal warmth of this relationship (a warmth capable of both delight and anger). It is found most clearly in Hosea, but also in later prophets (Is 54:1-8, Jer 3, Ezek 16, Mal 2:10-16), as they articulate the twin messages that the distance between Israel and their God is the result of Israel's sin, and that there is yet a way back into reconciliation. If a man can divorce his wife for any reason, God can divorce his people — but he will not. The marriage metaphor depicts Israel's relationship with God as an educational, transformative relationship. As, no doubt, ancient husbands disciplined their wives into submission, God can be angry and punish Israel for their faults; yet God does so not out of selfishness, but out of love (Is 67:9). But when God's anger is not evident, that is not (as so often in human terms) a sign of foolish indulgence or sullen resentment, but God's loving forgiveness (Hos 11:8; Am 3:2).

In these terms the prophets disclose God's passionate love of his people, and they do so in ways that ought to shock us. In Hosea we read that God has cast off his people, like an adulterous wife abandoned to her lovers. But he cannot overcome the love in his heart for this his people, and so he will take Israel back. He will do what Deuteronomy 24:1-4 forbids an Israelite to do: abounding in love, God overrides the Law. He also overrides the law of shame. The scandal of having an adulterous wife assaults the husband's honour as a man among men, that honour which is intricately bound up with wealth and status. In terms of ancient Near-Eastern culture, to take back a wife who has subjected one to dishonour is to add further dishonour. To do so for 'love' is to prefer the 'inner' world of women, associated with feeling, sexuality and shame, to the 'outer' world of men, associated with responsibility, property and honour, and is to 'lose face' beyond measure. But Yahweh shows his boundless love for Israel in choosing that disgrace (Hos 1-2, Jer 3).

This image of covenant as marriage must revalue the idea of marriage as a covenant. Indeed, with Malachi 2:10-16, it is hard to distinguish the theological description of God's accepting love from the ethical instruction: 'let no one be faithless to the wife of his youth'. Although it is not a lesson that the Old Testament draws out very often, we cannot avoid seeing that, in these mature texts, marriage is understood as a lasting bond of affection that shows itself both in strength of emotion and in willingness to make sacrifices for the beloved. The central value of *hesed*, loving-kindness or steadfast love, takes precedence over that of procreation ('Why is your heart sad?

Am I not more to you than ten sons?' the barren Hannah is asked by her husband in 1 Sam 1:8), and over the moral/economic world of honour — without, of course, displacing either. It is a bond which can subsist between friends, as we see with David and Jonathan (1 Sam 20:14-17); it is the unique status of the woman made from Adam's rib that she is 'a helpmeet fit for him' (Gen 2:18); it is one glory of the (by no means asexual) love celebrated in the Song of Solomon (Song 8:6f). What all these texts teach is that human relationship, including marriage, is fulfilled as it becomes a transformative bond, a growing together and towards each other in loving-kindness, which enriches and enlarges life. It is a growing into the inner reality of the mysterious 'one flesh' that leads into knowledge of the mystery of God.

The New Testament: Marriage and Celibacy in the new age
When the New Testament proclaims the fulfilment of Israel's great hope of knowing God, it makes use on several occasions of the metaphor of marriage. Jesus describes himself as the bridegroom (Mk 2:19f), and the image of the kingdom of God as marriage feast is found in several parables (Matt 22:2-12, 25:1-13; Lk 12:35-38). When John chooses to begin his account of Jesus' ministry, not with a synagogue service (like Mark and Luke), but with a wedding feast (Jn 2:1-11), he is, no doubt, saying the same thing. The Church is God's bride in Ephesians and Revelation (Eph 5:23-33; Rev 19:7-9, 21:2, 9). But aside from this kerygmatic metaphor, where do human love and the institution of marriage fit into the new age?

Jesus looks at marriage in the light of the divine ordering of creation and redemption. In what is his central and most distinctive pronouncement on the subject (Mt 19:3-8, Mk 10:2-9), he goes behind the Mosaic divorce permission (Deut 24:1-4), which he says was given 'because of your hardness of heart', to the mysterious union of 'one flesh' in Gen 2:24 (rightly understood as denoting indissoluble kinship rather than intercourse). He appeals to a law behind the Law, and reinstates the created order of marriage as establishing an unbreakable bond, even while recognising ('let no one put asunder') that, empirically, it is subject to disorder and decay. In this saying Jesus asserts a parable or mystery of human relating in the face of a less-than-ideal reality.

Jesus offers another kind of idealising vision in answer to the Sadducees' question about the (now defunct) practice of levirate marriage (Mk 12:18-27): if a man attempts to raise up children for his dead brother by marrying his brother's widow, whose property will the wife be 'in the resurrection'? An institution originally designed to preserve the kinship bond of 'one flesh' was now, in a more individualistic age (but cf. Gen 38:9), perceived as contradicting it. Jesus replies that 'when they rise from the dead, they neither marry nor are given in marriage, but are like the angels in heaven' (Mk12:25). Here the union of man and woman is subsumed, in the new age, into a higher union with God, a union which, unlike the union of 'those dying generations',[11] contains all ages at once, for God is simultaneously 'the God of Abraham, the God of Isaac and the God of Jacob' (Mk 12:26).

Elsewhere, Jesus expresses an explicit critique of marriage in the light of the kingdom's demands. Marriage is a part of created life which is under judgement and will not continue in the new age, for it was those who died in the Flood who were giving priority to 'eating and drinking, marrying and giving in marriage', heedless of the doom that was to befall them (Matt 24:38f). He holds at arm's length the pervasive demands of family: those who wish to proclaim the kingdom must make its ways their choice, not pause to discharge family obligations (Lk 9:60-62). Jesus came to divide households (Lk 12:51-53) and, as regards his own family, he proclaims: 'My mother and brothers are those who hear the word of God and do it' (Lk 8:19-21).

Such radical, eschatological teaching is not unmixed, however. In Jewish circles, discussion of marriage centred largely, in Jesus' day, around the boundary question of divorce, no doubt under the influence of Hellenistic practices that were making marriage much more fluid. So understood, marriage becomes less an order of being and more a restriction of sexual access. In some sayings, Jesus (or the evangelist) appears to align himself with such conservative trends in Israel, assuming the permissibility of divorce (on the basis of Deut 24:1-4), but limiting the criteria. Thus, according to Matt 19:9, Jesus allowed divorce, but only on one ground, 'because of unchastity'; Matt 5:31f adds to this that remarriage of a divorced woman is 'adultery'; Mk 10:10-12 seems to envisage a Roman setting in which women as well as men could initiate divorce, and allows this, but prohibits the remarriage of either party, which would constitute 'adultery'.

Such pragmatic legal interpretations are a world away from the eschatological vision that informs Jesus' characteristic teaching, and they alter profoundly the way his teaching was received. Looked at from this point of view — understood as a legal pronouncement — Jesus' parable of marriage as 'one flesh', and his command that 'what God has joined, let no one put asunder' (Mk 10:9) dictate a very strict marital regime, stricter than the Law of Moses, in setting aside its compassionate provision of divorce, or allowing only one exception. Is such a regime possible except in the kingdom of God? Yet does the kingdom have any place for marriage of any kind?

The prospect of marriage without divorce ('except for unchastity') and without remarriage caused Jesus' disciples to say that in that case 'it is better not to marry': better not to marry at all than to be bound to a wife for life, or released only by the shame of a wife's adultery. And Jesus offers this as the mysterious teaching, that 'there are eunuchs who have made themselves eunuchs for the kingdom of heaven' (Matt 19:10-12). For although eunuchs are forbidden to enter the assembly of Israel (Deut 23:1), paradoxically those whom God calls to 'eunuchise themselves' by standing outside the world's way of 'marrying and giving in marriage' have by implication a high place in the kingdom.

Thus celibacy becomes the way to make actual the marriage-less life of the kingdom within the bounds of this age. In line with this, the typical disciples of the Gospels, 'the Twelve', are depicted as an asexual community of men (with female associates) who have given up houses, wives, parents and children for the sake of the kingdom (Mk 10:28-30) — albeit with the promise of receiving these back, in some sense, a hundredfold in the kingdom. While the actual nature of their continuing kinship ties cannot be reconstructed, in the texts they model a new community outside the old order of procreation and property, as does the Jerusalem church described in idealised terms in Acts 2:42-47, 4:32-5.

Paul, likewise, envisages celibacy as the higher calling of the Christian. In 1 Corinthians 7 he urges those who are unmarried to remain so (7:8, 37, 39f), but acknowledges that marriage is a defence against uncontrolled sexual activity and need (7:2, 5, 9, 36f). The opening words ('It is well for a man not to touch a woman', (7:1)) are most probably to be taken, not as his own, but as those of his correspondents, so that Paul's reputation for misogyny on this score is unfounded. His view of marriage includes both a positive view of the dimension of care and a negative perception that care is anxiety (1 Cor 7:32f). But this negativity is a factor of his conviction (7:29) that 'the appointed time has grown short' and, therefore, the union of 'one flesh' should give way to devotion to Christ (7:32-35).

If Paul, in his central teaching, is ambivalent about marriage and sexuality, he is, like Jesus, very positive about love, which he understands as a way of living modelled on Christ, in dynamic union with Christ, and leading to a true humanity in which God's kingdom is tasted. This is the burden of the hymn of love in 1 Corinthians 13, and equally of the Christ hymn in Philippians 2:5-11, preceded by the instruction to 'be of the same mind', 'look not to your own interests but to those of others' and so 'let the same mind be in you that was in Christ Jesus...' (Phil 2:1-5). It is this which Paul means by 'the Body of Christ' (1 Cor 12; Rom 12), the 'new creation' (2 Cor 5:17), the new being in which 'there is no longer Jew or Greek, there is no longer slave or free, there is no longer male and female' (Gal 3:28) — a new humanity revealed in a renewed community.

Thus eschatological convictions led the New Testament writers, following Jesus, to develop models of non-procreative sociality. But other texts reflect the fact that, even in the Christian community, life went on, with its 'eating and drinking, marrying and giving in marriage' expressed in the hierarchical structure of the household: 'Wives, be subject to your husbands.... husbands, love your wives and never treat them harshly' (Col 3:18f; cf 1 Tim 2:12-15; 1 Pet 3:1-8). Wives are exhorted to show not only obedience, but also modesty of behaviour and dress (1 Tim 2:9-11; cf 1 Pet 3:3-6). Anyone called to the office of overseer must be 'above reproach, husband of one wife' (1 Tim 3:2), meaning 'not divorced and remarried'? 'not widowed and remarried'? 'not keeping a concubine'?

This tendency may appear to be a mere compromise with the institutions of the old age but, in various ways, the writers express the conviction that this form of life, although a part of 'the world' can, when practised by Christians, express a radically different purpose. 1 Corinthians 7:4 envisages a married mutuality in which, just as all Christians should 'be subject to one another out of reverence for Christ' (Eph 5:21; cf Phil 2:4f), a husband and wife may give to each other authority over their bodies. 1 Peter 3:5f appeals to an idealised picture of wifely submission in the patriarchal household of Abraham and Sarah, while 1 Timothy 2:12-15 seeks the same motif in the priority and (implausibly!) the undeceivedness of Adam in Genesis 2-3. Colossians 3 claims wifely submission is 'fitting in the Lord' (3:18) and, more substantially, urges the whole community to be filled with 'the peace of Christ' (3:15), 'the word of Christ' (3:16) and, in general, to seek 'the things that are above where Christ is' (3:1). In Ephesians and 1 Corinthians 11, such submission is regarded as equivalent to devotion to Christ (1 Cor 11:3; Eph 5:22-24), while a husband's love can be an image of Christ's self-giving love for the Church (Eph 5:23-33).

So the outward form of the Hellenistic household was preserved, in hope that whatever was oppressive and life-denying in the subordination of wives to husbands, and slaves and children to fathers, was able to be transformed by the Spirit. The Christian household, as a part of the Christian community, was to be a model of the kingdom of God. To this end, all those forms of behaviour which display disordered spirits and threaten the stability of the community were to be shunned: 'fornicators, idolaters, adulterers, *malakoi*, *arsenokoitai*,[12] thieves, greedy, drunkards, revilers, robbers...' (1 Cor 6:10), 'those who kill their fathers and mothers, murderers, fornicators, *arsenokoitai*, slave traders, liars, perjurers' (1 Tim 1:9f), 'dogs and sorcerers and fornicators and murderers and idolaters and everyone who loves and practices falsehood' (Rev 22:15).

In time these remarks about the Christian household, when purged of eschatological elements and supplemented by (de-polygamised) material drawn from the Old Testament, came to be the basis of an image of Christian marriage, buttressed by moral exclusions and reinforced by Jesus' divorce-sayings understood as laws. Meanwhile the eschatological thrust of the New Testament was expressed in the image of celibacy, virginity, eunuchs for the kingdom, the single state of Jesus, John the Baptist, Paul and the Twelve. In marriage and celibacy, two ways of Christian living were set side by side. The covenant ideology of love, made concrete in Christ, was borrowed by both to express the fact that, just as 'our citizenship is in heaven' (Phil 3:20), so also is our kinship.

Living between the Ages

The New Testament, in its references to sexuality, shows evidence of striving to be true to the new age of the kingdom opened by Christ and also to cope adequately with the demands of the life of the old age still continuing. The clearest message to emerge is that in God's kingdom both marriage and sexuality will be transcended, and therefore celibacy is the best preparation for that state — not to be understood as deprivation, but as celebration of marriage with God. What might have been possible for many for a short time became, in due course, transmuted into a lifelong vocation for a few, for those who would be 'perfect'. Monastic communities (and later a celibate priesthood) have set forth down the ages the image of a life apart from the common way of procreation and property, in devotion to God. Celibacy, in its many forms, remains one way of witnessing to a Christian sexuality in our day.

But if marriage continued, was that a mere compromise between the values of the new age and the old? What would make marriage good enough to be a vehicle of kingdom living? The answer which emerged was to treat divorce and all alternative forms of sexuality as excluded by law, while setting before married people the vision of living in unity and love enjoined in the New Testament on the whole Christian body. The resulting institution has remained in some tension. Does this, at its best, enact the prelapsarian creation order of living as 'one flesh', or is it only the old (fallen) Adam (and Eve) given permission to indulge themselves within limits? When, in recent years, churches have allowed the possibility of divorce and remarriage, even for Christians, thus reinstating the Mosaic permission (Deut 24:1-4), has this recognition of humanity's 'hardness of heart' been a fall from grace or an act of Christian compassion? Can the vision of kingdom living survive without support from law? Or again, if marriage is claimed to be a distinct 'order of life', is that only reaffirming the old central worldly structures of procreation and property, so that 'Christianity' and 'Family Values' can sound to some like code-names for the ideology of bourgeois capitalism, or of heterosexism?[13]

The image of mutuality in marriage is expressed very strongly in a few significant texts cited above and, no doubt, examples can be found from all ages of couples for whom that has been real. But how possible has it been in a society that takes as normal inequalities of status and regard in all other areas of life? Rowan Williams suggests that, if one kind of sexual perversion is the practice of 'asymmetrical' acts which do not depend on the desire of the other (such as rape, paedophilia, bestiality), then indeed 'in a great many cultural settings, the socially licensed form of heterosexual intercourse is a 'perversion'.[14] If today Christians as well as others can expect to find mutual regard in marriage, that situation owes far more to changes in women's status through movements of education and social reform, and to the novels of Flaubert, George Eliot and D.H. Lawrence, than to a distinctively Christian vision of marriage.

Likewise, if it is a commonplace today for Christians to say that 'sex is good', we have to be clear that this is not what Christians have usually said,[15] and that the current ambivalence on this score derives from the ambivalence of the founding text — less from the Old Testament, which takes sex for granted except in its dangerous elements, than from the New Testament. It is a lesson Christians learned, like everyone else, from secular movements in biology and psychology. And along with everyone else, they learned that 'good' means 'as much as possible' and 'however you like' — at least, for those not inhibited by 'old-fashioned' concepts like 'fornication' and 'adultery'. Christians are caught trying to affirm the goodness of sex, at least in theory, or within limits, while the fun lies in the practice, not the theory; and while it becomes apparent that, however much fun is being had, the dominance of sexuality is blowing society apart — not only promiscuity and the growth of uncommitted relationships but, more recently, the recognition of the shocking incidence of child abuse within families.

The ambivalence of the New Testament about marriage has left Christian theology impressionable to new secular movements, for good in some cases and for ill in others. Its ambivalence lies in protecting sexuality, procreation and (by implication) property as a godly order without being clear where God is to be found in them. It has been insufficiently theological.

Putting God at the centre of reflection on sexuality reveals that the heart of what the Bible and the Christian tradition have to say about relationships is that God is a covenanting God and that human beings are made to live in covenant relationships of fidelity and loving-kindness. And because God is endlessly generous, this order is a gift and not a restriction of human fullness. Marriage that intends the other unconditionally and for life is a response to God's grace that enables a relationship of trust to grow. Love, it must be insisted, is not that fickle and fleeting thing made of feelings that Romanticism has discovered — powerful and sometimes delightful as it is — but the lifelong practice of caring, which may create (but does not presuppose) mutuality.

A theology of covenant that has responsibility at its centre is concerned with sociality in its widest sense, from friendship to the ordering of a whole society. But, specifically, it answers the 'Does God really care whom I sleep with?' syndrome in the affirmative. The goodness of sex and its capacity to open up human beings at many levels cannot be separated. Through sexuality and the vulnerability it brings, there are so many possibilities of transformation — in trust, creativity and delight, but also in betrayal, depersonalisation and disease.

It is in this context, and from this perspective, that the current debate calls the Church to consider whether it does more harm than good by refusing to recognise the possibility of good and godly relationships among gay and lesbian people. Humans need security in order to learn to trust, and that security is hugely buttressed by public symbolic acts of commitment, of affirmation and acceptance. If loving-kindness is also possible for homosexuals, it is a value the Church should be promoting, against the culture of promiscuity and rootlessness to which they are constantly subject. Can they not also realise the vision of becoming 'one flesh'?

The question has to be asked because, despite claims often made to the contrary, heterosexual monogamy and the intercourse it entails are not 'the biblical norm' of human relating. The procreative community that is marriage is recognised and affirmed in the Old Testament and again in the New Testament. But its social manifestations, though in some ways protected, are also criticised: challenged to become the ground of the enlarging of human relating and knowing in faithfulness and loving-kindness. In each testament, there is a vision of a new possibility of relating to God and therefore to each other: in the Old Testament, marriage remodelled on the covenant-love that God desires with Israel, and, in the New Testament, celibate devotion anticipating the transcendence of sexual being in God's kingdom. Compared with these, marriage 'as it is' is at best second best.

So it has at least to be explored whether another form of embodied but non-procreative relationship may, for some, have as good a claim to be a place where love can be actual and God can be known. Gay and lesbian people hear the Church saying that they are uniquely under judgment and in need of healing, in a way that heterosexuals are not. It may be positive to note that the standard by which we are all judged, and towards which we are all called to be transformed, is not the sublime but tarnished institution of Christian marriage, but the love of God.

Endnotes

1 A convenient survey of the importance of honour and shame in Biblical thinking about marriage is provided by B. L. Malina in The New Testament World — Insights from Cultural Anthropology, rev. ed. (Westminster/John Knox Press, Louisville, 1993).

2 W. Shakespeare, *King Lear,* III. iv.

3 P. Trible, *God and the Rhetoric of Sexuality* (Fortress Press, Philadelphia, 1978), 80.

4 Plato, *Symposium,* trans. W. Hamilton (Penguin Books, Harmondsworth, 1951), 58-65 (188e-193e).

5 J. A. Dearman, 'Marriage in the OT', in R. L. Brawley, ed., *Biblical Ethics and Homosexuality* (Westminster/John Knox Press, Louisville, 1996), 55.

6 W. Shakespeare, *Othello,* I, i.

7 Jacob's entry into Laban's household, first as kinsman and then as son-in-law (Gen 29:13-30) is not a true exception.

8 C. Westermann, *Genesis 1-11* (SPCK, London, 1984), 233f; G. Wenham, *Genesis 1-15,* Word Biblical Commentary 1 (Word Books, Waco, 1987), 71.

9 J. Milgrom, 'Sex and Wisdom — What the Garden of Eden Story is Saying', *Bible Review 10/6* (1994), 21.

10 Westermann, 275f.

11 W. B. Yeats, 'Sailing to Byzantium', *Collected Poems,* 2nd ed. (Macmillan, London, 1950), 217f.

12 For the meaning of these terms, see chapter 5 below.

13 For example, R. Cleaver, *Know My Name — a Gay Liberation Theology* (Westminster/ John Knox Press, Louisville, 1995), 75-83, 99-101; D. B. Martin, 'Heterosexism and the Interpretation of Romans 1:18-32', *Biblical Interpretation 3* (1995), 332-55.

14 R. Williams, 'The Body's Grace', in C. Hefling, ed., *Our Selves, Our Souls and Bodies* (Cowley Publications, Cambridge, MA., 1996), 61.

15 For an argument that the Elizabethan Puritans, despite their dour reputation, were one group who did say this, see D. Doriani, 'The Puritans, Sex and Pleasure' in A. Thatcher and E. Stuart, *Christian Perspectives on Sexuality and Gender* (Gracewing, Leominster, 1996), 33-51.

Bibliography

Books and articles

Adam, A.K.M. 'Disciples, Together, Constantly' in Seow, C.-L., ed., *Homosexuality and Christian Community.*
Louisville: Westminster/John Knox Press, 1996, 123-32

Anchor Bible Dictionary.
New York: Doubleday, 1992

Barton, S.C. 'Is the Bible Good News for Human Sexuality? Reflections on Method in Biblical Interpretation', in Thatcher, A. and Stuart, E., *Christian Perspectives on Sexuality and Gender.*
Leominster: Gracewing, 1996, 4-13

Bird, P. 'The Place of Women in the Israelite Cultus', in Miller, P.D. et al., ed., *Ancient Israelite Religion.*
Philadelphia: Fortress Press, 1987, 397-419

—— 'To Play the Harlot', in Day, P.L., *Gender and Difference in Ancient Israel.*
Minneapolis: Fortress, 1989, 75-94

Brawley, R.L., ed. *Biblical Ethics and Homosexuality.* Louisville: Westminster/John Knox Press, 1996

Cleaver, R. *Know My Name — a Gay Liberation Theology.* Louisville: Westminster/ John Knox Press, 1995

Davies, M. 'New Testament Ethics and Ours — Homosexuality and Sexuality in Rom 1:26-27', *Biblical Interpretation 3* (1995), 315-31

Day, P.L. *Gender and Difference in Ancient Israel.*
Minneapolis: Fortress, 1989

Dearman, J.A. 'Marriage in the OT', in Brawley, R.L., ed. *Biblical Ethics and Homosexuality.*
Louisville: Westminster/John Knox Press, 1996, 53-68

Doriani, D. 'The Puritans, Sex and Pleasure' in Thatcher, A. and Stuart, E., *Christian Perspectives on Sexuality and Gender.*
Leominster: Gracewing, 1996, 33-51.

Douglas, M. *Purity and Danger.*
London: RKP, 1966

Fewell, D.N. and Gunn, D.M. *Gender, Power and Promise.*
Nashville: Abingdon, 1993

Goodfriend, N. 'Prostitution in the OT', *Anchor Bible Dictionary.*
New York: Doubleday, V, 507-9

Grenz, S.J. *Welcoming but Not Affirming.*
Louisville: Westminster/John Knox Press, 1998

Hays, R.B. 'Awaiting the Redemption of Our Bodies æ the Witness of Scripture concerning Homosexuality', in Siker, J.S., ed. *Homosexuality in the Church.*
Louisville: Westminster/John Knox Press, 1994, 3-17

Hefling, C., ed. *Our Selves, Our Souls and Bodies.*
Cambridge, MA: Cowley Publications, 1996

Henshaw, R.A. *Female and Male — the Cultic Personnel.*
Allison Park, Pa.: Pickwick, 1994

Malina, B.L. *The New Testament World -Insights from Cultural Anthropology,*
rev. ed. Louisville: Westminster/John Knox Press, 1993

Martin, D.B. 'Heterosexism and the Interpretation of Romans 1:18-32', *Biblical Interpretation 3* (1995), 332-55

—— 'Arsenokoites and Malakos: Meanings and Consequences', in Brawley, R.L., ed. *Biblical Ethics and Homosexuality.*
Louisville: Westminster/John Knox Press, 1996, 117-36

Melcher, S.J. 'The Holiness Code and Human Sexuality', in Brawley, R.L., ed. *Biblical Ethics and Homosexuality.*
Louisville: Westminster/John Knox Press, 1996, 87-102

Milgrom, J. 'How Not to Read the Bible', *Bible Review* 10/2 (1994), 14

—— 'Sex and Wisdom — What the Garden of Eden Story Is Saying', *Bible Review* 10/6 (1994), 21.

Miller, P.D., Hanson, P.D. and McBride, S.D., eds.
Ancient Israelite Religion.
Philadelphia: Fortress Press, 1987

Plato. *Symposium*, W. Hamilton, trans. Harmondsworth: Penguin Books, 1951

Rogers, E.F. *Sexuality and the Christian Body.* Oxford: Blackwell, 1999

Sedgwick, T.E. 'The Transformation of Sexuality and the Challenge of Conscience', in C. Hefling, ed. *Our Selves, Our Souls and Bodies.* Cambridge, MA: Cowley Publications, 1996, 26-42

Seow, C.-L. 'Textual orientation' in Brawley, R.L., ed. *Biblical Ethics and Homosexuality.* Louisville: Westminster/John Knox Press, 1996, 21-24

—— ed. *Homosexuality and Christian Community.* Louisville: Westminster/John Knox Press, 1996

Siker, J.S. 'Gentile Wheat and Homosexual Christians — NT Directions for the Heterosexual Church' in Brawley, R.L., ed. *Biblical Ethics and Homosexuality.* Louisville: Westminster/John Knox Press, 1996, 137-51

—— ed. Homosexuality in the Church. Louisville: Westminster/John Knox Press, 1994

Stone, K. 'Gender and Homosexuality in Judges 19 — Subject-honor, Object-shame?' JSOT 67 (1995) 87-107

—— 'The Hermeneutics of Abomination — on Gay Men, Canaanites and Biblical Interpretation', *Biblical Theology Bulletin* 27 (1997), 36-41

Thatcher, A. and Stuart, E. *Christian Perspectives on Sexuality and Gender.* Leominster: Gracewing, 1996

Trible, P. *God and the Rhetoric of Sexuality.* Philadelphia: Fortress Press, 1978

Wenham, G.J. The OT attitude to Homosexuality, *ExpT* 102/12 (1991) 359-63

—— *Genesis 1-15*, Word Biblical Commentary 1. Waco: Word Books, 1987

Westermann, C. *Genesis 1-11*. London: SPCK, 1984

Williams, R. 'The Body's Grace', in C. Hefling, ed. *Our Selves, Our Souls and Bodies*. Cambridge, MA: Cowley Publications, 1996, 58-68

CHAPTER FOUR

Homosexuality in the Old Testament

John Dunnill

It has to be admitted that the Old Testament (like the New) does not say very much about homosexuality. It is not mentioned at all in the psalms, the prophets or the wisdom writings; its appearance in the historical writings is contested, as we shall see; and among the laws it occurs only in two verses in one very specific context. However, such material as there is in the Hebrew Bible is more varied in kind than that in the Christian New Testament, a factor which must be taken into account in assessing its meaning and implications.

This chapter will look at material relating to homosexuality under four headings:

1. There is a pair of stories (Gen 19, Judg 19) concerning attempted homosexual rape;
2. There is the story of the friendship of David and Jonathan;
3. There is a group of possible references to male cultic prostitutes;
4. There are two verses in the Holiness Code condemning homosexual activity.

In addition to these passages from the Hebrew Scriptures, there are several references in the Deuterocanonical literature, Pseudepigrapha and other ancient texts which should be noticed.

Gibeah and Sodom

In Judges 19 and 20 is told the story of a Levite who, with his servant and his concubine, came at nightfall to the Benjaminite town of Gibeah and was offered shelter by an Ephraimite sojourner (resident alien). Then a crowd of male inhabitants came demanding that the Levite be handed over to them 'that we may know him'. Rather than allow this sexual assault, the Ephraimite offered his virgin daughter and the Levite's concubine instead, but this offer was refused. Then the Levite put his concubine out to them; she was subjected to rape all night and was found dead in the morning. The Levite took her body away and, reaching his home, cut the body into twelve pieces and distributed it throughout the tribes of Israel, demanding collective revenge on Gibeah.

Although this horrible story has at its centre a rape, it is only incidentally about sexual activity. Its primary theme is the disorder that results from denying the duty of caring for strangers. The Levite has avoided a city of Jebusite foreigners, preferring the safety of Gibeah, an Israelite city (19:10-18); the Ephraimite responds to the men's demands by protesting, 'since this man is my guest, do not do this vile thing' (19:23); the hideous demand is contrasted both with the kindly welcome offered earlier by the Ephraimite (19:16-21) and with the elaborate and extended hospitality shown earlier by the concubine's father (19:3-9).

This is not a quest for homosexual experience for, despite their demand to 'know' the man, it is the woman who is raped. The purpose of the rape is, in any case, not sexual pleasure, but the dishonouring of the stranger.[1] Therefore, the Gibeathites refuse the offer of two women, but accept one, the Levite's concubine, through whom (as his property) he can be dishonoured. Confirmation of this reading is found in that, when the tale is told to the tribes of Israel who answer his summons, he makes no mention of himself as a sexual object, but reports: 'they intended to kill me and they raped my concubine until she died' (20:5).

The much-better-known story in Genesis 19 is, in many ways, a parallel to this. Two angels came at evening to the city of Sodom, and were given hospitality by the sojourner Lot (19:1-3); the people of Sodom came to the door demanding access to the strangers 'that we may know them'; Lot offered instead his two virgin daughters. At this point the stories diverge, because there is no available subordinate to substitute for the angels, so the crowd's anger turns instead against the resident alien, Lot, who is then rescued by the angels. They send a mysterious blindness upon their attackers, and warn Lot and his whole family to escape from God's planned destruction of the city.

The fact that the Sodomites' attention is deflected from the angels (also described as 'the men') not onto Lot's daughters, but onto Lot himself, gives greater prominence to the homosexual motif. But the parallel passage should enable us to identify the primary theme as the lack of hospitality, or, better expressed, the 'homicidal xenophobia'[2] of the people of Sodom. It demonstrates the disorder that results from denying the duty of care for strangers. Once again, the word 'know', with so many possibilities of social and personal relating, is reduced to a parody: subjection to the kind of violent sexual assault meted out to prisoners of war.[3] Once again, the behaviour of the citizens is contrasted with the welcome extended by a sojourner (19:2-3) and with a preceding example of elaborate hospitality (that shown to the angels by Abraham in the previous chapter (18:1-8).

Excursus: What was the sin of Sodom?

In numerous passages of Scripture, Sodom and Gomorrah are a byword for sinfulness, but this reputation is not derived from the event narrated in Genesis 19: it is already presupposed by this story. In Genesis 13:13 we read: 'Now the people of Sodom were wicked, great sinners against the Lord'; and in the build-up to the Lot story we read: 'The Lord said, "Shall I hide from Abraham what I am about to do?... How great is the outcry against Sodom and Gomorrah and how very grave their sin"' (Gen 18:17, 20). The divine judgement is already planned, and does not depend on what happens in this incident. In fact, in contrast with the later tradition, sexual crime is not regarded in the Hebrew Bible as the typical sin of Sodom. What, then, was their sin?

<u>A. Great wickedness</u>

In Isaiah 1:10-17, the cities are criticised (as Israel is elsewhere) for failing to accompany their fervent practice of religion by social justice:

> What to me is the multitude of your sacrifices?... I cannot endure solemn assemblies with iniquity...Wash yourselves, make yourselves clean...Seek justice, rescue the oppressed, defend the orphan, plead for the widow.

In Jeremiah 23:14, the wickedness of the prophets of Jerusalem is compared to that of Sodom and Gomorrah:

> They commit adultery and walk in lies;
> they strengthen the hands of evildoers
> so that no one turns from wickedness.

In Ezekiel 16:49f, we read:

> This was the guilt of your sister Sodom: she and her daughters had pride, excess of food and prosperous ease, but did not aid the poor and needy. They were haughty and did abominable things before me; therefore I removed them when I saw it.

In Zephaniah 2:9f, Moab is promised a destruction equal to that of Sodom:

> This shall be their lot in return for their pride,
> because they scoffed and boasted
> against the people of the Lord of hosts.

A similar attribution of sinfulness, but without any special reference to sexual sins, is found in the intertestamental writings. Thus, in Sirach 16:8, we read:

> [God] did not spare the neighbours of Lot whom he loathed on account of their arrogance.

In Wisdom 10:6-8, Lot is identified as a righteous man, rescued by Wisdom from the fire that fell on the cities:

> For because they passed wisdom by,
> they not only were hindered from recognizing the good,
> but also left for humankind a reminder of their folly,
> so that their failures could never go unnoticed.

In Wisdom 19:13-17, language reminiscent of the events of Gen 19 (indicated here by underlined text) is used to describe the punishment of the Egyptians for mistreating the Israelites when they were 'strangers' among them:

> They justly suffered because of their wicked acts;
> for they practiced a more bitter *hatred of strangers*.
> Others had *refused to receive strangers when they came to them,*
> but these made slaves of guests who were their benefactors.

> And not only so — but, while punishment of some sort will come upon the former
> for *having received strangers with hostility,*
> the latter, having first received them with festal celebrations
> afterwards afflicted with terrible sufferings
> those who had already shared the same rights.
> They were stricken also *with loss of sight*
> *— just as those were at the door of the righteous man —*
> when surrounded by yawning darkness
> all of them tried to find the way through their own doors.

In Jubilees (2nd century BCE), we read:

> As the children of Sodom were taken away from the earth,
> so will all those who worship idols be taken away (22:22).[4]

The theme of mistreatment of strangers is echoed in Jesus' words to his disciples:

> If anyone will not welcome you or listen to your words, shake off the dust from your feet as you leave that house or town. Truly I tell you it will be more tolerable for the land of Sodom and Gomorrah on the day of judgement than for that town. (Matt 10:15;cf. Lk 10:12)

These passages show that while Sodom is uniformly a symbol of great wickedness and the fate that befalls it, the character of that wickedness is not explicitly derived from this narrative. The closest would be the references to 'adultery' in Jeremiah and 'abominable things' in Ezekiel, but more frequent are references to arrogance and failure to help the needy. In Hebrew Scriptures and early Jewish tradition, therefore, the story of Sodom functions as a parallel to that of Noah: a tale of terrible destruction visited upon general wickedness and rebellion against God.

B. Intercourse with angels

In the second and first centuries BCE, interest in the figure of Enoch caused attention to focus on the union of the sons of God and the daughters of humans in Gen 6:1-3, a union of humans with fallen angels (called 'Watchers') resulting in a race of 'Giants'. Here a *union of different kinds*, or miscegenation, is posited as the primal evil, as restated in 1 Enoch 6-7.[5] It was recalled that at Sodom, also, a union of different kinds was attempted: in this case, of human males with angelic beings. So in Sirach 16:7, preceding the verse cited above about the neighbours of Lot, it is said, "He did not forgive the ancient giants who revolted in their might'. So also in Job 20:5 we read:

> And he told them of the judgement of the Giants and the judgement of the Sodomites, just as they had been judged on account of their evil. And on account of their fornication and impurity and the corruption among themselves with fornication they died.6

In the Testaments of the Twelve Patriarchs (1st century BCE), we read that when people indulge in adultery, prostitution and marriage to gentile women, their 'sexual relations will become like Sodom and Gomorrah (T. Levi 14:6f); for 'Sodom did not recognise the Lord's angels and perished forever' (T. Asher 7:1).[7] Once, the sin of Sodom is described as 'changing the order of nature', but this is explained in terms of the monstrous 'Watchers' and the idolatry of the gentiles:

> The gentiles, because they wandered astray and forsook the Lord, have changed the order, and have devoted themselves to sticks and stones... But you, my children, shall not be like that: In the firmament, in the earth and in the sea, discern the Lord who made all things, so that you do not become like Sodom, which departed from the order of nature. Likewise, the Watchers departed from nature's order; the Lord pronounced a curse on them at the Flood. (T.Naphtali 13:4f)[8]

This is the context underlying the Letter of Jude which, in v. 14f, quotes 1 Enoch 1:9, apparently as Scripture, and following a reference to the Watchers, 'the angels who did not keep their own position but left their proper dwelling', continues:

> Likewise Sodom and Gomorrah and the surrounding cities which, in the same manner as they, indulged in sexual immorality and went after other flesh, serve as an example by undergoing a punishment of eternal fire (vv. 6f).

'Other flesh' (*sarkos heteras*) is rendered literally as 'strange flesh' by AV, but with a misleading vagueness by modern translators as 'unnatural lusts' (NEB, RSV, NRSV), or 'perversion' (NIV, TEV). It is not plausibly interpreted as a reference to same-sex activity. The great sin identified here is miscegenation, the unnatural union of humans and angels. The same perspective lies behind the combined reference to angels, Noah, Sodom and those who practice 'defiling lust' in 2 Peter 2:4-10.[9]

In short, neither the mainstream of biblical allusions nor the use of this passage as a part of the theodicy of early Judaism permits us to conclude that it was same-sex intercourse or anal intercourse that was the besetting sin of the Cities of the Plain. The mythological character of the concept of 'intercourse with angels' renders it hard to make use of today, but that, according to one tradition, is the horror of which Sodom was guilty. According to another tradition, its sinfulness without limit was particularly expressed in violent mistreatment of strangers. Only in the anti-Hellenistic anxiety of the period from 200 BCE onwards did this story eclipse the wider tradition, causing the sexual aspect of Sodom's sinfulness to come to the fore.

It is important to recognise that the reputation of Sodom is not tied to the particular event related in Gen 19, because this passage with its vivid narrative and lurid imagery of destruction has exercised a disproportionate hold upon the mind of later generations of Jews and Christians. More than any other passage, it is responsible for the association of same-sex activity with brutality and violence, and its characterisation as especially deserving of divine punishment. But the isolation of the same-sex motif to this one passage should cause this venerable misreading to be suppressed, together with the misleading terms 'sodomy' and 'sodomite'.[10]

David and Jonathan

In 1 and 2 Samuel, we find an intense friendship between David and Jonathan, the son of his master Saul:

> When David had finished speaking to Saul, the soul of Jonathan was bound to the soul of David, and Jonathan loved (*'aheb*) him as his own soul....Then Jonathan made

> a covenant with David because he loved him as his own soul (1 Sam 18:1-3).

After Jonathan's death in battle, David laments:

> I am distressed for you, my brother Jonathan;
> greatly beloved were you to me;
> your love (*'ahabah*) to me was wonderful,
> passing the love of women (2 Sam 1:26).

The intensity of the language raises for some a question about the nature of this 'love passing the love of women' between the two men. There is no mention at all of any sexual component to the friendship. Nor, although there is a disparity in the two men's ages, does it conform to the usual paedophilic pattern of active 'lover' and passive 'beloved'. We should note that the document in which their story is told is rich in the language of strong and changing affections: Saul is said to have 'loved David' while he served him as armour-bearer (1 Sam 16:21) and, at other times, hated him (1 Sam 18:8-11, 29); his daughter Michal, who was married to David, is also said to have loved him (1 Sam 18:20) and showed great fidelity in protecting him (19:8-17), but later 'despised him in her heart' (2 Sam 6:16).

In 1 Sam 20:30, Saul denounces his son as:

> You son of a perverse, rebellious woman! Do I not know that you have chosen the son of Jesse to your own shame, and to the shame of your mother's nakedness?

Is this a reference to a sexual relationship between the two men, a relationship that would be as shaming to Saul as the rape or adultery of his wife? The implication of Jonathan's preference for David is that he will help him to take his father Saul's throne, as indeed he does, thus preferring the chosen and private bond of friendship to the given obligations of kinship and blood. That situation, named in the next verse (1 Sam 20:31), is sufficient on its own to explain the violence of Saul's language and its reference to what shames and destroys Saul's house.[11]

In 2 Sam 6:16, what causes Michal to despise David is his semi-naked and unrestrained dancing before the Lord as the Ark is brought into Jerusalem: is he here behaving like a male temple prostitute, a *kadesh*? However, we shall see that implications of same-sex activity in the temple are not supported by evidence. What is shameful here is 'uncovering himself before the eyes of his servants' maids' (2 Sam 6:20). The context of this exchange, as in other examples of David's disordered sexuality (2 Sam 11-12), is entirely heterosexual.

The reason for including this topic here is not to imply that intense love between two mature men can only have a basis in sexual attraction (whether owned or not), but to record that the Old Testament does give evidence of a mutual 'knowing' outside marriage, which some modern homosexuals would recognise as expressing an experience close to their own. Whether or not it is physically expressed, such a love has at least as close a relevance to the issue of homosexuality as the data concerning cultic or violent sexuality upon which reflection has mainly been based.

Cultic prostitutes

A key theme in the Deuteronomic literature (Deuteronomy itself and the historical books of Joshua, Judges, Samuel and Kings) is the duty laid on the rulers of Judah and Israel to distinguish the true worship of Yahweh from the religion of the native inhabitants of Canaan. In 1 and 2 Kings, this is envisaged as the centralisation of Israel's worship (cultus) at Jerusalem, with destruction of all other shrines and abolition of their typical practices:

> For they also built for themselves high places, pillars and sacred poles on every high hill and under every green tree; there were also *kedeshim* in the land. They committed all the abominations (*to'ebath*) of the nations that the Lord drove out before the people of Israel (1 Kg 14:23f; see also 1 Kg 15:12, 22:46; 2 Kg 23:7).

The word *kedeshim* in these texts is frequently translated as 'male temple prostitutes' (NRSV), or 'sodomites' (AV). This derives from a theory that Canaanite fertility religion included the practice of cultic prostitution, usually understood as a form of 'sympathetic magic' ensuring the fertility of the land through sexual intercourse. In a few places, the female term *kedesha* clearly means 'prostitute'

(Gen 38:21f, Hos 4:14), and from this follows the rendering of the masculine *kadesh* as 'male temple prostitute'.

There is what appears to be an explicit prohibition of such activity:

> None of the daughters of Israel shall be a temple prostitute (*kedesha*); none of the sons of Israel shall be a temple prostitute (*kadesh*). You shall not bring the fee of a prostitute (*zona*) or the wages of a male prostitute (*keleb*, literally dog) into the house of the Lord in payment for any vow, for both of these are abhorrent (*to' ebath*) to the Lord your God (Deut 23:17-18 NRSV).

However, scholars today question whether, in fact, this practice ever existed, either in Israel or in the religion of other peoples of the ancient Near East. It is true that, in some cases, the activity of female prostitutes seems to have taken place in the environs of the temple or at feast times, but there is no clear relation to the temple ritual. Likewise, references to public homosexual activity in Mesopotamia and elsewhere cannot be linked to the cultus. The evidence for the cultic activity (or even the existence) of male prostitutes is, therefore, extremely slender, since it is dependent on a linguistic inference from the existence of the female. In any case, the function of (necessarily non-procreative) same-sex activity in a fertility cult is far from clear.

The word *kadesh* has the basic sense of 'sacred', and may in principle describe any cultic official or institution. Further, these may be either men or women, since the masculine form may be indeterminate (see 1 Kg 14:23f, above). The worship of the temple of Yahweh at Jerusalem, under the later monarchy, had only ancillary roles for women, and its male hierarchy may well have looked with suspicion on the active participation of women in the worship of other local deities (for example, as singers and dancers) and their presence on the edge of Israel's cultus.[12] So these people are denounced, in the biblical perspective, as servants of the worship of foreign deities, and what is forbidden to members of Israel is participation in this worship. The sexual references should, therefore, be understood as pejorative rather than descriptive. Even the abusive term 'dog' (*keleb*), which has been thought to refer explicitly to same-sex intercourse, is more probably referring (contemptuously) to the 'faithful ones' who serve in the sanctuary of the false gods, and not to be taken literally.

It is, therefore, unlikely that there was a practice of prostitution (male or female) connected to the worship of Canaan or Israel or any socially and religiously sanctioned form of homosexuality in ancient Israel.

Legal prohibitions

A prohibition is pronounced in Leviticus 18:22:

> You shall not lie with a male as with a woman; it is abomination (*to'ebah*)

In Leviticus 20:13, a punishment is pronounced on this activity:

> If a man lies with a male as with a woman, both of them have committed an abomination (*to'ebah*); they shall be put to death; their blood is upon them.

These verses form part of the Holiness Code (Lev 17-26), a section of the Priestly document that prescribes the conditions of purity needed for the worship of Yahweh. In accord with the need to distinguish Israel from the worship of Canaan (18:2), numerous offences are named. In contrast to the earlier law codes, a major emphasis here falls on ritual defilement, and on the defilement that proceeds from various kinds of sexual relations, including: incest, intercourse during menstruation, bestiality (Lev 18:19f, 23). Other ritual sins include giving offspring to Molech (18:21), consumption of blood, recourse to wizards, ritual lamentation, giving daughters as prostitutes (19:26-31). Other social sins include oppressing the alien, slander and cheating in trade (19:13-16, 33-37), but these are not described as defiling. The sexual sins are, therefore, to be understood as part of a system of ritual holiness, and it is significant that the earlier laws, which show less interest in issues of ritual purity, are silent on the subject of homosexuality.[14]

The prohibition of homosexual acts refers only to males (unlike the proscription of bestiality for both men and women in Lev 18:23). The emphasis in 20:13 on the guilt of both parties implies an unequal relationship involving (as was usually the case) an active and a passive partner, but the language does not distinguish acceptable from unacceptable forms. It is not clear what constitutes 'lying with'.

Although other literature assumes as standard the anal penetration of a slave or prostitute, with seminal emission, no doubt other forms of activity could come under this heading. This alone is identified in the Holiness Code as *to'ebah* ('abomination'), a term always connected with idolatry (e.g. 1 Kg 14:23f (see section 3 above), Jer 7:30). Of bestiality a different word is used: *tebhel* ('mixing' or 'confusion'). The death penalty puts this action on the same level of seriousness as adultery and incest (Lev 20:10-12, 16), but there is no record of the punishment being inflicted.

The Jewish and Christian communities have always sought to understand the rationale underlying these and other portions of the Levitical regulations. For the Letter of Aristeas (c.170 BCE), the food laws were parables of right living;[15] for Maimonides in the 12th century CE, they were based in concepts of hygiene — a view of the Bible as anticipating the discoveries of modern medicine (including a pre-scientific genetics expressed in the kinship rules), which was very popular in the 19th century, but is now discredited. More common today is an understanding of the elements of this code as signs within a symbolic system, a system that expresses, by means of the metaphor of the body (what goes into it, what comes out of it, what touches it), an understanding of the identity of Israel.[16]

One recent example of this semiotic approach focuses attention on the significance given to features like 'flesh' (i.e. kinship, Lev 18:6, 12) and the limits of sexual activity; the male control of female 'nakedness' (i.e. sexuality, Lev 18:6ff) in a patriarchal society; the importance of 'seed' (18:21, 20:2-5), the rights of the male seed-giver and the avoidance of waste (one interpretation of *tebhel* , 18:19, 21-23); the undefiled body, standing for the undefiled 'land' (18:24-30; 20:22-26).[17] On this analysis, the body in this patriarchal metaphor is a male body, whose integrity ('holiness') is threatened by the very idea of homosexual intercourse and all it implies: uncontrolled 'nakedness', wastage of 'seed', the penetrator penetrated. Such anxiety about the 'defiling' of maleness, an anxiety seen also in the tale of Sodom, may be sufficient to explain the force of the exclusion here.

There are, of course, other ways of construing the meaning of the Holiness Code. Such reflections are necessarily provisional and part of the ongoing work of interpretation. But the task is not optional, for the meaning of the parts depends on the meaning of the whole context in which they are placed. Although the terms of these two verses are clear, prohibiting sexual intercourse between males, the effect of their placement within a system of ritual holiness and under the concept 'abomination' raises questions about how they are to be applied. Do they apply only in cultic contexts? Or only when signifying idolatry? And why does the ban specify intercourse only between males?

Since the text, notoriously, offers no clear answer to such questions, the verses cannot be simply plucked out of their context and enforced as laws. It is necessary to seek to understand the meaning of the whole legal and symbolic system, before evaluating the ethical status of any individual rule.

More generally, when some parts of Israel's ritual law are carried over into the New Covenant, and others not, the authority for Christians of any particular law must be assessed and not assumed. As a starting point, what these texts say now must be examined in the light of their putative use in the New Testament.[18]

Conclusion

Perhaps the most surprising conclusion of this chapter, for many people, will be that 'Sodom' has nothing to do with the subject of homosexuality. This conclusion is arrived at by a close reading of the story in Genesis 19 with its parallel in Judges 19, and by comparison with all the other biblical references. These show that in the Biblical tradition about the wickedness of Sodom, sexual sin, usually unspecified, has a small place and, when it is specified, it relates either to general promiscuity or to intercourse with angels rather than to same-sex issues. The story is about the violent mistreatment and humiliation of strangers, and should be excluded from the debate about homosexuality.

Note that this conclusion follows simply from a reading of the relevant texts. The same method was used to examine the stories relating to David and Jonathan, with the conclusion that what is presented is probably a non-erotic friendship.

Sometimes other methods have to be used. When we looked at cultic prostitution we had to ask historical questions about the institutions of Israel and its neighbours, and concluded that, despite much ancient and modern opinion, there probably never was such a practice. In relation to the prohibition of homosexual activity in the Holiness Code, we noted various approaches to understanding just what is meant by 'holiness', and why this particular activity, for males only, is excluded.

The purpose of this chapter is to describe, not to determine. The Old Testament informs the Christian understanding and the Christian imagination at many levels. Its laws and narratives, with their different kinds of ambiguity, are material in our day, as in the past, for the construction of Christian ethical positions on homosexuality, in the light of the Gospel.

Endnotes

[1] Stone, K., 'Gender and Homosexuality in Judges 19: Subject-honor, Object-shame?' *JSOT*, 67. (1995), 87-107.

[2] Milgrom, J., 'How Not to Read the Bible', *Bible Review*, 10/2 (1994), 14.

[3] Wenham, G.J., 'The OT Attitude to Homosexuality', *ExtT*, 102/12 (1991), 361.

[4] J. H. Charlesworth, ed., *The Old Testament Pseudepigrapha* (Doubleday, New York, 1983), II, 99.

[5] Charlesworth, I, 15-16.

[6] Charlesworth, II, 94.

[7] Charlesworth, I, 793, 818.

[8] Charlesworth, I, 812.

[9] R. J. Bauckham, 'Jude, 2 Peter', Word Biblical Commentary (Word Books, Waco, 1993), 50-54, 248-55.

[10] C.-L. Seow,, 'Textual Orientation', in R. L. Brawley, ed., *Biblical Ethics and Homosexuality* (Westminster/John Knox Press, Louisville, 1996), 21-24.

[11] For a different assessment of this friendship, see D. N. Fewell and D. M. Gunn, *Gender, Power and Promise* (Abingdon, Nashville, 1993), 148-51.

[12] P. Bird, 'The Place of Women in the Israelite Cultus', in P. D Miller et al., eds., *Ancient Israelite Religion* (Fortress, Philadelphia, 1987), 397-419; P. Bird, 'To Play the Harlot', in P. L. Day, *Gender and Difference in Ancient Israel* (Fortress, Minneapolis, 1989), 75-94; R. A. Henshaw, *Female and Male — the Cultic Personnel* (Pickwick, Allison Park, Pa., 1994).

[13] N. Goodfriend, 'Prostitution in the OT', *Anchor Bible Dictionary* (Doubleday, New York, 1992) V, 507-9.

[14] S. J. Melcher, 'The Holiness Code and Human Sexuality', in Brawley, *Biblical Ethics and Homosexuality*, 87-102.

[15] Letter of Aristeas, 128-171, in Charlesworth, II, 21-24.

[16] M. Douglas, *Purity and Danger* (RKP, London, 1966), ch. 1-3.

[17] D. N. Fewell, and D. M. Gunn, *Gender, Power and Promise*, 102-8; Melcher, Op. cit.

[18] Seow, Op. cit., 17-21.

CHAPTER FIVE

Homosexuality in the New Testament

Glenn Davies

The evidence of the New Testament affirms the creation intentions for humankind as set forth in the Old Testament. Man and woman, as image bearers of God, are created for sexual union in the context of marriage, which is the lifelong, exclusive union between a male and a female. While marriage is the norm, not everyone will enjoy the benefit of being married. Some will remain single, either by choice or circumstances. Moreover, the New Testament countenances no provision for any sexual activity outside of marriage, whether that activity be heterosexual or homosexual in nature. The prohibitions on homosexuality are not limited merely to cultic homosexuality or promiscuous homosexuality. Rather, Paul's condemnation of homosexual practice appears absolute. It is against nature for two women to be involved in sexual intercourse as it is for two men. In fact, Paul declares that such behaviour excludes one from an inheritance in the kingdom of God. However, this is not to suggest that homosexual behaviour is somehow more heinous than other sins. For all unrepented sin excludes one from God's kingdom. In this regard, homosexual activity is just one of a number of sins that are inconsistent and incompatible with the Christian life. The New Testament, accordingly, does not countenance the persecution of homosexuals that arises from a homophobia which does not recognise the validity and integrity of homosexuals as men and women made in the image of God.

However, it is not impossible, according to the apostle Paul, for homosexuals to change their behaviour. By God's grace, they can be set free from their sin and sanctified in the name of the Lord Jesus and in the power of the Holy Spirit. There is hope for those who want to live God's way. Fidelity to the teaching of the New Testament will always extend hope and mercy to all those who love God and seek to keep his commandments.

Jesus

The teaching of the New Testament concerning sexuality assumes the understanding of marriage as the bond between a man and a woman, in accordance with the creation accounts of Genesis 1-2. Jesus' teaching on this subject reinforces the permanency and exclusivity of the sexual bond between a man and a woman (Matt 5:27-32; 19:1-12). Moreover, Jesus condemns all kinds of sexual impurity as evils to be avoided, including *porneiai, moicheiai* and *aselgeia* (Mark 7:20-23). The third term in this list suggests sexual licence or debauchery beyond the norm. Otto Bauernfeind[1] suggests it characterises Sodom and Gomorrah (citing 2 Pet 2:7) and the pagan world generally (Eph 4:19), with a special sense of sexual excess (Rom 13:13; 2 Cor 12:21; 2 Pet 2:2,18). Although it may not be possible to establish a specific reference to homosexual practice, the semantic range of *aselgeia* is inclusive of homosexual practice.

Jesus does not specifically address the question of homosexuality, but two points are worthy of attention. First, in the discussion of divorce in Matthew 19:1-12, the disciples' response to Jesus' high standards concerning marriage is to question whether it is better not to marry at all. However, Jesus' reply suggests that apart from marriage, the only other viable state is celibacy. Such celibacy may be the result of one being born a eunuch (the impotent), being made a eunuch (the castrated) or making a voluntary decision not to marry. It would, therefore, appear that Jesus did not contemplate homosexual union as a viable alternative of sexual expression for those who would be members of the kingdom of God. On the contrary, he reaffirmed and reinforced the teaching of the Old Testament with respect to sexual union (Matt 19:4-5; cf. 5:17).

Second, Jesus affirmed loving relationships between his disciples. Apart from the oft-cited commandment to love one another (John 13:34), Jesus also evidenced a special love relationship with other men. Lazarus is described as one whom Jesus loved (John 11:36); a special relationship is evident between Jesus and the trio of Peter, James and John; and the author of John's Gospel also describes himself as the 'disciple whom Jesus loved' (John 13:23; 19:26; 22:7; 21:20). Moreover, Jesus described his followers as 'friends', suggesting a greater degree of intimacy than that conveyed by the term 'servants'

(John 15:15). Although there is no warrant to infer any sexual union by such descriptions of intimacy, it is important to note that the Gospel records do give ample testimony to the promotion of genuine, loving and caring relationships between people, beyond the marriage bond.[2]

Paul

When we turn to the Pauline writings, we find specific references to the practice of homosexuality and, in each instance, the behaviour is viewed negatively. In Romans 1:26-27, Paul describes the kind of behaviour that is characteristic of the wicked, those who by their wickedness suppress the truth. The central concern of Paul's indictment of the wicked, however, is their rejection of God the creator. This rejection is exemplified by idolatry and results in God giving them up to all kinds of aberrant behaviour. Such behaviour includes a range of sins listed in verses 28-32, as well as that of homosexual practice discussed in verses 26-27. Homosexual behaviour, therefore, is not singled out above all others as worthy of special condemnation. Nonetheless, same-sex union is, according to the apostle, unnatural (*para physin*); by way of contrast, sexual relations between a man and a woman are natural (*physikê*). In verse 26 Paul highlights the dishonour of sexual acts that are contrary to the created order of male/female relationships.[3] He first makes mention of sexual intercourse between females,[4] and then draws attention in greater detail to similar homosexual activity between men. Such same-sex activity is part of God's judgment upon the wicked, whether they be Jew or Gentile, in that they have rejected the one true God.

The depiction of homosexual activity as 'against nature' (*para physin*) is, according to John Boswell, not a generalised statement about all homosexuality, but a reference to homosexual behaviour between heterosexual males.[5] For them it would be against nature, but not for those with a homosexual orientation. However, such a distinction is difficult to maintain in a first-century world, which knew nothing of the concept of describing homosexuality as a condition as opposed to a behaviour (compare fornication or adultery). It is against nature because it is against God's created order for human beings ('contrary to the intentions of the creator', Cranfield, 125).[6] Similarly, despite the attempts by some to deduce a philosophy of natural law, it is more likely that Paul was following the principles laid down in the Old Testament which prescribe marriage between a man and a woman as the only appropriate context for sexual union.

As B G Webb says:

> So *physis*, 'nature', in this context clearly denotes the world as God has made it, the created order. Paul has something more in mind than custom. He is appealing to what, in terms of the Bible's own theology, is prior to all culture: the will of God for human relationships expressed in the way he made us 'from the beginning' (Matt 19:4). Again we are back at Genesis 1-2.[7]

Nonetheless, it is also important to note that we all share in the fallenness of this present world order. For that reason, homosexual behaviour is not more heinous than other sins, which reflect the world in opposition to God. Accordingly, there is no justification for the persecution of such persons, who still bear the image of God, despite their sinful behaviour.

As Helmut Thielicke so long ago observed:

> The predisposition itself, the homosexual potentiality as such, dare not be any more strongly depreciated than the status of existence which we all share as men in the disordered creation that exists since the Fall. Consequently, there is not the slightest excuse for maligning the constitutional homosexual morally or theologically. We are all under the same condemnation and each of us has received his 'share' of it. In any case, from this point of view the homosexual share of that condemnation has no greater gravity which would justify any Pharisaic feelings of self-righteousness and integrity on the part of us 'normal' persons.[8]

A second reference to homosexual practice is found in a catalogue of vices in 1 Corinthians 6:9-10. In this list Paul describes those persons who will be excluded from the kingdom of God. Such persons are generally described as the wicked or unrighteous (*adikioi*), and then specifically included are the sexually immoral (*pornoi*), adulterers (*moichoi*), male prostitutes (*malakoi*) and homosexual offenders (*arsenokoitai*). Gordon Fee comments:

> The word *malakoi* has the basic meaning of 'soft' (cf. Matt 11:8; Luke 7:25), but became a pejorative epithet for men who were 'soft' or 'effeminate', most likely referring to the younger, 'passive' partner in a pederastic relationship — the most common form of homosexuality in the Greco-Roman world.[9]

Yet, since *malakos* was not the usual word for such a person,[10] Fee admits to some difficulty in being certain of its designation in this list, if it were not for the appearance of the following word *arsenokoitai.*[11] This is the first time the word appears in preserved literature, and has most likely been coined by Paul to describe the sexual union of two males (cf. *arsenes en arsesin,* Rom 1:27): a compound of male and intercourse (literally 'bed').[12] The LXX of Leviticus 18:22 (*meta arsenos ou koiméthésé koitén gynaikeian*) is the most likely source for Paul's neologism which, for both Old Testament Israel and new covenant Corinth, was something to be avoided by the people of God. Although Paul does not reflect upon any homosexual orientation of the person as such, what he does make plain is that those who practise homosexual acts, along with those who practise other forms of sexual immorality, will be excluded from the kingdom of God (1 Cor 6:10).[13] In a similar vein, Paul's instructions to Timothy indicate that the *arsenokoitai* (those who commit acts of homosexual behaviour) behave contrary to sound doctrine and contrary to the gospel (1 Tim 1:10-11). As Greg Bahnsen concludes:

> In ancient culture homosexuality was commonplace with certain distinctions customarily drawn between homosexuality as an ideal expression of love (e.g. in Plato's *Symposium*) or as an aid to military prowess (e.g., in Spartan propaganda) and homosexuality in the form of prostitution or indiscriminate infatuation. The one was encouraged, the other discouraged. By contrast, Paul, who was well versed in the culture of his day, drew no such distinctions but categorically condemned homosexuality without exception.[14]

Earlier in his letter to the Corinthians (chapter 5), Paul wrote of his outrage upon hearing that one of the members of the congregation was living with his father's wife. Although Paul argues that such behaviour was not even found among the pagans, it is universally recognised that his ethical stance is governed by the prohibitions of Leviticus 18:7-8. Such prohibitions are still in force under the new covenant.[15] Paul does not explore the level of commitment of the couple involved. He does not examine the evidence as to whether they truly love one another. In the face of such strong apostolic denunciation, there is no defence — it is condemned by God and requires the church to take action against it.

Nonetheless, it ought also to be noted that Paul does not consider that homosexual activity is so ingrained in a person's behaviour that there is no escape. The triune God is able to wash, sanctify and justify in the name of the Lord Jesus and by the Spirit of God. 'That is what some of you were', Paul reminds the Corinthians (1 Cor 6:11). A history of homosexual behaviour, therefore, does not prevent a person from coming to Christ. Yet it is also true that homosexual behaviour should not continue for the person converted to Christ. This is not to suggest that such persons will be free from all temptations and inclinations to revert to homosexual conduct. However, as in all cases of temptation to sin, there is a way of escape for the disciple of Christ (1 Cor 10:13).[16]

Moreover, those who once took part in homosexual behaviour are not to be shunned because of their past offences. On the contrary, like all other sinners who have been saved by grace, they are to be welcomed as part of the body of Christ (Rom 15:7; 2 Cor 2:5-11).[17]

Jude

The reference to *sarkos heteras* in Jude 7 could, as has been argued by John Dunnill above, refer to miscegenation, the (unnatural) union of angels and humans. However, one cannot be dogmatic about this interpretation. Apart from alternative interpretations of Genesis 6:4, it is to be noted that Jude accuses not only Sodom of 'other flesh' activity, but also the surrounding towns. Even if the sin of the city of Sodom was an attempt to have intercourse with angels (did they know of the angelic origin of these strangers?), we are hard pressed to find evidence of angel/human union occurring in the surrounding towns. Moreover, the men of Sodom did not have intercourse with the angels. Certainly there was the sin of lack of hospitality, but it is also the sin of sexual immorality (*ekporneuein*), embracing a wide range of sexual misconduct, which is condemned by the writer. Nonetheless, if Jude had wanted to single out homosexual activity as a specific sin, he could easily have done so by the use of a more specific word. The fact that he did not prevents us from drawing any specific application from this text to the issue of homosexuality. All that can be said is that sexual immorality was part of the sin of the people of Sodom, who thereby serve as an example of those who suffer the punishment of eternal fire (cf. 2 Pet 2:6).

Summary

The teaching of the New Testament concerning sexual union between humans is consistent with the teaching of the Old Testament. The male-female union within the bond of marriage is the only sexual union sanctioned by God. The New Testament writers regularly cite occurrences of sexual immorality in the Old Testament as behaviour to be avoided. However, within this strict moral guideline, the New Testament also acknowledges the weakness of the flesh and the power of God's grace. While homosexual activity is clearly described by the apostle Paul as sin, it is not the only sin, nor the worst sin. There is no justification, therefore, in persecuting homosexuals in the name of Christian piety.

Christians will never be free from sin in this world. Occasions of homosexual behaviour do not, therefore, exclude one from the kingdom of God any more than occasions of theft or murder. What is imperative for Christians, however, is the acknowledgment that such acts are sinful and deserve God's judgment. Unless they repent of all sinful activity, they will be excluded from the kingdom of God. God's grace is sufficient to renew and sanctify all who turn to Christ, even those who fall into sin, time and time again. However, for those who choose to disobey God's commandments wilfully and deliberately, there no longer remains a sacrifice for sins (Heb 10:26). The Christian faith will be true to the New Testament when it affirms both the purity of God's ways and the forgiveness that is available to those who truly repent.

Endnotes

[1] *TDNT*, 1., 490.

[2] The reference to the centurion whose servant was very dear (*entimos*) to him (Luke 7:2) is a reflection of the honour in which the centurion held his servant (or the value he was to him). However, it would be straining the text to consider that the description of 'being dear' suggested the existence of a sexual relationship between the two men. Cf J. Duncan M. Derrett, *Law in the New Testament* (Darton, Longman & Todd, London, 1970), 174.

[3] 'The use of the adjectives meaning 'female' and 'male', rather than the words *gunê* and *anêr*, is appropriate here, since it is the sexual differentiation as such on which attention is specially concentrated (cf. Gen 1:27; Mat 19:4=Mk 10:6; Gal 3:28).' Cranfield, 125.

[4] The use of *chrêsis* for sexual relations is well attested. (BAG, 894).

[5] J Boswell, *Christianity, Social Tolerance and Homosexuality* (Chicago University Press, Chicago, 1980), 110-12. L. William Countryman extends Boswell's thesis with a more detailed examination of the terminology of Romans 1:26-27, deducing that Paul is using same-sex union as an example of Gentile 'uncleanness' which suggests a cultic distinction rather than a moral distinction. For a convincing rebuttal of this view, see T. E. Schmidt, 'Romans 1:26-27 – The Main Text in Context', *Striving for Gender Identity: Homosexuals and Christian Counseling. A Workbook for the Church*, C R Vonholdt, ed.,(Reichenberg Fellowship, Reichelsheim, 1996), 36-59. Cf R. B. Hays, 'Relations Natural and Unnatural: A Response to John Boswell's Exegesis of Romans 1', *Journal of Religious Ethics*, 14 (1986), 184-215; J. B. De Young, 'The Meaning of "Nature" in Romans 1 and Its Implications for Biblical Perspectives of Homosexual Behavior', JETS, 31 (1988), 429-47.

[6] LSJ explain *para* as having three main senses: I. *Beside, near, by*; II. *along*; III. *Past, beyond.* The idea of 'contrary to' is located under III. Their entries under III suggest a sequence of development along the lines: *past, beyond...over and above...in excess of... in transgression of, in violation of.* This is similar to the idea of 'trans' in transgress, i.e., 'to go across/past/beyond the bounds of', etc. (Latin *trans = across*). Note Cranfield's reference to the use of *para* plus the accusative (in reference to v 25) as giving the meaning of 'rather than', 'in preference to', 'instead of' (124). For further references to the use of *para physin* in contemporary literature, see the articles by Schmidt, Hays and De Young above.

7 B. G. Webb, 'Homosexuality in Scripture', *Theological and Pastoral Responses to Homosexuality*, B. G. Webb, ed., (Open Book, Adelaide, 1994), 87. Although J A Fitzmyer considers Paul's thinking to be

coloured by Hellenistic philosophy, 'in the context of vv 19-23, "nature" also expresses for him [Paul] the order intended by the Creator, the order seen in the function of sexual organs themselves, which were ordained for an expression of love between man and woman and for the procreation of children', in *Romans* (Doubleday, New York/London, 1992), 286. See also the insightful analysis of G Bahnsen, *Homosexuality: A Biblical View* (Baker, Grand Rapids 1978), 53-61.

[8] H. Thielicke, *The Ethics of Sex*, J W Doberstein, trs. (James Clarke & Co., London, 1964), 283.

[9] G. D. Fee, *The First Epistle to the Corinthians* (Eerdmans, Grand Rapids, 1987), 243; so also C. K. Barrett, *A Commentary on the First Epistle to the Corinthians* (Harper & Row, New York, 1980), 140. More generally, Dennis Prager states: 'Indeed, for all intents and purposes, Judaism may be said to have invented the notion of homosexuality, for in the ancient world sexuality was not divided between heterosexuality and homosexuality. That division was the Bible's doing. Before the Bible, the world divided sexuality between penetrator (active partner) and penetrated (passive partner),' 'Judaism's Sexual Revolution', *Striving for Gender Identity: Homosexuals and Christian Counseling. A Workbook for the Church*, C R Vonholdt, ed. (Reichenberg Fellowship, Reichelsheim, 1996), 17. See also Bahnsen, 50.

[10] The pejorative sense of the word has been found in a third century BC papyrus from Egypt (P. Hib. I (1906) 54, reproduced by A. Deissmann, *Light from the Ancient East*, L.R.M. Strachan, trs., (G.H. Doran Co., New York, 1927, 164). In a letter to Ptolemaeus, a police official, Demophon, a wealthy Egyptian, writes: 'Send us also Zenobius, the effeminate, with tabret and cymbals and rattles. For the women have need of him at the sacrifice'. Deissmann comments: 'The word [*malakos=effeminate*] is no doubt used in its secondary (obscene) use, as by St. Paul in 1 Cor 6:9. It is an allusion to the foul practices by which the musician eked out his earnings'. In Modern Greek the word *malakos* also describes a person easily manipulated. However, the sexual connotations of the word group can be seen in the contemporary translations of *malakia* (masturbation) and *malaka* (wanker).

[11] The 1946 edition of the RSV translated the two Greek words by the one English word 'homosexuals' and, in the second edition (1971), by the phrase 'sexual perverts', whereas the NEB (1961) chose the phrase 'homosexual perversion'. Most other translations use two different words, e.g., 'male prostitutes, homosexual offenders' (NIV); 'self indulgent, sodomites' (JB); 'male prostitutes, sodomites' (NRSV).

[12] Note the use of the word *paidophthoros* ('corrupter of boys') which, while not used by the New Testament writers, is found in Barnabas, Justin Martyr, Clement of Alexander and other classical writers.

[13] In Paul's extensive discussions concerning singleness, marriage and divorce in 1 Corinthians 7, it is clear that he, like Jesus, only contemplates two states of life: either as a married person, entailing an exclusive sexual union between husband and wife; or as a single person, living a celibate life.

[14] Bahnsen, 50.

[15] The applicability of these prohibitions has long been recognised by Anglicans, as evidenced by the printing of the Table of Kindred and Affinity in the Book of Common Prayer.

[16] Of course, knowing the way of escape and choosing it are not synonymous (Gal 5:16-26). However, the distinguishing mark of Christians is that they recognise sin to be sin, even though they may still succumb to temptation. For a recent clinical approach to the opportunities of change for male homosexuals, see Joseph Nicolosi, *Reparative Therapy of Male Homosexuality: A New Clinical Approach* (Jason Aronson Inc., Northvale, NJ/London, 1997).

[17] Christian organisations such as Courage (Roman Catholic), Exodus Ministries (Interdenominational) and Sydney Liberty (Interdenominational) specialise in assisting those homosexuals who want to change their lifestyle.

Bibliography

Books and articles

Bahnsen, G. *Homosexuality: A Biblical View.*
Grand Rapids: Baker, 1978.

Boswell, J. *Christianity, Social Tolerance and Homosexuality.*
Chicago: University Press, 1980.

Countryman, L. W. *Dirt, Greed and Sex.*
Philadelphia: Fortress, 1988.

Cranfield, C. E. B. *A Critical and Exegetical Commentary on the Epistle to the Romans, vol 1,* ICC.
Edinburgh: T & T Clark, 1975.

De Young, J. B. 'The Meaning of "Nature" in Romans 1 and Its Implications for Biblical Perspectives of Homosexual Behavior', *JETS 31* (1988), 429-47.

Fee, G. D., *The First Epistle to the Corinthians.* NIC.
Grand Rapids: Eerdmans, 1987.

Fitzmyer, J. A, *Romans.* Anchor Bible.
New York/London: Doubleday, 1992.

Hays R. B. 'Relations Natural and Unnatural: A Response to John Boswell's Exegesis of Romans 1', *Journal of Religious Ethics* 14 (1986), 184-215.

Nicolosi, J. *Reparative Therapy of Male Homosexuality: A New Clinical Approach.*
Northvale, NJ/London: Jason Aronson Inc, 1997.

Prager, D. 'Judaism's Sexual Revolution', *Striving for Gender Identity: Homosexuals and Christian Counseling. A Workbook for the Church.*
C R Vonholdt, ed. Reichelsheim: Reichenberg Fellowship, 1996, 14-27.

Schmidt, T. E. 'Romans 1:26-27 – The Main Text in Context', *Striving for Gender Identity: Homosexuals and Christian Counseling. A Workbook for the Church*, C. R. Vonhold, ed.
Reichelsheim: Reichenberg Fellowship, 1996, 36-59.

Schmidt, T. E. *Straight or Narrow? Compassion and Clarity in the Homosexuality Debate.*
Leicester: IVP, 1995.

Scroggs, R. *The New Testament and Homosexuality. Contextual Background for Contemporary Debate.*
Philadelphia: Fortress, 1983.

Thielicke, H. *The Ethics of Sex*, J W Doberstein, ed.
London: James Clarke & Co., 1964.

Webb, B. G. 'Homosexuality in Scripture', *Theological and Pastoral Responses to Homosexuality.* Explorations 8.
Adelaide: Openbook, 1994, 65-103.

Wold, D. J. *Out of Order. Homosexuality in the Bible and the Ancient Near East.*
Grand Rapids: Baker, 1998.

CHAPTER SIX

Natural Law and Homosexuality

Cathy Thomson and *Don Edwards*

Our purpose in this paper is to examine whether — and, if so, in what ways — taking account of natural law contributes to a Christian understanding of homosexuality. This involves an inquiry into the value of natural law now and its applicability to sexual morality. It transpires that it also leads into an investigation of how natural law relates to Scripture, and how current concerns with what is 'natural' might affect Christian attitudes to homosexuality.

What is natural law?

Johannes Gründel has spoken of natural law as 'the order of things assigned to man by his creator for the development of his human qualities. This order is to be rationally known and used as the basis for free action.'[1] Gründel goes on to say that the function of the study of natural law is to describe the dignity of the person, human rights, and give them validity in social life.[2] Charles E. Curran goes so far as to claim that, from the viewpoint of moral theology or Christian ethics, anyone who admits human reason as a source of moral wisdom adopts a natural law perspective.

David Brown has argued helpfully that natural law is based on the view that human nature has been so fashioned by God that it is only by leading a moral life that certain basic demands of this nature can be satisfactorily realised. 'Natural law is thus the attempt to read off from those basic demands of human nature what the moral imperatives set by God in creating man might be.'[4] This, of course, leaves open what might be discerned to be the moral life in particular circumstances.

Karl Barth has put forward this view:

> By 'natural law' we mean the embodiment of what humanity is alleged to regard as universally right and wrong, as necessary, permissible and forbidden 'by nature', that is, on any conceivable premise. It has been connected with a natural revelation of God, that is, with a revelation known to humanity by natural means.[5]

The figure of Thomas Aquinas looms large in the development of natural law within Christianity. Clearly when he posited a natural law based on Augustinian theology and Aristotelian philosophical categories, his main purpose was to affirm that there was indeed an eternal law (a law that is of God – 'eternal, objective and universal'[6]); that human beings have that law inscribed on their hearts; and that they are capable of knowing that law through conscience and the exercise of reason. Human beings by their nature are thus understood to be capable of participating in this eternal law of God which, in Thomistic terms, is understood to be a reliable source of objective truth. Theoretically, then, under the aegis of natural law and by the proper use of reason, all people ought to be led to the same apprehension of eternal truth.

It is interesting that the word 'natural' with respect to natural law primarily refers to the faculty of reason, which was understood to be natural within each human being, and which would lead them to a full participation in the fundamental truths about God and about human existence. It is undeniable that, if these 'truths' are held to be present, they have moral significance for the individual who apprehends them. Indeed, one can argue by implication that the gnoseological dimension of natural law (its affirmation of the human ability to apprehend eternal truth) has, as a logical concomitant, an ontological dimension, namely that there are acts (or 'behaviours', to use a more contemporary word) that have a quality of either naturalness or unnaturalness about them,[7]... and, by extension, that there are acts which are intrinsically good or evil.

Natural law: a critical evaluation

However, three less-than-sure presuppositions undergird this proposal: firstly, that it is valid to make the leap from natural law to a claim for 'naturalness'/'unnaturalness' in terms of what does or does not truly pertain to human nature in a scientific sense; secondly, that it is appropriate to make the transition from general moral standards that represent a 'consciousness' almost, to a set of valorisations and prohibitions with respect to particular acts; and thirdly, that the 'natural' is coextensive with the good; the 'unnatural' with the bad.

Joseph Boyle, a prominent Catholic theologian, attempts to answer the first case, that it is valid to make the leap from natural law to a claim for 'naturalness'/'unnaturalness'. Boyle suggests that this is not a valid move because the objectivity claimed for natural law as a standard or norm written on the human heart is derived qualitatively from its originating within God's own truth, and that it is not the same kind of objectivity that is relied upon in empirical processes which may be aimed at the establishment of a clear understanding of human nature. He maintains that 'knowing the natural law, therefore, has little similarity with knowing the laws of nature in scientific inquiry'.[8]

It is now necessary to answer the second case: that it is appropriate to make the transition from general moral standards to a set of valorisations and prohibitions with respect to particular acts. Aquinas himself, it can be argued, never intended his writings on natural law to be used in the development of definitive moral stances on a range of specific human acts or practices. He clearly understood natural law as that which 'suffices for the ordering of all human affairs', so that 'any human law is needless'.[9] Thomas Gilbey emphasises the distinction between reason and particular rules for conduct:

> Law is here taken in no limited legalistic sense, as though good morals were conformity to a pattern for conduct imposed by human authority, civil or ecclesiastical, or to developed social custom. It is taken according to its specific sense in philosophical theology, namely an ordinance of reason, for the common good, made by the ruling authority, and promulgated to its subjects.[10]

Aquinas did, however, develop some primary propositions, which led to the establishment of general standards for human moral thought and action. These can be summarised as follows: that 'all human beings seek to preserve their own lives, procreate and educate their young, live in society with others, and know the truth about God'.[11]

The difference seems to reside in Aquinas' desire to understand natural law inductively rather than deductively: namely to begin with the human faculties, as the locus of exploration of divine truth, and not to move from general truths to particular practices. This conflicts with the tendency within later theology to use the term 'natural law' as a synonym for formulated Christian moral teaching. It can be seen that in order to establish such teaching, natural law was utilised deductively: which means that general rules were derived from the primary propositions expressed above, namely that it is wrong to take a life, that procreation is the only proper purpose of sex etc., and that these were then applied to particular cases — which, in turn, led to the understanding that there are human acts which, irrespective of circumstances, are inherently evil (e.g. abortion).

Notwithstanding the above arguments against the misapplication of 'objectivities' and against the wrong-headed move from the general to the particular, it is clear that a fixed moral concomitant of natural law is prevalent within Catholic moral theology, and that it is discernible from the scholastic era to the present day; it is this very moral law which clearly undergirds the Roman Catholic approach to ruling on questions of sexual ethics such as abortion, contraception, and the validity of homosexual acts.

However one more case calls for an answer. Caught up into the web of forming Christian moral theology is the presupposition that the 'natural' is necessarily the good; the 'unnatural', the bad.

Janet Radcliffe Richards examines closely what she calls the issue of the 'natural' and, in doing so, she acknowledges indebtedness to the work of the philosopher John Stuart Mill. She firstly tries to ascertain the character of the natural, and concludes that this is an impossible task. Is the natural to be derived from the nature of an entity uninfluenced by anything outside of it? If this is so, Richards argues, we have merely established an absurdity, as no such uninfluenced entity exists; if we seek a definition of the natural by setting it against the miraculous or supernatural, there is no possibility of this sense of the natural being invoked as the basis of moral decision-making, as humans have no choice but to act 'naturally'. Alternatively, if 'natural' means that which is set over against the human, i.e., that which 'takes place without the voluntary and intentional agency of man'[12], the natural is a self-defeating concept, once more unable to be the basis of moral decision-making, which does depend on the agency of human consciousness.

Well then, is it possible to 'follow' or 'copy' nature? Richards thinks yes, but that this will scarcely lead human beings unequivocally to the good. Again quoting Mill, she suggests that 'In sober truth, nearly all the things which men (sic) are hanged or imprisoned for doing to one another are nature's everyday performances.'[13]

Richards identifies three traditional expressions of a rationale for desiring that human beings act according to nature. These are that it is wrong to upset the balance of nature, wrong to invoke the wrath of God, wrong to make people frustrated and unhappy. However, Richards indicates that even if we accept these attempts to provide a rationale to justify acting according to nature, we are still left with the question of 'how' to do so. Epistemologically, this reverts back to the previous question of what the 'natural' or 'nature' is. It is this kind of circularity which undermines any attempt to utilise ideas of the 'natural' to justify or condemn within a Christian moral theology specific human acts or practices.

Richards is thrown back to the conclusions of Hume, Mill and Moore that the 'natural' can mean many different things, and that it is impossible on the basis of any one of these to provide guidance on how to distinguish good from bad. She argues, further, that since the idea of the 'natural' usually implies an intention of a moral agent to preserve a certain attitude or practice from undue intervention or influence of outside factors, this practice of intentionality determines that 'what is to count as natural or unnatural is entirely context dependent.'[14] The natural can, therefore, in no wise be understood as implying the good.

It would seem that in the development of Christian moral theology, the 'natural', originally intended to refer to the inherent qualities of human conscience and reason, has been misappropriated to refer to specific human acts or practices, and that this transference of meaning has been less than true to Thomas Aquinas' original intention for the development of an idea of natural law.

It is very difficult now within Christian moral theology to use conceptions of the 'natural' as a foundation upon which to posit justification or condemnation of particular human acts or behaviours. The feminist revisionist approach to Christian ethics in the work of Lisa Sowle Cahill agrees with the assertion of Janet Radcliffe Richards that 'all claims about what is natural to persons arise out of limited, partisan and provisional experiences'.[15] And Cahill points out that, particularly in the area of the relationship between sex and gender, the ability to discern a clear law of nature has been radically called into question.[16]

It is important to take account of criticisms of a natural law approach to moral issues even from within traditions that have hitherto championed it. Though he goes on to question objections to natural law, Bruno Schüller begins his theological discussion with the comment that anyone these days who still resolutely supports the doctrine of natural law must be regarded, now even among Catholic theologians and jurists, as stuck behind the times or reactionary.[17] And of course there are theologians from other Christian traditions who also find a natural law approach far from compelling.

Stanley Hauerwas identifies a series of difficulties in the natural law starting point for ethics. For instance, he finds that it confuses the claim that Christian ethics is an ethic that we should and can commend to anyone with the claim that we can know the content of that ethic by looking at the human. It fails to appreciate that there is no actual universal morality; we live in a world of many moralities. It seems to entail a strong continuity between Church and world, and so fails to provide the critical perspectives the Church needs to recognise and deal with the challenges presented by our societies and the inherent violence of our world. It ignores the narrative character of Christian convictions. And it attempts to coerce those who disagree with us, since its presumptions lead us to believe that we always occupy the high ground in any dispute.[18]

Hauerwas sharpens this critique by suggesting that part of the difficulty with the moral reasoning supporting some of the Church's sexual ethics is that by attempting to give them a natural law basis devoid of their theological basis, they appear arbitrary and irrational and so require authoritarian imposition.[19]

Hauerwas finds the traditional distinction between natural knowledge of God and revelation to be misleading. All knowledge of God is at once natural and revelatory. But, like all knowledge, it depends on analogical control. And analogies derive their intelligibility from paradigms that draw on narratives for their rational display. Hauerwas adds that our knowledge of God is also moral. For instance, we aver that God's perfection is that of a being with complete integrity. There is no underside to God's intentions. 'That God is moral in this sense is the basis for our confidence that we are more nearly ourselves when we are like God. Christian morality, therefore, cannot but require us to become faithful imitators of God.'[20]

Hauerwas argues that we Christians are not called to be 'moral', but faithful, to the true story, the story that we are creatures under the lordship of a God who wants nothing more than our faithful service. By such service we become not 'moral', but holy. He points out that the New Testament is not self-interpreting. Each of the four Gospels has its own particular emphasis. Interpretation requires not only careful historical research but, even more, our willingness to be morally formed in a manner appropriate to the claims of those texts. The diversity of Scripture is actually at the heart of Christian life insofar as it requires that we be a community capable of allowing those differing texts to be read among us with authority. To know what Scripture means finally is to look to those who have most nearly learned to exemplify its demands through their lives.[21]

One thing that militates against a natural law approach in our time is the sense that it tends to make universal claims that fail to take serious account of context and particularity. This is brought out in Hauerwas' critique: it fails to appreciate that there is no actual universal morality; we live in a world of many moralities.[22]

Possibilities in a natural law approach now

This critical evaluation of natural law does not mean that it has ceased to have relevance for moral theology. Clearly, its claims need to be examined; yet there may be value in considering it along the lines Aquinas intended.

Gründel affirms the Church's right to speak authoritatively in questions of natural law, but observes that the theologian needs to examine the notion of nature supposed in such declarations and test its validity in the light of the results of the human sciences. Schüller also points to the continuing significance of natural law. He finds the revealed moral message does not render reflection and argumentation based on natural law superfluous, but makes them required. "The gospel as criterion of value offers no alternative to knowledge of the moral based on natural law because there can be no such alternative."[24]

Obviously there are differing views on the value and applicability of natural law in recent Christian moral theology. And this debate may have implications for Anglicans. Brown argues that, in so far as Anglicanism has had any moral theology of its own, all its leading figures have adopted a Catholic approach, irrespective of whether they were Catholic in their general doctrinal disposition. The reason for this he finds, hardly surprisingly, in the influence of Aquinas.[25] Brown himself finds doubts concerning reliance on natural law and conscience to be unfounded. Contrary to common misconceptions, natural law has nothing to do with law in the sense of specific injunctions to action, or with nature in the wider sense. It has to do with God's fashioning of human nature in such a way that realisation of this nature requires leading a moral life.[26] Not all Anglicans would agree with Brown on the place of natural law within moral theology, but he puts a case for taking the natural law tradition seriously within Anglicanism.

One strength of a natural law approach is its positing a point of contact between Christian morality and other moralities by which people live. Christians may well cooperate with other people of good will in seeking the good of a society. There can be value in seeking common ground in matters of morality, as well as indicating where Christianity is distinctive in such matters. A view of natural law that does not over-generalise and does not claim too much can still have possibilities.

Aquinas has observed that the first principle for the practical reason is based on the meaning of good, namely that it is what all things seek after. And so the first commandment of law is 'that good is to be sought and done, evil to be avoided'. All other commands of natural law are based on this. 'Accordingly, then, natural-law commands extend to all doing or avoiding of things recognised by the practical reason of itself as being human goods'.[27] It may be that if we hold to natural law now, it will not be concerned with a detailed list of prescriptions.

William Temple argues that we find in our experience of the world in some situations an obligation to act, or not to act, in certain ways. This sense of obligation is uncompromising. The types of conduct are different in different regions or in different periods of history. This variety has sometimes been used to discredit the consciousness of obligation. The conscience certainly derives much of its actual content from its social environment. But this does not account for the imperative note in the sense of obligation. And the most imperative demands of conscience are demands that the individual should defy their social context.[28] The emphasis here on obligation may indicate a way of taking up an element of natural law theory without denying or overlooking the diversity in different cultural settings and life experiences.

Hauerwas concedes that emphasis on the distinctiveness of Christian ethics does not deny that there are points of contact between Christian ethics and other forms of the moral life. He contends, though, that while such points frequently exist, they are not sufficient to provide a basis for a 'universal' ethic grounded in human nature *per se.* Attempts to secure such an ethic result in a minimalist ethic and often one that gives support to forms of cultural imperialism.[29] Hauerwas and Charles Pinches also observe that learning to note what marks Christians off from others does not prevent communication and genuine dialogue, but creates its very possibility.[30]

John Macquarrie goes further than Hauerwas in seeking a common ground between Christian and non-Christian morals. He finds in what has been called natural law (for want of a better name) a firm basis for moral cooperation and community between Christians and non-Christians. It allows us to see moral obligations in a new depth, as ontologically founded. It safeguards against moral subjectivism and encourages moral seriousness by locating the demand of moral obligation in the very way things are.

Cahill, too, maintains the value of natural law as a component of ethical discourse. She notes that it emphasises a human being's 'innate inclination towards what promotes human fulfilment.'[32] Thus it is of lasting value today in that it 'grounds an experiential morality while holding to an ideal of shared human truth, and manifests a confidence that God's will for persons is revealed in creation as an ongoing process of discovering God in human life.'[33] She also affirms the capacity of natural law morality to build a 'community of moral discourse that transcends cultures and unites individuals and societies.'[34]

Notwithstanding Cahill's cautious support of natural law as providing a basis for moral theology, she nevertheless acknowledges that the trend within Catholic moral theology of the past three decades has been towards establishing a moral foundation at once 'more biblical, more historically conscious, and in some ways more flexible.'[35] A feminist ethical stance with respect to the use of Scripture in determining ethical systems emphasises that Jesus' teachings may be at odds with 'the most obvious conclusions of rational, objective ethical teaching.'[36] (It could be argued that loving one's enemies challenges the rational ethical position of Just War.) Feminist ethics is also clear that the Bible takes sides. It suggests that Jesus establishes a radically inclusive community in which 'the sinner, the poor, the outcast and the marginal have a new place and are even preferred in God's eyes.'[37] Thus natural law is de-emphasised within feminist Catholic moral teaching, where the moral test of any teaching is the impact it has on people's lives.[38]

So, despite holding to natural law as valid for ethical discourse, Cahill nevertheless supports an ethical feminist stance that diverges in the direction of consequentialism. She is directly critical of certain aspects of natural law ethics such as its emphasis on the rational, and she emphasises the 'consciously experiential' within ethics, which implies there are sources of insight for ethics in addition to reason.[39]

It is problematic to find in natural law a detailed set of prescriptions holding good for all social and historical contexts. The criticisms made of such a proposal are telling. However, we may be able to argue with conviction that God has created us human beings in God's own image, and that, even in our sinfulness, we have some sense of an imperative to act in responsible ways in particular situations. As Christians we would hold that the imperative is to act in ways that are in keeping with the God who has made us. Of course, human beings often fail to live up to the demands placed on us.

Still, Christians and the Church do not always live up to the claims God makes on us through the incarnation, ministry, cross and resurrection of Jesus Christ, and the sending of the Spirit. This in itself does not disprove the transformation that life in Christ brings. Nor do our failures as human beings negate the imperative that being human brings with it. Augustine could speak of a *cor inquietum* in humanity.[40] And yet it is only in Christ that the heart finds peace.

Pannenberg speaks of an openness of humanity to the world, which signifies ultimately an openness to what is beyond the world, to God.[41] For him, human limitation can only be understood against the background of our constitutional openness. And our innate and implicit openness to God is present to the consciousness only in retrospect, in the light of historically concrete experience of God. As such, it underlies different forms of explicit belief, and is also a condition of the possibility of unbelief and existential closure against God.[42] It may be that we can also identify a 'moral' imperative in human beings. We dare not idealise this. It can be trivialised, distorted or ignored. Still, it is sometimes respected and acted on.

Hauerwas and Pinches are right in refusing to separate theology and ethics.[43] Speaking in terms of moral theology may help bring out the interrelatedness of theology and morals for Christians. It may also rule out conforming Christian morality and holiness to a general human morality. Still, many Christians seek points of contact with non-Christians. There can be significant cooperation in matters of morality, personal and social, and it is important to explore the grounds for such cooperation, as well as what limits might be set to it. Discussions among Christians and by Christians with non-Christians on matters such as this are pertinent to us as we engage with moral issues.

Scripture and natural law

As we examine natural law and attempt to discern whether it has anything to offer to a Christian understanding of homosexuality, one issue that arises concerns how it relates to Scripture.

It seems sometimes as if natural law and Scripture constitute alternative sources for moral theology. Basil Mitchell sees in those who rely on Scripture and those who rely on natural law 'two different streams of the tradition which do not always mingle'.[44]

There are many instances of approaches to ethics, both at a theoretical level and in relation to particular issues, that take account of Scripture but show little or no concern with natural law.

A very different approach is that of Gerard Hughes who, while not disputing the use of Christian tradition in ethics, seeks to dispute the claim that Christian revelation functions as the ultimate court of appeal in morals.[45] He contends that the problems of hermeneutics show that 'the application of the New Testament to our own ethical problems would be quite impossible in default of other moral assumptions which could be defended on independent grounds'.[46] In examining the way moral issues are introduced into the New Testament writings, he questions arguments for the individual moral assertions in the New Testament being salvation-truths rather than the opinions of the writers offered in the course of reinforcing the general truth that our moral behaviour is intimately connected with the Kingdom. Hughes does not suggest that a natural law theory of ethics, or indeed any moral philosophy, is independent of God and God's grace. However he does contend that such moral theory does not ultimately depend on knowledge of the way in which God has revealed Godself in Christ, as that knowledge is mediated to us by the tradition of Christian belief.[47]

Not all approaches set natural law and Scripture over against each other. Some find Scripture taking account of natural law. Schüller, for example, argues that 'if by natural law is understood the totality of ethical norms that can be known at least in principle in logical independence of Scripture', then Romans offers proof that such a natural law actually exists.[48] Alan F. Johnson finds warrant in both Old and New Testaments for believing that the authors either directly or indirectly taught that there is some sort of universally accessible moral knowledge of the divine will for humanity, at least in principle. There is also evidence the authors recognised that these moral principles are related to the way human beings are made and to the nature of human social relations.[49]

With respect to homosexuality in particular, there is pertinence in James Barr's conclusion from the terminology in Romans that for Paul, 'nature' is a theological criterion. Barr holds that Paul views homosexual relations as a climactic manifestation of evil. The reason he gives is not because they are forbidden by God or are disapproved in the Old Testament, though doubtless Paul thought both reasons to be valid and sufficient. The reason he actually gives is 'that these relations are against 'nature'.'[50] Barr finds a clear implication of a 'natural' order in creation that it is wrong to override.[51]

Others, too, find in Scripture an authoritative statement of what is natural, and specifically what is natural in terms of sexuality. Tony Higton, for example, finds grounds for distinguishing what is 'natural' from what is 'unnatural' in what Scripture says about creation and creation order. He argues that sexuality is created by God and is an aspect of creation that God called 'very good' (Gen 1:31). He adds that the regulation of sexual relations in marriage is a creation ordinance, and the most fundamental contradiction of the idea that homosexual practice is acceptable is found in the creation narratives. Similarly, in the context of a discussion of creation, Paul speaks of both female and male homosexual practice as contrary to nature.[52]

A detailed exposition of attitudes to sexuality in Scripture is not part of the brief of this paper. There is continuing value in the General Synod Doctrine Commission paper, *A Christian Discussion on Sexuality*, which examines the scriptural evidence and works with it in putting forward a view on human sexuality, including homosexuality.[53] It is good that that paper and more recent articles set homosexuality within the broader framework of human sexuality, and attempt to discern how in Scripture references to homosexuality relate to what is said about God's creation, human sinfulness and God's work of reconciliation in Jesus Christ. It is problematic at best to focus on homosexuality as being against nature while leaving aside other aspects of human existence which Scripture also identifies as out of keeping with our being created by God. For instance, Romans 1:26f. may well open up a discussion of what is natural and what is unnatural in relation to human sexuality, but this needs to be set in the context of 1:18-32 overall.

Theology requires interpretation of Scripture, and that involves relating Scripture to its own contexts and to the context of interpreters. In our setting, this can mean that natural law theories and attempts to define what is 'natural' through Scripture must ask what can and should be considered 'natural' now.

What counts as natural?

It is hardly controversial to suggest that in examining the question of homosexuality, Christian theology does well to take account of the natural and human sciences.[54] Many Anglicans would be in sympathy with Ann C. Lammers's claim that experience complicates necessarily the three mediating authorities in Anglican thought: Scripture, tradition and reason. Respect for the authority of experience in moral discourse entails attending to the findings of empirical science and the witness of subcommunities in the Church.[55] There is further support from another tradition for taking experience seriously. In his study of Job, Gustavo Gutiérrez finds that for Job a dividing line is drawn by personal experience, which sometimes brings a painfully acquired closeness to God that untouched theologians (Job's friends) do not know. Gutiérrez contends that the language we use depends on the situation we are in. 'Job's words are a criticism of every theology that lacks human compassion and contact with reality; the one-directional movement from theological principles to life really goes nowhere.'[56] A concern with results of research and practice is evident in *A Report on Homosexuality*, produced by the Diocese of Melbourne Social Questions Committee in 1971, which sought a consensus of professional opinion as to the incidence of homosexuality in its deliberations.[57]

Other disciplines cannot provide a ready resolution of difficulties confronting moral theology, but they provide important discussion partners. Of course, there are differences among researchers in similar fields; for instance, over essentialist and constructivist views of homosexuality.[58] There are divergences sometimes across fields as well.[59] Nevertheless, there is a multidisciplinary study involved here, and theology does well to be involved in it by listening and contributing.

Research over some decades suggests that a division of human sexuality into two or three categories (heterosexual, homosexual, with the addition of bi-sexual) is problematic. For one thing, it takes insufficient account of differences between men and women. It is more a matter of 'vague, permeable, and potentially shifting "locations" along the continuum'.[60] John P. De Cecco concludes that sexual orientation is 'a tapestry far richer and more intricate than we have imagined'.[61] He argues also that homosexuality is not limited to a small proportion of individuals, but seems to be an integral aspect of human sexuality.[62]

There is much scientific discussion about the causes of homosexuality, though there is by no means any common mind about the results or the value of the research at this point. Researchers point to many interacting factors. These may be identified as genetic and environmental or more fully biological, psycho-dynamic and environmental causes.[63]

Why causation occupies so much attention is addressed by Janis S. Bohan, who finds here remnants of the view of homosexuality (or homophilia, as she prefers to call it) as a disease. She herself finds an enormous array of elements that comprise sexual orientation, and so it is reasonable to expect that the origin and development of sexual orientation vary widely among people, with various components contributing differentially and at different times to the course of each person's evolution.[64]

Simon LeVay indicates how important and how dangerous such research into causality can be. It is a social and political enterprise, as well as a scientific one. Rightly or wrongly, it affects people's lives by influencing medicine, law, religious teaching and attitudes. He considers that attitudes toward gays and lesbians are inextricably tied up with beliefs about what causes them to be homosexual. This requires taking account of bias in scientific research, and also minimising the effects of bias.[65]

In terms of natural law approaches, causes of homosexual orientation can be related to whether such orientation is to be seen as 'natural' in some sense, or is purely the result of choice and so 'unnatural'. It would seem that there is an increased unwillingness among a number of researchers to speak of homosexual orientation as unnatural. Bohan, for instance, examines arguments that homosexuality does not occur in non-human species, does not lead to reproduction, and does not conform to the obvious intentions of the sexual organs. These arguments she considers flawed. Furthermore, arguments from evolutionary biology might now lead to a view of homosexuality as a variation in human experience that serves some purpose for the species, and so is natural.[66] LeVay examines possible occurrences of homosexuality in other species and suggests that bi-sexuality may be the predominant mode of animal sexuality. He finds scientific studies challenge one particular sense of the dogma that homosexual behaviour is 'against nature': 'the notion that it is unique to those creatures who, by tasting the fruit of the tree of knowledge, have alone become morally culpable'.[67]

Some Christians continue to argue that homosexuality is thoroughly unnatural. Evidence is sometimes presented to show that, with counselling and support, there are at least some Christian homosexuals who can change.[68] To be sure, there are questions about the effectiveness and even the ethics of attempts to cure or change homosexual orientation.[69]

There are other Christians who have come to a view that homosexuality is not at all unnatural, and argue that the Church should allow for and regulate the marriage of gay and lesbian couples.[70] This too provokes significant disagreement, as one might expect.

Between those two ends of the spectrum, there is a range of conclusions that Christians come to as they attempt to relate teaching from Scripture and tradition, and in some instances natural law, to our present context.

Higton is willing at least to consider the possibility that Paul in Rom 1:25 uses the word 'unnatural' in a relative sense, though he concludes that this would not in itself justify homosexual behaviour on the part of those for whom it was (relatively) natural. 'After all, there are various undesirable weaknesses and behaviour patterns which are 'natural' for some people, but are hardly justified morally.'[71]

On the other hand Cahill contends that in the case of homosexuality, only a nuanced judgment and not a simple condemnation or approval is possible. Heterosexual marriage is the normative context for sexual acts for the Christian. And yet it is possible to judge sexual acts in other contexts as non-normative, but objectively justifiable in the exceptional situation, including that of the confirmed homosexual.[72]

Basil Mitchell's discussion of an English Report on homosexuality has points of contact with Cahill's conclusions. Mitchell argues that natural law tradition is relevant to the discussion of homosexuality, because the question concerns the purpose of sexual relationships, and about this that tradition speaks. He notes that those who prepared the report reaffirmed an essentially traditional doctrine of marriage as providing the norm for sexual relations. This involved rejecting the claim of homosexual equality, and holding that it is wrong for anyone to engage in homosexual activities if he or she were capable of a normal heterosexual relationship. In going further, the Report is in line with other studies on ethical questions. There is a basic pattern of Christian tradition yielding a strong moral imperative, and then the question arising whether there can be any justifiable exceptions. In this case, the working party came to the conclusion that certain exceptions were permissible.[73] Criticisms of this report from various perspectives do not preclude its providing some help in taking further the discussion of issues under examination here.

There is need for continuing interaction between Christian moral theology and human and natural sciences on homosexuality, if Christianity is to speak with integrity and credibility on this question now. Stephen Barton adds a further dimension with his claim that the social sciences can help us see that conflicts about morality have a social function and that the moral imagination is an integral expression of how a group identifies itself.[74]

Issues natural law raises now for Christian views of homosexuality

Re-examining natural law in relation to human sexuality does not threaten theological convictions concerning the significance of heterosexual marriage between an adult man and an adult woman for the expression of sexuality among Christians. John R.W. Stott certainly argues persuasively for the centrality of marriage. If some of us nevertheless find ourselves not entirely in agreement with him in the way he expounds human sexuality, there is value in his refusal to single out homosexual intercourse for special condemnation.[75]

There is a significant debate going on in the Church concerning human sexuality, including homosexuality. This debate has risks attached to it. It could alienate and exclude people whose sexuality is presented as unacceptable. It can be seen as jeopardising our loyalty to the Gospel. It affects our identity as a Church and, as such, has implications for our unity. And yet it also involves shared reflection and a seeking together for what is God's will for us, even as we acknowledge how deep our differences may be.[76] We are not campaigning for state legislation against homosexual acts in private between consenting adults. We are discussing Christian morality: what might be encompassed within it and what may be excluded by it. We can agree that anyone with a homosexual orientation can be a Christian, and that being a Christian means for all of us the acceptance of moral demands, or arguably demands to be holy. On the other hand, we recognise how difficult Scripture, tradition and some accounts of natural law make it to allow for any expression of such an orientation within the life of the Church.

Given that this paper has a focus on natural law, two considerations arise at this point. The first is that an expression of what natural law contributes to any issue in a particular context requires examination of that context. The second is that taking account of natural law in our context requires an investigation not only of Scripture and tradition, but of the place of natural law in Scripture and tradition. It is worth looking more closely at each of these in turn.

First of all, in the Australian context, our theological stance is informed not only by Scripture and tradition, but also by pastoral practice, experience and engagement with insights from recent studies of humanity and human sexuality. This process can be painful as we have new evidence presented and, at times, somewhat unexamined viewpoints challenged. Viewpoints can harden when some people of homosexual orientation apparently prey on others who are uncertain of their own sexuality. And yet there are also encounters with close, loving relationships between single-sex couples who commit themselves to each other for life. Some of those in such relationships will tell us that they consider themselves irreversibly homosexual (though not by choice). In upholding marriage as fundamental to expressions of sexuality among human beings, at least some of us find ourselves compelled to admit the possibility of certain other expressions.

Secondly, the place of natural law in tradition, and particularly in that part of tradition that finds expression in the Christian canonical Scriptures, is significant to our present discussion. A digression may illustrate this. Barr has given attention to the 'ban' in the Old Testament, the ritual destruction of the population of conquered Canaanite cities. It is not certain that the ban (or holy war) was actually practised by Israel; the problem is that Scripture commends this ritual destruction, and no passage explicitly states disapproval of it or denies that it was commanded by God.[77] Barr goes on to say:

> It is here that a critical ethical voice can be heard: this cannot be justified as the picture of a moral deity. How can it be reconciled with what we otherwise know and believe of God? Quite possibly, natural theology or natural morality cannot settle the question: but they do succeed in insisting that the question should at least be raised. By contrast, biblical theology, through its general, if not universal, ignoring of natural theology, has led to a position where the issue is not raised at all...[78]

The pertinence of this digression is the fact that Leviticus not only forbids homosexual relations (18:22), but prescribes the death penalty for them (20:13). This aspect of the scriptural evidence seems not to play a large part in many of our Christian discussions of homosexuality. There is anecdotal evidence that some Christians are prepared to follow the injunction in Leviticus quite literally, but the notion is unthinkable and abhorrent to the vast majority in the Church, the Anglican Church included. This leaves open the question of what we are to do with this particular piece of scriptural evidence.

For Anglicans, Article VII of The Articles of Religion may point to a resolution of this issue. It says, in part:

> Although the Law given from God by Moses, as touching Ceremonies and Rites, do not bind Christian men, nor the Civil precepts thereof ought of necessity to be received in any commonwealth; yet notwithstanding, no Christian man whatsoever is free from the obedience of the Commandments which are called Moral.[79]

This could suggest that the moral commandment against homosexual relations holds good for us, while the death penalty can be omitted from our code of law. And there are doubtless other ways to solve this hermeneutical and practical problem. In any case, it is possible for Christians to continue to reject homosexual relations (perhaps while not seeking legal penalties for those who engage in them). It is possible also to accept people of homosexual or bisexual orientation and expect them to be celibate in the case of the former and to be celibate or to marry in the case of the latter.

Still, the moral conscience that now finds affronting the penalty Scripture imposes (and does not rescind) on those having homosexual relations may also feel compelled to examine closely the grounds for holding those relations to be unnatural or against God's will and so being liable to that penalty. Another possibility (in addition to those identified in the previous paragraph) is to hold marriage to be the norm for expressions of human sexuality within Christianity, but to allow for exceptions to the norm. This takes account of homosexual orientation apparently occurring naturally, or at least not being the conscious choice of many who are homosexual. It also asks what expressions of such orientation are permissible, and what are the limits to such expressions.

Barr himself asks bluntly whether the natural theology of the Bible is right. How did homosexual practices arise from idolatry?[80] Of course this is related to Barr's denial of any absolute distinction between revelation and natural theology. It is related also to his view that the Bible 'properly' is 'not revelation coming from God to humanity but the Church's (properly: Israel's and the Church's) response to and interpretation of that revelation'. And this response and interpretation 'derive from, and depend on, natural theology and other kinds of "natural" knowledge.'[81] As has become obvious, our differing views of Scripture play a major role in the ways we are prepared to proceed at this point.

Conclusion

If one agrees with the tendency within contemporary thought to deconstruct the concept of the 'natural', a result is that it becomes problematic to suggest that homosexuality *per se* can be coined either 'natural' or 'unnatural', either good or bad. Where such an evaluation is made, it is context-driven and cannot be regarded as an absolute.

Natural law in itself cannot provide clear, absolute and assured answers to the moral questions facing us. Perhaps it may speak, more or less adequately, of a moral imperative which is innate in the human person, but which finds expression and becomes effective only in concrete situations. That moral imperative may militate against engaging in promiscuity (heterosexual or homosexual), even if what constitutes promiscuity is found to vary in different settings. To 'use' another person for our own gratification is a misuse of our sexuality. It can militate against a heterosexual or bisexual person engaging in homosexual activity. However, if someone is innately homosexual, it is not self-evident that that imperative rules out a close exclusive relationship between two adults of the same sex. Where a person becomes a Christian, the moral imperative must come to terms with additional expectations and accountability within the community of the Church. The debate now is whether Christian norms of morality or holiness rule out any expression of homosexuality.

The following is a list of new emphases within Christian moral theology that impact on the Christian response to homosexuality:

- Natural law is still valued as that which emphasises the possibility of discovering God in an ongoing way in the life of the Christian person and community.
- The biblical basis for moral theology acknowledges Jesus' tendency to challenge accepted norms in the act of establishing a radical inclusive community in which the marginalised are shown special concern.
- The human consequences of ethical decisions have to be taken into account.
- Relationships, rather than isolated moral acts, need to be emphasised for moral decision-making.

One consequence of these more flexible approaches to Christian ethics is the suggestion that it is not necessarily inconsistent as a faith community to seek moral ideals whilst acknowledging that Jesus had a special concern to establish an inclusive community within which the marginalised were welcomed and respected. Also, that when the Church is attempting to develop moral teaching about sexuality, methodologically, there are grounds for contextualising moral acts and taking account of the relationships within which these 'acts' take place.

This new emphasis could facilitate the full inclusion of homosexual people in Christian communities; it could also lead to the emergence of a set of moral ideals consistent with the lives of faith of both heterosexual and homosexual Christians. This set of ideals could eradicate the anomalous situation which, it could be argued, exists at the moment, whereby at the level of moral discourse, homosexual Christians are held by the Church to be more accountable morally for their sexual acts than any heterosexual Christian. The establishment of new ideals founded on a principle of godly relationality means that all within the Body of Christ become accountable equally for the quality of their relationships.

The debate going on in the Church concerning sexuality, and homosexuality in particular, will require great sensitivity. Pastoral care for those who feel themselves the focus of attention, and for those who feel their Christian identity under threat, will be needed. Importantly, the St Andrew's Day Statement of 1995[82] affirms that, at the deepest ontological level, there is not 'a' homosexual or 'a' heterosexual, but 'there are human beings, male and female, called to redeemed humanity in Christ, endowed with a complex variety of emotional potentialities and threatened by a complex variety of forms of alienation.'[83] It is vital that we do not resort to abstractions as we explore how we can be true to our humanity, and to Scripture and tradition in bearing witness to God's will for human beings. We are speaking of and to real people who are loved and valued by God.

Endnotes

[1] 'Natural law', in *Encyclopedia of Theology: a Concise Sacramentum Mundi*, Karl Rahner, ed. (Burns and Oates, London, 1975), 1017.

[2] *Ibid.*

[3] 'Foreword' to *Moral Theology, no. 7,* Charles E. Curran and Richard A. McCormick, eds. (Paulist Press, New York, 1991, 1.

[4] *Choices: Ethics and the Christian* (Blackwell, Oxford, 1983), 31.

[5] 'The Christian Community and the Civil Community', in *Karl Barth: Theologian of Freedom,* Clifford Green, ed. (Fortress Press, Minneapolis, 1991), 276f.

[6] Joseph Boyle, 'Natural Theology', in *The New Dictionary of Theology,* J.A. Komonchak, M. Collins and D.A. Lane, eds. (Gill and MacMillan, Dublin, 1990), 705. Also, Thomas Aquinas, 'Universal Knowledge of the Natural Law Which Naturally Belongs to Men (sic) and to Some Degree Directs Men to What Is Good'. *Summa Theologica,* XV, 1(a), 51.

[7] This terminology is used by Jacques Maritain, who attempts to make sense of natural law within his existentialist theological schema. 'Natural law and moral law', in *Four Existentialist Theologians,* Will Herberg, ed. (Doubleday, New York, 1958), 80.

[8] *Op. cit.,* 705.

[9] Thomas Aquinas, *Summa Theologica,* Vol. XXVIII, 1(a) 2ae, 25.

[10] Thomas Gilbey, 'Appendix X: The Form of Moral Good', in *Summa Theologica,* Vol. XVIII, 1(a) 2ae, 163.

[11] Lisa Sowle Cahill, 'Feminism and Christian Ethics', in *Freeing Theology,* Catherine Mowry LaCugna, ed. (Harper, San Francisco, 1993), 215.

[12] *The Sceptical Feminist* (Penguin, Harmondsworth, 1980), 70. (Original quotations from John Stuart Mill, 'On Nature', one of his 'Three Essays on Religion, in *The Essential Works of John Stuart Mill,* Lerner, ed., 370.)

[13] *Ibid.,* 70. (Mill, 'On nature', 381.)

[14] *Ibid.,* 69.

[15] 'Feminism and Christian Ethics', 217.

[16] Ibid., 224.

[17] 'A Contribution to the Theological Discussion of Natural Law', in *Moral Theology No. 7,* 72.

[18] 'Nature, Reason, and the Task of Theological Ethics', in *Moral Theology No. 7,* 58.

[19] *Ibid.,* 58f.

[20] *Ibid.*, 61f. He points out that this is a familiar biblical concern, and quotes as examples: Leviticus 19:1-4 and 11-12. He does not refer here to the penalties for violations of holiness in Leviticus 20, which include death for various sexual sins, including homosexual acts.

[21] *Ibid.*, 64-66.

[22] *Ibid.*, 58.

[23] *Op. cit.*, 1022.

[24] *Op. cit.*, 92f.

[25] *Op. cit.*, 25f.

[26] *Ibid.*, 30f. Brown finds here the basis for a solution to Plato's Euthryphro dilemma: does God will something because it is good, or is something good because God wills it? See *Ibid.*, 33f.

[27] *Summma Theologiae*, Vol. 28 (1a.2ae. 90-97), Latin text and English translation, Blackfriars, 94, 2, 81.

[28] *Nature, man and God* (London: Macmillan, 1934), 169.

[29] 'Nature, reason and the task of theological ethics', 55.

[30] *Christians among the virtues: theological conversations with ancient and modern ethics* (Notre Dame: University of Notre Dame Press, 1997), xi.

[31] 'Rethinking natural law', in Moral theology no. 7, 221, 244.

[32] 'Feminism and Christian ethics', 214.

[33] *Ibid.*, 215.

[34] *Ibid.*

[35] *Ibid.*, 212.

[36] *Ibid.*, 220.

[37] *Ibid.*, 221.

[38] *Ibid.*, 214.

[39] *Ibid.*, 219.

[40] *Confessions*, I, 1. To be sure, Moltmann finds the true source of this in the 'promisio inquieta': *Theology of Hope*, J.M. Leitch, trs. (SCM, London, 1967), 88.

[41] *Anthropology in Theological Perspective* (Westminster, Philadelphia, 1985), 41ff., 69f.

[42] *Systematic Theology*, vol. 2., G.W. Bromiley, trs. (Eerdmans, Grand Rapids, 1994), 229.

[43] They even consider the distinction between theology and ethics problematic: *Op. cit.*, x.

[44] 'The homosexuality report', *Theology*, 83 (693), 1980: 184-190.

[45] 'Christian tradition and natural law', in *Readings in Moral Theology, No. 7,* 19.

[46] *Ibid.*, 32f.

[47] *Ibid.*, 34-40.

[48] *Op. cit.*, 80.

[49] 'Is There a Biblical Warrant for Natural Law Theories?' *Journal of the Evangelical Theological Society,* 25 (2), 1982: 185-199.

[50] *Biblical Faith and Natural Theology.* The Gifford Lectures for 1991. (Clarendon, Oxford, 1993), 51.

[51] *Ibid.*, 69.

[52] *What Does the Bible Say on Homosexual Practice?* (ABWON), 3, 10.

[53] *A Theology of the Human Person,* M. Rodgers and M. Thomas, eds. (Collins Dove, North Blackburn, Vic., 1992), 83-100.

[54] In addition, Barry D. Adam puts a case for taking account of the tools of analysis provided by political economy (construed broadly) in 'Structural Foundations of the Gay World', in *Social Perspectives in Lesbian and Gay Studies: A Reader,* Peter M. Nardi and Beth E. Schneider, eds. (Routledge, London, 1998), 220-229. Reprinted from *Comparative Studies in Society and History* 27:4 (October 1985): 658-71.

[55] 'The Complications of Experience', *Anglican Theological Review,* 75 (1), 1993: 10-33.

[56] *On Job: God-talk and the Suffering of the Innocent,* Matthew J. O'Connell, tr. (Orbis, Maryknoll, 1987), 30 and cf. 28-30.

[57] Page 28.

[58] In *Psychology and Sexual Orientation: Coming to Terms* (Routledge, New York, 1996), Janis S. Bohan considers that from an essentialist perspective, 'sexual orientation exists as a freestanding quality of individuals, present whether or not it is acknowledged by the individual, observed by others, or given meaning by the culture' (6). The constructionist approach suggests that sexual orientation is not a trait or quality of individuals, but 'a socially constructed notion that imbues certain acts and experiences with a particular meaning: they are taken as expressions of an identity grounded in (what we term) sexual orientation' (7). She also points to a merger of these views that sets the role to be played by psychology: 'to develop an understanding of how individuals and society come to terms with those phenomena

we understand as manifestations of sexual orientation in a culture that construes sexual orientation as an intrinsic aspect of individual identity' (10).

[59] For instance, Jim McKnight points to a sharp divergence between social science and biology. *Straight science? Homosexuality, Evolution and Adaptation* (Routledge, London, 1997), 4, 173-7.

[60] Bohan, *Op. cit.*, 25, and cf. 27; McKnight, *Op. cit.*, 5.

[61] 'Definition and Meaning of Sexual Orientation', in *Nature and Causes of Homosexuality: a Philosophic and Scientific Inquiry*, Noretta Koertge, comp./ed., *Journal of Homosexuality*, 6.4 (Summer 1981): 64.

[62] *Ibid.*, 57.

[63] See Michael Ruse, 'Are There Gay Genes? Sociobiology and Homosexuality' in *Nature and causes of homosexuality*, 28-32; , Simon Le Vay, *Queer Science: the Use and Abuse of Research in Homosexuality* (The MIT Press, Cambridge, MA, 1996), 281, respectively.

[64] *Op. cit.*, 63, 74.

[65] *Op. cit.*, 2-5, 281-3.

[66] *Op. cit.*, 32f.

[67] *Op. cit.*, 208-9, and cf. 195-209.

[68] Tom Minnery, 'Homosexuals Can Change', *Christianity Today*, 25 (3), 1981: 172-177; William Consiglio, 'Doing Therapy in an Alien Culture with Christians Overcoming Homosexuality', *Journal of Pastoral Counselling*, 28, 1993: 66-75.

[69] Already in 'Report on Homosexuality', Diocese of Melbourne Social Questions Committee, 1971, 31. More recently LeVay has discussed a number of treatments and therapies for 'conversion'. He finds it impossible to assess the validity of psychoanalytic 'cures'. *Op. cit.*, 79 and passim. In *Psychology and Sexual Orientation*, Bohan discusses a range of treatments, including those in a spiritual context, and questions the effectiveness and ethics of such treatments (18-21).

[70] Note Chris Peck, 'What is Natural?' *Modern Churchman*, 31 (11), 1989: 25-29; Robert Williams, 'Toward a Theology for Lesbian and Gay Marriage', *Anglican Theological Review*, 72 (2), 1990: 134-157; Louis Weil, 'The Church Does Not Make a Marriage', *Anglican Theological Review*, 72 (2), 1990: 172-174.

[71] *Op. cit.*, 10f.

[72] 'Moral Methodology: A Case Study', *Chicago Studies*, 19 (2), 1988: 171-187.

[73] 'The Homosexuality Report', 186-190.

[74] 'Homosexuality and the Church of England: Perspectives from the Social Sciences', *Theology*, 92 (747)m 1989: 175.

[75] 'Homosexual "Marriage"', *Christianity Today*, 29 (17), 1985: 21-28.

[76] Rowan Williams has identified the pain and tension of Christian disagreement over moral questions, and rightly observed that living in the body of Christ is profoundly hard work. 'Making Moral Decisions', in *The Official Report of the Lambeth Conference 1998* (Morehouse Publishing , Harrisburg, PA, 1999), 338, 342.

[77] *Op. cit.*, 207-211.

[78] *Ibid.*, 212. To be sure, Barr then notes a growth of serious discussion of this question in recent years.

[79] *A Prayer Book for Australia.* (Broughton Books, Sydney, 1995), 826.

[80] *Op. cit.*, 147.

[81] *Ibid.*, 197, and note 195, and elsewhere on revelation and natural theology.

[82] Text available from website: www.episcopalian.org/cclec/paper-st-andrews-day-htm

[83] *An examination of the theological principles affecting the homosexual debate.* Quoted in Section 1 Report, *The Official report of the Lambeth Conference 1998,* 94f.

Bibliography

Books and articles

Aquinas, Thomas. *Summa Theologica,* (Vols 18 and 28):
Westminster: Blackfriars, 1970

Augustine. *Confessions.* R.S. Pine-Coffin, trs.
Harmondsworth: Penguin, 1961

Barr, James. *Biblical Faith and Natural Theology.*
The Gifford Lectures for 1991.
Oxford: Clarendon, 1993

Barton, Stephen. 'Homosexuality and the Church of England:
Perspectives from the Social Sciences', *Theology,* 92 (747) 1989: 175-181.

Bohan, Janis S. P*sychology and Sexual Orientation: Coming to Terms.*
New York: Routledge, 1996

Boyle, Joseph. 'Natural Law', in J. A. Komonchak, M. Collins, and D. A.
Lane, eds. T*he New Dictionary of Theology.*
Dublin: Gill and MacMillan, 1990)

Brown, David. *Choices: Ethics and the Christian.*
Oxford: Blackwell, 1983

Cahill, Lisa Sowle. 'Feminism and Christian Ethics', in C. M. LaCugna, ed.
Freeing Theology.
San Francisco: Harper, 1993

Cahill, Lisa Sowle. 'Moral Methodology: A Case Study', *Chicago Studies,*
19 (2), 1988. 171-187

Consiglio, William.'Doing Therapy in an Alien Culture with Christians
Overcoming Homosexuality', *Journal of Pastoral Counselling,* 28, 1993. 66-75

Curran, Charles E. and McCormick, Richard A., eds. *Moral theology no. 7.*
New York: Paulist, 1991

*Examination of the Theological Principles Affecting the Homosexual
Debate.* Quoted in Section 1 Report, *The Official Report of the Lambeth
Conference 1998.*
Harrisburg, Penn.: Morehouse Publishing, 1999. 94f

Gaden, John A. *Vision of Wholeness,* Reid, D., ed.
Sydney: E.J. Dwyer, 1994

Gilbey, Thomas. 'The Form of Moral Good' (Appendix 10) in *Summa Theologica* (Vol 18).
Westminster: Blackfriars, 1970

Green, Clifford, ed. *Karl Barth: Theologian of Freedom.*
Minneapolis: Fortress, 1991

Gründel, Joseph. 'Natural Law', in *Encyclopedia of Theology: A Concise Sacramentum Mundi*, Karl Rahner, ed.
London: Burns and Oates, 1975, 1017-1023

Gutiérrez, Gustavo. *On Job: God-talk and the Suffering of the Innocent.* Matthew J. O'Connell, trs.
Maryknoll: Orbis, 1987

Hauerwas, Stanley and Pinches, Charles. *Christians among the Virtues: Theological Conversations with Ancient and Modern Ethics.*
Notre Dame: University of Notre Dame Press, 1997

Higton, Tony. *What Does the Bible Say on Homosexual Practice?* (ABWON)

Johnson, Alan F. 'Is There a Biblical Warrant for Natural Law Theories?' *Journal of the Evangelical Theological Society*, 25 (2), 1982, 185-199

Koertge, Noretta, comp. and ed. 'Nature and Causes of Homosexuality: A Philosophic and Scientific Inquiry', *Journal of Homosexuality*, 6.4, Summer, 1981

Lammers, Ann C. 'The Complications of Experience', *Anglican Theological Review*, 75 (1), 1993, 10-33

LeVay, Simon. *Queer Science: The Use and Abuse of Research into Homosexuality.*
Cambridge: Mass.: The MIT Press, 1996

McKnight, Jim. *Straight Science? Homosexuality, Evolution and Adaptation.*
London: Routledge, 1997

Maritain, Jacques. 'Natural Law and Moral Law' in Will Herberg, ed. *Four Existentialist Theologians.*
New York: Doubleday, 1958

Minnery, Tom. 'Homosexuals Can Change', *Christianity Today*, 25 (3), 1981: 172-177

Mitchell, Basil. 'The Homosexuality Report', *Theology*, 83 (693), 1980: 184-190

Moltmann, Jürgen. *Theology of Hope*, J.M. Leitch, trs. London: SCM, 1967

Nardi, Peter M. and Schneider, Beth E., eds. *Social Perspectives in Lesbian and Gay Studies: A Reader.*
London: Routledge, 1998

Pannenberg, Wolfhart. *Anthropology in Theological Perspective.*
Philadelphia: Westminster, 1985

____. *Systematic Theology.* 3 vols. G.W. Bromiley, trs. Grand Rapids: Eerdmans, 1991, 1994, 1998

Peck, Chris. 'What is Natural?' *Modern Churchman*, 31 (11), 1989: 25-29

A Prayer Book for Australia. Sydney: Broughton Books, 1995

Report on Homosexuality. Diocese of Melbourne Social Questions Committee, 1971

Richards, Janet Radcliffe. *The Sceptical Feminist.* Harmondsworth: Penguin, 1980

Rodgers, Margaret and Thomas, Maxwell, eds.
A Theology of the Human Person.
North Blackburn, Vic.: Collins Dove, 1992

Stott, John R.W. 'Homosexual "Marriage"', *Christianity Today*, 29 (17), 1985: 21-28

Temple, William. *Nature, Man and God.*
London: Macmillan, 1934

Thomas Aquinas. *Summa Theologiae.* Vol. 28 (1a.2ae. 90-97).
Latin text and English translation.
London: Blackfriars, 1966

Weil, Louis. 'The Church Does Not Make a Marriage', *Anglican Theological Review*, 72 (2), 1990: 172-174

Williams, Robert. 'Toward a Theology for Lesbian and Gay Marriage', *Anglican Theological Review*, 72 (2), 1990: 134-157

Williams, Rowan. 'Making Moral Decisions', in *The Official Report of the Lambeth Conference 1998.*
Harrisburg, PA: Morehouse Publishing, 1999, 334-344

CHAPTER SEVEN

Science and the Meaning of Homosexuality

Sean Mullen

As the Church considers the question of homosexuality and the implications of the phenomenon of same-sex sexuality in the world and amongst her members, it makes sense to establish clearly what exactly we mean when we speak of homosexuality or homosexual people. Two questions present themselves. First, how do we define homosexuality and its related terms? Second, what is the etiology, or cause, of homosexuality?

To state the obvious, these questions are important because ultimately we are not talking about a scientific phenomenon, but about people – creatures of God's own making for whom Christ came into the world, died and rose to new life. For centuries now, the various disciplines of science have informed the doctrines and attitudes of the Church – sometimes uncomfortably. As science teaches us more and more about the complexity of human biology, psychology, and sociology, we marvel at the wonder of God's work, at the same time that we are perplexed by it.

Semantics Of Sexual Identity

Although most of us use terms like 'homosexuality', 'gay', 'lesbian', and 'bi-sexual' with the presumption that these terms have clearly understood, shared meanings, literature on the subject is quick to point out that 'defining homosexuality is a fiendishly difficult task'.[1] The difficulty lies both in the variety of types and circumstances of same-sex sexual activity that have been documented in history and throughout the world, and in the variety of sexual behaviours, ideologies and identities in the modern Western world. Does the gay couple living together in a terrace house in Melbourne for the past twenty years have anything to do with the inter-generational same-sex relationships characteristic of initiation rites in Melanesia? Can they be categorised together?

Sociological and anthropological research has documented a wide variety of same-sex relationships, famously in ancient Greek culture, but more recently among several tribes of Native Americans, in Papua New Guinea, Melanesia, Mexico, China, and Africa, to name a few.[2] In each case, the nature and cultural context of the sexual behaviour is different, although the particular acts involved may be similar. Are we to understand and evaluate these cultural behaviours in the same way?

Even if we could categorise behaviours in such a way as to define clearly what constitutes homosexuality and what does not, could we categorise people so easily? As Janis Bohan points out, 'The very notion of sexual orientation as "the distinguishing characteristic of a particular kind of person" (Weeks, 1981, p. 81) is a recent construct... Until at least the 18th century, homosexual acts were seen simply, as acts, and not as defining one's identity.'[3]

Today it is suggested that we may need to distinguish between three categories, at least: sexual behaviour, orientation, and identity. Behaviour defines the act, orientation defines the inclination to categories of behaviour, and the concept of identity includes not only a predilection to a certain type of sexual-emotional relationship, but the labelling of one's self as gay, lesbian, or bi-sexual, and the attendant process of 'coming out', which constitutes claiming an identity based on sexual orientation.[4]

For some people behaviour, orientation and identity do not all correspond neatly. What are we to make of the married man who has never had a same-sex sexual encounter, but whose sexual fantasies predominantly feature sex with other men? How do we define the common adolescent experimentation of boys? What of the young woman who deliberately chooses a lesbian relationship for political reasons, although a sexual relationship with a man would be physically and emotionally satisfying? Are these people homosexual?

The famous research of Alfred Kinsey in the middle of the twentieth century called into question the whole notion that the web of sexual behaviour, fantasy, orientation and identity can accurately be classed in dichotomous terms as either homosexual or heterosexual. Kinsey challenged the long-held presumption that 'homosexuality and heterosexuality are two mutually exclusive phenomena emanating from fundamentally and, at least in some cases, inherently different types of individuals.'[5] The so-called Kinsey Scale places people on a continuum between 0 and 6, where 0 represents a pattern of exclusive heterosexual orientation and 6 a pattern of exclusive homosexuality, with room for variations on the points between. Kinsey's research placed the majority of people somewhere along the continuum, between the defining poles. By no means is the Kinsey Scale universally accepted but, despite recent harsh criticisms of Kinsey's work, this perspective of human sexuality has profoundly affected the way culture and science think about sexual orientation and has called into question the usefulness of classifying people in strictly dichotomous terms.

The semantics of terminology and categories are sufficiently complex that we can appreciate Bohan's comment: 'The one certainty is precisely the uncertainty of the meaning of sexual orientation and the impossibility of identifying individuals or groups that actually reflect the separate, internally homogenous, and stable categories we use in everyday language.'[6]

All the same, there is surely some intuitive level at which we are able to speak broadly of homosexuality and homosexual orientation. The lines of definition may be blurry, but not so blurry that we are unable to make any sense of it at all.

Whether driven forward by the questions of definition or confounded by them, we find ourselves inevitably confronting the question of etiology: the cause of homosexuality.

Etiological Arguments

While there are those who believe that any inquiry into the cause or causes of homosexuality begs the question of the cause or causes of heterosexuality, we can reasonably argue that from a statistical basis alone, heterosexual orientation is the norm for humans and most other species. Homosexuality is a variance from the well-established norm. With the rarest exception, the vast majority of species reproduces sexually: perpetuation of the species fairly demands that heterosexuality, which produces offspring, should be normative.

Typically, the arguments about the cause of homosexuality are laid out in dichotomous terms: nature versus nurture; biological or psychological; essentialist or constructionist. Each of these dichotomies presents a different set of choices. In the debate of nature versus nurture, the question seems to be: were you born that way or were you raised that way? The biology versus psychology debate asks those questions, too, but in a nuanced way, since psychology is not unrelated to biology. The essentialist versus constructionist debate, however, casts the question in an entirely different light. In the essentialist point of view, sexual orientation is 'a trait or attribute intrinsic to individuals'.[7] The constructionist viewpoint suggests that 'homosexuality, or more particularly, the "homosexual", is not something waiting out there in the real world, ready to be described and explained.... According to this school, the homosexual does not exist in reality at all. The homosexual is rather an artefact, a "social construction".'[8]

While the questions asked in this paper may not depend on an essentialist point of view, clearly they presume that sexual orientation is more than a social construction, i.e., that it is an observable, occurring phenomenon that yields to inquiry.

Psychology

Freudian Theory

Sigmund Freud's theory of human behaviour emphasised the importance of early childhood events. Naturally, his understanding of homosexuality was built on this principle, too. Generally speaking, 'Freud understood homosexuality (for males at least) as arising from an aberrant childhood experience, poor resolution of a sexual conflict, and the relentless playing out of this conflict in adulthood'[9]. His theories were perpetuated, in one form or another, in the field of psychoanalysis, of which he is the father. Among the most widely accepted derivatives of Freudian theory on homosexuality is the notion that 'male homosexuality is the product of an over-protective mother and a distant father'. This general notion has left a powerful impression on both the professional and public consciousness about homosexuality. The theory, however, has never really been demonstrated in careful scientific study.[10]

A number of recent writers are at pains to point out that Freud himself never classified homosexuality as a pathological behaviour.

A famous letter he wrote to a woman who had asked for his help with her homosexual son reads in part:

> Homosexuality is surely no advantage but it is nothing to be ashamed of, no vice, no degradation, it cannot be classified as an illness; we consider it to be a variation of the sexual function produced by a certain arrest in development.... It is a great injustice to persecute homosexuality as a crime and cruelty too.[11]

Earlier, Freud had written, 'I am of the firm conviction that homosexuals must not be treated as sick people for a perverse orientation is far from being a sickness. Homosexuals are not sick, but they also do not belong in a court of law!' (1903).[12] Nevertheless, it seems clear that Freud regarded the norm of heterosexuality as a more desirable, more healthy state. Regardless of his own views, however, the psychoanalytical field generally did subscribe to a theory of mental disease to explain homosexuality, and it predominated for years.

Contemporary Psychological Approach

By 1952, when the American Psychiatric Association published its first edition of the Diagnostic and Statistical Manual (DSM), homosexuality was listed as a sociopathic personality disorder. This assessment was the controlling paradigm for some years. In subsequent editions, homosexuality was variously listed as a sociopathology, a mental disorder, or a sexual deviation. It may be that the Stonewall riot of 1969, which marked the beginning of the gay rights movement, and the shift in cultural attitudes that it signalled, played a role in the progress of thinking in the field of psychology and sexual orientation. Whatever the impetus, research in the 1970s confirmed earlier findings that there was no noticeable difference in the psychological adjustment of homosexual and heterosexual men.[13] In 1973 the American Psychiatric Association (APA) removed homosexuality from the DSM altogether. On its current website, the APA has information available about homosexuality that explains the thinking behind the change:

> The action was taken following a review of the scientific literature and consultation with experts in the field. For a

> mental condition to be considered a psychiatric disorder, it should either regularly cause distress or regularly be associated with clinically significant impairment of social functioning. ...homosexuality does not meet these criteria.[14]

The trend in contemporary psychological and psychiatric care seems to be in helping individuals who are troubled by questions of sexual identity to come to terms with that identity and cope with the attendant feelings and social stigmas that may be associated with it.[15]

Reparative Therapies

The idea that homosexuality is a mental disease naturally has as a corollary the possibility of a cure. Certainly, reparative therapies of many kinds have been employed in search of a cure. These therapies range from long-term psychotherapy to castration, implantation of 'normal' testes, lobotomy, electro-shock therapy and others. Studies that support the success of conversion or reparative therapy have been called into question. For instance:

> Pattison and Pattison's (1980) study of 'ex-gays' reported successful treatment 'in a spiritual context' of eleven gay men. However, these eleven individuals were from an initial pool of 300 'dissatisfied' gay men, of whom thirty were studied in the research project. There is no explanation of why the other 270 (of the initial 300) were excluded, nor why the other nineteen from this sample were not followed. Although success was defined by these authors as a complete shift in sexual orientation, of the eleven 'successes,' only three (of eleven, of thirty, of 300) reported no lingering same-sex fantasies.[16]

While Bohan asserts that the various psychological disciplines are generally and gradually abandoning the notion that 'nonhetero-sexuality is in need of a cure', she acknowledges that 'not all psychologists and psychiatrists have participated in this shift'[17]. Indeed, an organisation called The National Association for Research and Therapy of Homosexuality (NARTH) maintains a large website. The stated purpose of the organisation is 'to provide psychological understanding of the cause, treatment and behaviour patterns associated with homosexuality.... Professionals who belong to NARTH comprise a wide variety of men and women who *defend the right to pursue change of sexual orientation*'[18] (emphasis original). The case put forward on NARTH's web page actually has very little to say about psychological theories of the cause of homosexuality or its treatment. It is aimed at debunking arguments for biological causes of homosexuality still to be discussed in this paper. The website points out that claims for biological causes of homosexuality are far from unequivocal, and it amasses a string of qualifying statements that together undermine the thrust of a biological argument. It is noticeable, however, that NARTH does not seem to be promoting any research of its own. One scholar responding to NARTH points out that their 'research has not been published in peer-reviewed scientific journals. Instead, it has been summarised in the media and on the World Wide Web. But science isn't conducted by press releases.'[19]

It is important to point out that the official position of the American Psychiatric Association is that:

> There is no published scientific evidence supporting the efficacy of 'reparative therapy' as a treatment to change one's sexual orientation. It is not described in the scientific literature... There is no evidence that any treatment can change a homosexual person's deep-seated sexual feelings for others of the same sex.[20]

In light of these various viewpoints, Bohan, who has a bias toward what she considers the more prevalent and progressive attitude, summarises the current climate by saying that 'attitudes within psychology toward the topic of sexual orientation remain ambivalent at best'.[21]

Biology

Biological explanations for the cause of homosexuality are not a recent innovation. The study of eugenics, which looked to heredity for an explanation for many social behaviours, including homosexuality, flourished in the late nineteenth and early twentieth centuries.[22] The subsequent range of biological explanations of homosexuality is too vast and too complicated to cover in detail, but we can get an idea of the larger picture and most significant arguments.

Hormones

The discovery of distinct male and female hormones led to the examination of the possibility that homosexuality is the result of an adult hormonal imbalance. That is, homosexual behaviour in men is the result of low testosterone levels and unusually high oestrogen levels, and vice versa for women. However, 'a summary of this research concluded that the bulk of evidence demonstrates no relationship between adult hormone levels and sexual orientation.'[23]

A strong link has been suggested, however, between pre-natal hormones and sexual orientation. It is well established that pre-natal hormones play an important role in determining the gender of a foetus.[24] The theory goes that as these hormones determine the physical development of sex organs, so they also affect brain development in crucial areas that might be involved in sexual orientation. Various theories place the hormonal effect on either the structure or organisation of the brain. One writer summarises the theory this way, 'There is so much evidence linking the effects of prenatal hormone levels to adult sexual orientation that one cannot help but be curious as to the nature of the links'.[25] Even those who are eager to link prenatal hormones to sexual identity, however, acknowledge that 'hormone levels are only part of the story'.[26]

Genetic Determinism

The work of Franz Kallman in the 1940s and 1950s marks the beginning of modern genetic studies of homosexuality.[27] Kallman studied groups of monozygotic (identical) and dizygotic (fraternal) twins. Monozygotic (MZ) twins are the result of a single fertilised egg and, therefore, genetically identical. Dizygotic (DZ) twins, the result of two fertilised eggs, share only the same genetic similarity as any other non-twin siblings. Naturally, if homosexuality is genetically determined, one would expect to find a high level of homosexuality in pairs of MZ twins. Indeed, Kallman's study found a 100% concordance rate for MZ twins (i.e. in every case, both twins of the pair were homosexual). Kallman's study, however, has been widely criticised for methodological deficiencies and, despite efforts, no other study has been able to replicate his results.[28]

In 1991 and 1993, Michael Bailey and Richard Pillard conducted a new series of studies with twins. Their results showed a concordance rate of 52% in MZ twins and 22% with DZ twins. As the result of their work, they concluded that 'the high concordance rate for MZ twins strongly supported a genetic hypothesis' of the cause of homosexuality.[29]

The Gay Gene

Encouraged by research suggesting a genetic cause of homosexuality, Dean Hamer led a group of researchers at the National Institute of Health in the United States who, in 1993, published a paper which claimed a link between male homosexuality and a particular region of a particular chromosome. Hamer and his colleagues also worked with pairs of brothers (not necessarily twins). Rather than observing behaviour in order to compile statistical analysis, they began looking at the DNA of their subjects. Specifically, they were looking for a genetic marker on the X chromosome of subjects drawn from a carefully selected pool. Their study claimed to have found such a 'marker,' or indicator, of a gene on a strand of DNA in a high percentage of the subjects. 'When the DNA markers on the X chromosome of these brothers were examined, it was found that thirty-three of the forty pairs shared markers at the tip of the long arm of the X chromosome in an area called Xq28.'[28] This high rate of concurrence suggests a possible correlation between the genetic marker and sexual orientation. A later study demonstrated a similar pattern and addressed some of the criticisms of the first study.

While Hamer's study was widely reported as lending weight to the increasing suggestion of a genetic cause of homosexuality – as indeed it does – several caveats need to be kept in mind. First of all, if homosexuality has a genetic cause, we might reasonably expect to find a 100% rate of concordance in twins with identical genetic material – which has not been demonstrated to be the case. Secondly (and perhaps in answer to the first point), genes do not exercise total, invariable control over human development. 'The genome [all the genetic material in an organism] is not a blueprint... but a set of instructions. The brain 'wires' itself – largely *after* birth – in response to information from the environment.'[31] This 'wiring' process is the process by which the brain, while genetically encoded for complex processes such as speech, actually develops the capacity to perform such processes after considerable environmental input. In the words of another researcher, 'simply finding a gene or two associated with a particular trait is likely to be only one piece of the complex of genes, prenatal biology, and postnatal environment that sum or interact to form the final product....'[32]

The notion that genes exercise a total, uncompromising control on human development persists, however, and this common misconception of how genes function bears further comment. Garland E. Allen says this:

> The view of genes as fixed blueprints has been perpetuated by most textbooks and other popular presentations of genetics for the past seventy-five years or more (Nelkin & Lindee, 1995). Yet any experienced geneticist will tell you that, of course, it is not strictly true that genes directly determine traits independent of environment. The phrase, 'the gene for' is just a 'shorthand', they say. Yet it is a shorthand that may ultimately conceal more than it reveals. This 'shorthand' has contributed significantly to the confusion surrounding human behavior genetics in the past five or more decades.
>
> ...What is clear is that genes contain information for the amino acid sequence of proteins. However, how that information is initially read out and ultimately transformed into an adult phenotypic trait [such as sexual orientation] is a multistage process, the complete sequence of which remains unknown for almost any trait, even simple ones such as hair colour or height.[33]

At the same time, however, we are reminded that 'a genetic hypothesis virtually requires that being gay and lesbian should run in families. All modern family studies show that this is true. Randomly recruited gay men have from two to five times as many gay brothers as a similar group of heterosexual men (Pillard, et al., 1981, 1982; Pillard & Weinrich, 1986; Hamer et al., 1993; Bailey & Bell, 1993).'[34]

So, while it must be said that no gay gene has been found (if such a thing could even exist), perhaps a marker for associated genetic material has been located. Genetic and statistical research has bolstered the genetic hypothesis for the cause of homosexuality. But it may also be important to remember that, genetically speaking, 'we differ from the chimpanzee by only one base pair out of a hundred – 1 percent – and from each other by less than 0.1 percent. The cultural lesson of the Human Genome Project could be that we are all very much alike....'[35]

The Gay Brain

Another study that received a great deal of attention in the 1990s was the work of Simon LeVay. LeVay conducted a post-mortem study on the brains of forty-one subjects. He found that a specific cluster of cells in a specific area of the hypothalamus (namely, the interstitial nuclei of the anterior hypothalamus, or INAH) was two to three times as large in heterosexual men as in homosexual men. LeVay's study is in line with other research (Swaab, Gooren and Hoffman, 1995; Allen and Gorski) that has identified physiological differences in the brains of gay men. These various studies, however, have all focused on different parts of the brain, and none has been independently replicated. Therefore, 'the findings of brain structural differences between homosexuals have to be considered even more tentative than the respective findings of differences between the sexes.'[36]

LeVay's work has been much discussed and contested, and he himself acknowledges that his findings are open to different interpretations. Pointing out the difficulty of drawing conclusions from the research, William Byne says:

> ...The human brain is relatively immature at birth, doubling in size during the first year of life and quadrupling by the end of the fourth. The major growth of the human brain, therefore, occurs at a time when it is in constant interaction with the external world.... The biology of the brain itself, therefore, is influenced by the early environment and experiences of the individual.[37]

This is an observation that LeVay might well accept. In his own book, he writes:

> I do not know – nor does anyone else – what makes a person gay, bi-sexual, or straight. I do believe, however, that the answer to this question will eventually be found by doing biological research in laboratories and not simply by talking about the topic, which is the way most people have studied it up to now.... Believing in a biological explanation for sexual orientation is not the same thing as insisting that sexual orientation is inborn or genetically determined.[38]

In all discussion of possible biological causes of sexual orientation, it is important to remember that the biological differences being observed are of the minutest nature. We do well to keep in mind that 'gay men and lesbians differ so slightly from their heterosexual counterparts in every respect aside from their sexual attractions that only the most sophisticated and precise investigations have been able to discover any differences at all between them'.[39] And, of course, even those differences that we think may have been measured are tenuous, debated, and unconfirmed.

Social learning theory

A small group of theories of the cause of homosexuality fall into what we may call Social Learning Theory. According to this point of view, homosexual behaviour and its correlating orientation are learned patterns that may have their origins in one of several powerful environmental factors. These factors might be heterophobia, or a fear of the opposite sex, perhaps based on performance anxiety or a fear of rejection; or a negative heterosexual experience that repels an individual from the opposite sex. Similarly, some would place the importance on the first sexual experience, which could more or less stamp a child or adolescent with the expectation that same-sex activity is normative for them.

Perhaps the most prevalent social learning theory is that of seduction or recruitment, which supposes that individuals (usually children) are recruited into a lifestyle of same-sex sexuality. Or, similarly, the theory of exposure and imitation purports that a homosexual identity might be 'contagious', so that its spread is a result of exposure to the lifestyle and behaviours of homosexual people. None of these explanations is supported by scientific research, and indeed most are undermined by what we know to be true about behaviour patterns of homosexual and heterosexual people.[40] In summary, while these theories do have some currency in popular culture, they are generally unsupported by scientific inquiry.

The big picture

In surveying the research into various theories of the cause of homosexuality, one point stands out: that the dichotomy between nature and nurture is probably a false dichotomy. Most of the scientists and scholars writing on the subject – even those with a particular investment in biological etiology – are in accord on this point. In LeVay's words, 'Nature alone, or nurture alone cannot provide an adequate explanation for our sexual identity.'[41] He makes the point that most others also want to make: 'We have seen that both nature and nurture are at work in the development of sexuality, and that to some extent at least the two factors have to interact during development.'[42] And just as the nature/nurture dichotomy seems false, so do other sharp distinctions in the debate. The question of causation does not, it seems, boil down *only* to genes, or *only* to hormones, or *only* to the brain, or *only* to environment. The research suggests that the development of human sexual identity, like so much else about us, is the result of a complex, even mysterious set of processes that takes place in body, mind, and household.

A few points about all this research still need to be made. First of all, no study is beyond critique, and studies are regularly criticised, especially for the difficulty in assembling a fair, healthy, stable, and representative pool of subjects, but for numerous other reasons as well. This science is not foolproof.

Additionally, many studies, particularly those looking into hormones, are conducted on laboratory animals, especially rats. Conclusions about humans are by inference. This method is not necessarily flawed; however, it does raise some questions about what we think we might be discovering. Bohan urges us to 'note that the definition of sexual orientation here is completely grounded in sexual behaviours, in contrast to the convoluted meaning of sexual orientation discussed previously. Consider the huge pragmatic, theoretical, and philosophical leap from the simple behaviours of mounting and lordosis [the receptive female mating position for rats] to the complexities of lesbian, gay, or bi-sexual identity.'[43] When rats are studied, note is taken of how one induces a male to assume the female mating position, but no one questions the male who then mounts its hormonally altered same-sex partners. The scientific environment reminds us that 'in these laboratory models it is what you do and not who you do it with that defines sexual orientation, whereas in humans, sexual orientation is defined not only by the motor patterns of copulation but by the gender of the individuals that arouse one's erotic interest.'[44]

It is notable that most of the research mentioned in this paper has to do with male homosexuality. In fact, this is a reflection of the research available, which deals primarily with male homosexuality. It does seem that studies in this direction are certainly more numerous, but it may well be that these studies are also more conclusive. Genetic studies, for instance, have consistently failed to demonstrate any genetic link to lesbianism.

The meaning of research and the meaning of sexuality

It has been suggested that 'no investigation of sexuality can be politically neutral.'[45] And while this proposition could be debated, it seems a helpful caution as we search for meaning in all this research. We are reminded, that 'neither biological nor environmental explanations of human behaviour have an inherent social meaning. Both forms of explanation can be used to justify liberal or conservative causes; both can be applied oppressively. And each can be used to promote greater human freedom.'[46] The broad spectrum of possibility for the interpretation of data moves Garland Allen to caution, 'Civil rights or any form of social justice should never hinge on biology'.[47]

It is easy to get caught up in the variety of possibilities suggested by the scientific research outlined in this paper. What might it all mean if we could put the pieces of the puzzle together? On the other hand, we might wonder how it can be that science so obscures simpler realities that are evident to us as common observers of life and as people of faith.

Indeed it is impossible to isolate one set of questions from another in the discussion of the cause of homosexuality. What happens in the lab can only, it seems, shed light on what is learned in the therapist's chair and what happens there only sheds light on what happens in the family kitchen, which in turn may well shed light on what is discovered in the researcher's office, which informs what happens in the lab. And all of this interaction is played out in a political atmosphere.

History has taught the Church that she ignores science and what it has to say at her own peril. It is worth saying that we look to science not so that we can undermine Scripture, but in order to bring a new dimension to our understanding of how God is at work in creation. So that when we accept, for instance, that science teaches us something very different about the origins and expanse of our universe than either of the Genesis accounts of creation, we need not conclude that the Bible is *wrong*. Rather, we understand anew the same truth as the biblical writers: that the God who created the heavens and the earth is marvellous in power and imagination. But we have a more sophisticated appreciation of the extent of the divine power and imagination because of what we have learned.

But the messages of science with regard to the question of homosexuality are far from clear.

If we think it is important to understand homosexuality as a phenomenon not only of nature, but of the human condition, which at least some Christians believe should be celebrated, then we have to accept that there is much that we simply do not understand about human sexuality in general. Why should sex be the means of procreation? Where do the 'primal urges' in humans come from? How can there be so many variations of physical sexual development, as well as sexual desire? And what is the meaning of that desire?

These questions are no more new to the Church than they were to the biblical writers. Perhaps science will provide some answers as it has for some of the perplexing questions about the universe we inhabit. Perhaps the answers science provides will only provoke new questions. No matter what, we should be aware that research and information can both be manipulated to serve various ends. In reviewing the research to the end of finding the meaning of homosexuality, we can best say that it is inconclusive at this time and is likely to be so in the foreseeable future. This makes it all the more difficult for us to know what to do with the varied and sometimes conflicting information and interpretation available to us. The one thing we know for certain is that we cannot ignore it any more than we can ignore the people whose story this research at heart tries to tell.

Endnotes

[1] Francis Mark Mondimore, *A Natural History of Homosexuality* (The Johns Hopkins University Press, Baltimore, 1996), 2.

[2] See Mondimore, 3 – 19, and Janis S. Bohan, *Psychology and Sexual Orientation; Coming to Terms* (Routledge, New York, 1996), 13 — 16.

[3] Bohan, *Op. cit.*, 16.

[4] Heino F. L. Meyer-Bahlburg, 'Psychobiologic Research on Homosexuality' in *A Queer World*, Martin Duberman, ed., (New York University Press, New York, 1997), 286.

[5] Kinsey, 1941, 425, quoted in 'Who Counts When You're Counting Homosexuals? Hormones and Homosexuality in Mid-Twentieth Century America', Stephanie H. Kenan in *Science and Homosexualities*, Vernon A. Rosario, ed. (Routledge, New York, 1997), 207.

[6] Bohan, *Op. cit.*, 30.

[7] Bohan, *Op. cit.*, 5-7.

[8] Michael Ruse, *Homosexuality: A Philosophical Inquiry* (Basil Blackwell, Oxford, 1988), 15.

[9] Mondimore, *Op. cit.*, 72.

[10] Bohan, *Op. cit.*, 77. Bohan cites the research of Bieber, et al. (1962), which she claims was flawed and was subsequently called into question by the work of Bell, Weinberg, & Hammersmith (1981).

[11] Sigmund Freud, 1935, quoted in Mondimore, *Op. cit.,* 76.

[12] Quoted in Richard C. Pillard, 'The Search for a Genetic Influence on Sexual Orientation' in *Science and Homosexualities* (Routeldge, New York, 1997), 227.

[13] Bohan, *Op. cit.*, 18 cites the work of Siegelman, 1972a, 1972b and Thompson, McCandless, and Strickland, 1971, in support of the work of Evelyn Hooker in 1957.

[14] Website of the American Psychiatric Association: www.psych.org, February 2000.

[15] Bohan, *Op. cit.*, 20-21.

[16] Bohan, *Op. cit.,* 20. Bohan also criticises the 1979 Masters and Johnson study on the basis of an ill-defined pool of subjects and poor follow-up.

[17] *Ibid.*, 20-21.

[18] Website of NARTH: www.narth.com, February 2000.

[19] Gregory M. Herek, PhD., in his article 'Attempts to Change Sexual Orientation', published on the Internet: http://psychology.ucdavis.edu/rainbow/html/facts_changing.html.

[20] Website of the APA, February 2000.

[21] Bohan, *Op. cit.*, 21.

[22] Garland E. Allen, 'The Double-Edged Sword of Genetic Determinism: Social and Political Agendas in Genetic Studies of Homosexuality, 1940-1994', in Rosario, *Op. cit.,* 245, cites the work of Richard von Krafft-Ebbing in the 1880s and Magnis Hirschfeld in 1936 as examples of biological studies in the period.

[23] Meyer-Bahlburg, 1984, 1995, quoted in Bohan, *Op. cit.*, 69.

[24] Mondimore, *Op. cit.,* 102-104, 120.

[25] *Ibid.*, 132.

[26] *Ibid.*, 133.

[27] It is worth noting that Kallman had been a member of the Nazi Party in pre-World War II Germany, where he worked under Ernst Rudin and Heinrich Himmler to draw up the 1933 German Sterilisation Law. He was forced to flee Germany because of partial Jewish ancestry. See Allen, *Op. cit.*, 246.

[28] Allen, *Op. cit.,* 249-250.

[29] *Ibid.*, 252.

[30] Mondimore, *Op. cit.*, 44. Hamer and colleagues used statistical analysis to determine which pairs of brothers had a high occurrence of homosexuality on their mother's side of the family (the X chromosome in males is inherited from the mother), helping narrow the search for genetic material to the X chromosome.

[31] Mondimore, *Op. cit.*,quoting Robert Wesson, 148.

[32] Pillard, *Op. cit.*, 231.

[33] Allen, *Op. cit.,* 259.

[34] Pillard, *Op. cit.,* 233.

[35] Dorothy Nelkin and M. Susan Lindee, 'Creating Natural Distinctions', in Duberman, *Op. cit.*, 316.

[36] Meyer-Bahlburg, *Op. cit.,* 293.

[37] William Byne, 'LeVay's Thesis Reconsidered', in Duberman, *Op. cit.*, 324.

[38] Simon LeVay, *The Sexual Brain* (MIT Press, Cambridge, MA, 1993), 108

[39] Monidmore, *Op. cit.,* 133.

[40] Bohan provides an outline and criticisms of these theories and others, *Op. cit.*, 78-82.

[41] LeVay, *Op. cit.*, 138. See also Bohan, *Op. cit.*, 28; Mondimore, *Op. cit.*, 147; Allen (in Rosario), *Op. cit.*, 244.

[42] *Ibid.*, 94.

[43] Bohan, *Op. cit.*, 71.

[44] Byne, *Op. cit.*, 321.

[45] Kenen, *Op. cit.*, 198.

[46] Nelken and Lindee, *Op. cit.*, 310.

[47] Allen, *Op. cit.*, 264.

Bibliography

Books and articles

A Queer World, The Centre for Lesbian and Gay Studies Reader, Martin Duberman, ed. New York: New York University Press, 1997

Bohan, Janis S. *Psychology and Sexual Orientation: Coming to Terms.* New York: Routledge, 1996

LeVay, Simon. *The Sexual Brain.* Cambridge, MA: MIT Press, 1993

Mondimore, Francis Mark. *A Natural History of Homosexuality.* Baltimore: The Johns Hopkins University Press, 1996

Ruse, Michael. *Homosexuality: A Philosophical Inquiry.* Oxford: Basil Blackwell, 1988

Science and Homosexualities, Vernon A. Rosario, ed. New York: Routledge, 1997

Tripp, C.A. T*he Homosexual Matrix,* 2nd ed. New York: Meridian, 1987

CHAPTER EIGHT

Friendship

Peter Carnley

Christians are inevitably faced with the phenomenon of homosexual relationships in contemporary society, and must come to terms with this reality. The first question to be addressed has to do with language: with what categories are homosexual relationships to be most appropriately described? How are such relationships to be understood and interpreted from a Christian point of view? The answer to these questions will condition both the Church's pastoral response to homosexual people and its assessment of what behaviours may be deemed to be appropriate within such relationships.

The increasingly vocal call in our time for homosexual relationships to be recognised, and legalised by the civic authority of the State, and for the Church to legitimise and even to bless them, has led the popular mind to the idea that such relationships might be considered as a form of marriage. Indeed, press reports of the blessing of homosexual relationships in various parts of the world regularly refer to such ceremonies as a form of 'marriage'.

A relationship between two people of the same gender, which is entered into with the intention of forming a life-long union, based upon a covenant or contractual commitment, effectively for the 'mutual support, help and comfort' of the parties, and designed to secure inheritance and property rights as well as social security benefits, might indeed, at least in these specific social and legal respects, resemble the institution of marriage. The need to recognise a homosexual partner as 'next of kin' in difficult pastoral situations, as for example, when a funeral has to be arranged, seems also to lead in the direction of institutionalising such a partnership as a kind of marriage. To speak of such relationships as a form of marriage is thus a natural and logical possibility. Indeed, some writers wish to argue very strenuously for the desirability of employing this category, even if, to the mind of many in the Church, as in the wider community, it may not be a possibility that can be positively accepted and embraced.[1] Stanley Hauerwas, for example, supports this kind of analogous comparison in describing homosexual relationships: 'I do not see why we cannot see this kind of relationship as analogous to what Christians mean by marriage.'[2]

Insofar as the *Book of Common Prayer* took over the traditional medieval doctrine of marriage, not just as a *sacramentum signum*, a sign of the steadfast bond between Christ and his disciples, but specifically as a *sacramentum vinculum*, a bond or pledge designed to save people from a life of faithless promiscuity and immorality, the concept of marriage may also commend itself for use with respect to homosexual relationships. In other words, the traditional theology of marriage as an effectual instrument against temptations to promiscuity, based on Paul's injunction that it is at least 'better to marry than to burn with passion', may ground the contention that permanent and exclusive relationships are socially and morally more acceptable than a serial string of casual sexual encounters. In this way, the theology of marriage may provide an analogy for assigning a positive value to a lifelong commitment of loyalty between partners of the same gender.

A permanent and exclusive commitment of lifelong loyalty and steadfastness may, at the very least, be seen as a better option for homosexual people than an entirely undisciplined life of promiscuity. Indeed, a permanent and exclusive commitment may be seen to have positive spiritual and saving value as a bulwark against the otherwise inescapable dangers to health and well-being that attach to an undisciplined life of faithless casual relationships.[3]

However, one of the chief purposes of marriage between heterosexual couples, as it is explicitly defined in the Anglican tradition, is the procreation and nurture of children. Marriage is thus intended explicitly for the setting up of an inter-generational family. In this sense a partnership, even a partnership that is intended to be permanent and exclusive between heterosexual couples, is not actually a family, though it may at least have the potentiality to become a family. Given that this important inter-generational element which flows from procreation within the context of marriage will normally and in principle be absent from same-gender relationships, it may not be really helpful to refer to such relationships by using the category of 'marriage'. Indeed, it may make more for confusion than for conceptual clarity. If the term 'marriage' were to be used of same-gender relationships, the Church would at least need to acknowledge that it was being used not literally, but in an extended, metaphorical sense. However, ultimately, it may not really be helpful for achieving what is desired by homosexual people themselves, given its potential to generate negative reactions in the community. While it is admitted that some writers wish to defend the use of the paradigm of 'marriage' for the characterisation of homosexual relationships[4] , those gay people in long-term committed relationships with whom the Doctrine Panel discussed the issue were clearly themselves of the view that the concept of marriage was not appropriate. The Church may, therefore, do well to avoid the use of the concept of marriage and to encourage others to do likewise.

While it has become fashionable in the secular world to speak of long-term committed relationships between people of the same gender as a form of 'marriage', it might be much more amenable and helpful from a Christian point of view to categorise such relationships by resorting to the concept of friendship. Indeed, Marilyn Friedman has proposed that 'friendship may emerge, in our culture, as the least contested, most enduring, and most satisfying of all close personal affiliations'.[5] It is a category that may be as important for defining a most desired aspect of the relationship between married heterosexual couples as it is for describing both sexually neutral same-gender relationships and explicitly homosexual relationships. Indeed, the concept of friendship may usefully transform even the Christian understanding of the marriage of heterosexual couples, in so far as it may help to transcend the rather more legal and contractual connotations of marriage by introducing nuances of mutuality and emotional warmth into the understanding of the relationship. In other words, the concept suggests that husbands and wives should love one another as friends on the model of the relationship of Christ with his Church.

Certainly, the concept of friendship suggests itself as a potentially useful one, given that it is hallowed by theological significance in

Scripture. John Inge has recently argued[6] that friendship might be thought of as a normative pattern for a Christian understanding of all human relationships, including both inter-human and human-divine relationships. For, while it is unambiguously clear in Scripture that the idea of friendship, like marriage, can appropriately be understood to characterise the relation of God with his people, it is an inclusive concept that is also used in Scripture with reference to both hetero-sexual and same-gender relationships. Indeed friendships, including same-gender friendships, appear to be accepted and celebrated in Holy Scripture.

Stanley Hauerwas has pointed out that Jesus' imperative is that his disciples should love one another *as he loved* them. It is by this love that all people will know and identify his disciples. And Jesus loved his disciples by making them his friends. This involved the intimacy of interpersonal sharing, and a sense of equality of status and mutuality, free of the power and control usually associated with the element of subordination that is inherent in the master-servant relationship: 'I do not call you servants any longer, because the servant does not know what the master is doing; but I have called you friends, because I have made known to you everything that I have heard from my Father'.[7]

Even when, in John 15:14, Jesus says: 'You are my friends if you do what I command you', we are not, therefore, to entertain the suggestion that Jesus somehow dominates and controls his disciples as subordinates. Rather, the response of obedience between Jesus and his disciples is the 'obedience of love'. It reflects the same kind of obedience that characterises the relationship between the Father and the Son. In that relationship the Son is not subordinate to the Father.[8] Rather, the Father finds his own will freely reflected back to himself by the Son, 'like an image in a mirror'. In the felicitous phrase of Basil of Caesarea, 'a coincidence of willing' thus characterises the relationship of perfect harmony between Father and Son. This means there is no sense of subordination, duress, or unwilling compliance in the relationship of the Son to the Father. Likewise, the obedience of the disciples to Jesus is a willing compliance in which the disciples themselves freely choose to do the will of the Son. The harmony of a 'coincidence of willing' is thus found between mutual friends.

In the Bible there are already some paradigms of same-gender friendships that operate as natural models for conceiving of an analogous friendship between humans and the divine. These provide the experiential grounding of the biblical doctrine of friendship. A classic example is the relationship of enduring friendship, characterised by a profound loyalty, commitment and love, between David and Jonathan.[9] There is certainly no sense in which this same-gender relationship is denigrated in the biblical text. Indeed, it is celebrated. David's love for Jonathan is said to have been 'wonderful, even greater than that of a woman'.[10]

The timelessly enduring qualities of the relationship of Ruth and Naomi, characterised by the celebrated values of loyalty and steadfastness of commitment that are expressed in the refrain 'where you go, I will go; where you lodge, I will lodge',[11] provides us with another example of an exemplary same-gender relationship.

In the New Testament, the example of the care expressed by the centurion for the servant 'who was dear to him'[12] and, above all, the intimacy of the relationship of friendship between Jesus and the twelve — and, within the number of the twelve, Jesus' special relationship with Peter, James and John, not to mention the 'disciple whom Jesus loved',[13] — encourage us to a positive view of same-gender relationships of friendship.

Moreover, the concept of friendship not only signals a degree of mutuality and respect that breaks down any sense of alienation or subordination of one party to the other, but is also an impulse of the saving work of Christ. The special relationship that allows Jesus to call his disciples not servants but friends, also grounds a willingness to sacrifice his life on their behalf. One characteristic of the commitment of friendship as a genuinely loving relationship is the element of self-sacrifice that overrides self-interest in the service of the ultimate good of the other: 'No one has greater love than this, to lay down one's life for one's friends' (John 15:13). It is clear that 'mutual society, help and comfort' to the point of willing self-sacrifice in the interests of the well-being of the other is quite properly found outside as well as within heterosexual marriage.

In classical literature a sustained reflection on the nature and value of friendship is to be found in Aristotle's *Nichomachean Ethics*.

Indeed, Aristotle is fully aware of the fundamental importance of friendship to human individuals: 'Nobody would choose to live without friends'.[14] But, for Aristotle, friendship also has a social value, for it is the bond that holds communities together.[15] At the same time it provides the context within which friends 'name together those activities that constitute virtue as well as vice',[16] for supportive friendship is a help to moral goodness.

Aristotle is also aware that there are various kinds of friendship. First, there are utility friendships, which are formed for the pragmatic purpose of achieving some goal. People might become friends in order to pursue some business deal, for example. Then there are what Aristotle calls pleasurable or erotic friendships. Finally, he speaks of perfect friendships. These are friendships based not upon motivations of self-interest, but on a genuine affection and respect for the other. While friendships based on some form of pragmatic self-interest tend to be passing and temporary, these friendships are more enduring. In this respect Aristotle's perfect friendships echo the sentiment of Proverbs 18:24: 'Some friends play at friendship, but a true friend sticks closer than one's nearest kin'.

More recently, in a classic analysis of friendship, Graham Little has highlighted its importance to individual self-identity: we come to know ourselves in relationship with others, and particularly in relation to those who respect and support us. Friendship provides a sacred space in which people may encounter one another, freed from the unreal expectations, assumptions and prejudices that tend to be imported into other relationships. In what Little calls 'communicating friendship', value is therefore seen in friendship as a means of self-discovery.[17] A friend accepts and respects one as oneself, and gives one support and the space to be. As a consequence, we become who we are as persons in relationship with others.

It is probably no coincidence that the very concept of a human person, as distinct from a mere human individual, appears to have emerged in the fourth century in the context of the development of the doctrine of the Trinity, in which the three, identifiable Persons are from all eternity found in relationship to one another and defined by their relationship to one another, in one Unity of Being. What Little calls 'communicating friendship' is, in a similar way, fundamental to the identity of human persons. The mutual interdependence of the Persons of the Trinity in the loving communion of fundamental friendship was described by John of Damascus with the term *perichoresis*. This denotes a cyclical movement in his theology of the Trinity, and is related to *perichoreuo*, which means to dance around. It conjures up a dynamic, non-hierarchical, equal, mutually-enriching relationship (a beautiful intertwining, unending dance, whose movement flows to and fro between the dancers).[18] This icon of friendship allows us to appreciate the importance of the relationality of persons to the development of personal self-identity in friendly communion with others.

Then there is the humanly redemptive effect of friendship. As George Santayana said, 'One's friends are that part of the human race within which one can be human.' One celebrated recent example of this kind of friendship is the relationship that developed between John McCarthy and Brian Keenan during the long period in which they were flung together in appalling circumstances as hostages in Lebanon. Of this Keenan wrote: 'The extraordinary bond that developed between John and myself was a bonding not just of two separate human beings caught up in a mortal whirlwind. It was also the bonding of our innermost selves or "people" in a manner which all of us perhaps deep down aspire to. John and I discovered not only a love for each other which transcended our divisions and backgrounds. We also discovered a renewed love for the world and its possibilities which, whilst nascent in us as children, had become buried by the accretions of the conscious worlds we had been brought up in'.[19] As a consequence of confinement together, Keenan and McCarthy grew together as intimate friends: 'There was no room in this place for any distance between us. We lay or sat side by side all day, every day. Like lovers in bed. There was little that could be withheld for long.'[20]

Not all Christian writers have portrayed friendship in such a positive light. C. S. Lewis, for example, in his fourfold analysis of love in *The Four Loves*, tends to downgrade the value of friendship in the interests of establishing a hierarchy in which the uniquely Christian love known as *agape* comes out on top. For Lewis, friendship does not have the interpersonal significance, for example, of Little's account of it. Rather, a somewhat doctrinaire agenda appears to provide the driving impulse for Lewis to elevate *agape* above *philia*, brotherly love, and this inevitably devalues friendship. Friendship, thus, is for him 'the least natural of loves; the least instinctive, organic, biological, gregarious and necessary'.[21] It is a kind of optional extra to being human. 'Both the individual and the community can survive without it'.[22] Thus, friendship is unnecessary, like philosophy, like art, like the universe itself (for God did not need to create).[23]

In contending that friendship is unnecessary for human survival and well-being, Lewis has entirely failed to appreciate its life-sustaining, life-changing potential. The importance of friendly acceptance, respect and interpersonal delight as the context in which one finds one's own true being and identity as a human person is entirely underestimated. Rather, for Lewis, friendships just happen to form around shared interests.[24] Thus, he writes, 'Lovers are normally face to face, absorbed in each other; Friends, side by side, absorbed in some common interest.'[25] Unfortunately, this tends to reduce friendship simply to a passing form akin to Aristotle's utilitarian type alone. It overlooks the rich and life-sustaining qualities of genuine, self-sacrificial friendship.

Lewis also, somewhat quaintly, imagines that for most of the time friendship will not exist between the sexes: 'For they will seldom have had with each other the companionship in common activities which is the matrix of Friendship'. Rather, the 'sexes will have met in Affection and Eros but not in this love.' It follows that for him it would not really be appropriate to speak of friendship within marriage.

At the other end of the spectrum, some contemporary feminist theologians raise friendship above marriage which, in the context of society marked by patriarchal structures, is held to be defective because of the element of male dominance that has come to be associated with it.[26] By contrast, friendship is said to admit of an affectionate mutuality and equality that is free of suggestions of power and control. But some feminist writers then go on to recoil from marriage, cast in the form of this stereotype, in favour of friendship. This leads to a tendency to treat marriage and friendship as polar opposites, even to the point of contending that friendships cannot be a one-to-one relationship. Rather, the contention is that a more diffused quality of friendly affection is always spread around amongst a larger number of people. This, however, fails to take account of the possibility of elevating one relationship of friendship above all others, such as is implicit in talk of one's 'best friend'.

In reality, human society is characterised by a network of various kinds of friendship, of differing levels of commitment and emotional intensity: there are those with whom we are 'just friends', and those with whom we are 'good friends', 'very good friends', or 'best friends'. It is logically impossible that every friend is one's 'best friend'. This seems to imply the ranking of some friendships above others, with a degree of intimacy denied to others. The category of friendship does not therefore exclude the possibility of a special relationship, one to one, to the exclusion of others. In this respect, friendship is both similar to marriage and found within marriage, rather than being its contrary.

The positive quality of friendship between two people of the same gender to the exclusion of others is explored by E. M. Forster in his novel *Maurice*, which appears in large part to be autobiographical. In the search for his own self-identity as a homosexual person, Forster seeks to define a middle way between the platonic ideal of a 'man-love' that is 'chaste with asceticism' and the more physical pull of lust, which was not entirely foreign to his own experience, even if he may not have necessarily succumbed to it. Forster allows Maurice to find an option with a greater all-embracing honesty between these two extremes: Maurice 'would not —and this was the test — pretend to care about women when the only sex that attracted him was his own. He loved men and always had loved them. He longed to embrace them and mingle his being with theirs.'[27] Indeed, clear scriptural echoes of the sacrificial qualities attaching to true friendship may be detected when Forster writes of Maurice: 'He could die for such a friend, he would allow such a friend to die for him; they would make any sacrifice for each other, and count the world nothing, neither death nor distance nor crossness could part them, because, this is my friend'.[28]

Elizabeth Stuart in *Just Good Friends*, a study of a theology of human relationships from a gay and lesbian perspective, has observed, 'People pushed to the edge, marginalised and oppressed, the victims of the survival-of-the-fittest world view, often appreciate that friendship is the only means to survive'.[29] It is thus understandable that the category of friendship is currently being favoured by homosexual people as a congenial and useful tool for characterising their experience. Michael Vasey speaks of homosexual relationships as examples of 'passionate friendship', in which interpersonal emotional attraction and involvement is an important defining feature.

What then, is to be the Church's view of faithful, long-term commitments within same-gender passionate friendships? Amongst heterosexual people, steadfast love and faithfulness are the signs of human relationships transformed by grace; such relationships reflect something of the character and presence of the God of hope, who is 'faithful to his promise'. This raises the question of whether steadfast love, enduring commitment, and loyalty are to be valued and celebrated, irrespective of any moral assessment that might be made of other qualities attaching to a relationship. Even amongst thieves and robbers, a glimmer of all that is good and beautiful in human friendship may show through, despite themselves, as it were, and be glimpsed, at least from time to time. Likewise, and irrespective of what conclusion might be drawn about physical behaviour within same-gender relationships, the element of loyal friendship and steadfastness of commitment may at least be celebrated and valued.

The Church may wisely avoid the concept of 'marriage' as a category for referring to same-gender relationships, even those of a long-term committed kind, given its normal purpose of procreation. The category of friendship may have much more to offer. However, the crucial question is whether the Church could bless a friendship expressed in some kind of covenant, or formalised life-long commitment secured by a solemn promise or contractual arrangement? There appears to be a biblical warrant for this possibility, given that, at one point in the David and Jonathan story, David is said to have 'made a covenant' with Jonathan,[30] and to have called on God to be witness to it. In other words, the implication is that God is called upon to look favourably on this covenant relationship, which is consciously and solemnly made in his presence, and to secure and sustain it. Indeed, the Spirit of God is understood to provide an ingredient essential to the permanence and stability of the relationship: Jonathan says to David, 'Go in peace, since both of us have sworn in the name of the Lord, saying, "The Lord shall be between me and you, and between my descendants and your descendants, forever"' (1 Samuel 20:42). It is clearly implied that this same-gender relationship of loyal friendship is essentially not just a good thing, but that it is appropriate to think that the 'go-between God' confers a positive 'blessing' upon it.

This classic paradigm raises the question of whether the Church might countenance the possibility of ministering to same-gender partnerships in the modern world in a similar way, by calling down God's blessing on a commitment to a permanent and exclusive, and thus special, one-to-one friendship. It seems unexceptionable that the Church could support law reforms to 'register' a relationship so as to secure social service benefits, pensions, and rights to property inheritance between partners of the same sex. The Church could also call down God's blessing on a household that is shared by friends. But, could it view same-gender friendships, not just with humane tolerance, but with a positive sense of acceptance, and could this acceptance be publicly expressed through some kind of formalised approval? In other words, could not the ministry of the Church publicly and solemnly witness this kind of covenant relationship in a way broadly analogous to the way that it furnishes a public witness to the marriages of heterosexual people? In this way the Church would be seen to be uncompromisingly saying 'No' to promiscuity by upholding the values of faithfulness and loyalty in a relationship of friendship intended to be permanent and exclusive. At the same time, by generating the expectation that the relationship will be exclusive and for life, it would provide concrete support that would make such relationships less likely to fail. Indeed, it could be argued that friendships of this kind 'participate in the divine nature' insofar as they show forth something of the steadfast love of the God who is always faithful to his promise.

On the other hand, given the polymorphous nature of human sexual activity, there is an obvious need to 'direct affections aright', in the interest of achieving social harmony and stability, avoiding the heartbreak of the trivialisation of relationships and securing the protection of people from hazards to health. In other words, the same good purpose outlined in the theology of marriage that affirms the value of marriage as a sacramental pledge, which has a salvific significance in so far as it is a help towards the avoidance of promiscuity in relationships, also operates in relation to same-gender friendships. The covenant form of the commitment would thus contribute to the saving of life from the health risk associated with the sin of promiscuity. Is there something positive to be said by the Church's affirming of 'stable committed relationships', both of a homosexual and heterosexual kind, and in a way that is entirely even-handed?

If so, what kinds of behaviour might be countenanced as appropriate within homosexual relationships, and what are the limits of touch? The physical expressions of friendship within same-gender relationships in contemporary society are familiar enough and apparently accepted. In particular, hugging is accepted as being appropriate between fathers and sons, and between football players celebrating a victory on the sporting field. But what does the Church have to say about genital activity within long-term committed homosexual relationships? There appear to be a number of options:

A regime of celibacy is to be advised, with strict, well-defined limits as to touch. Aelred of Rievaulx permitted the holding of hands amongst members of his Cistercian monastic community, but did not allow his charges to go any further than this. Certainly, the heroic life of the celibate is not to be undervalued or gainsaid. While many may say today that it is not a realistic option, the experience of many of a former generation is that they know that abstinence from sexual activity outside of marriage is an actual possibility. While the social pressure of today to conform to the values of permissiveness are much greater than a generation ago, the celibate life remains as a possibility. It is an option. The challenge to resist the pressure of the crowd and to maintain one's individual and personal integrity in a way that runs counter to the culture retains a positive attractiveness. The Church should commend this option.

Alternatively, it could be contended that the Church should say virtually nothing. In other words, it may prefer to bless a 'life-long commitment' simply as an acceptable form of human friendship, without enquiring into intimate private matters. This, it could be argued, is a matter that may be left to adult individuals to decide for themselves. This appears to be an option having a wide currency in contemporary culture, which is informed by Enlightenment values of individual autonomy, freedom and independence. The privatisation of moral values in the community at large is bound to spill into the life of the Church.

Given that the handful of biblical injunctions that have been brought to bear on the question of homosexual behaviour appear to be aimed primarily at promiscuity, and that it is assumed in the Bible that it is dealing with what we would call today undifferentiated heterosexually-orientated men (because homosexual orientation had yet to be defined),[31] there is inevitably no absolutely clear biblical teaching about behaviour that might be explicitly appropriate to homosexually-orientated persons. This is particularly the case in relation to the essentially modern question of homosexual people in what are intended to be long term-committed relationships. Certainly, there is nothing explicitly directed towards homosexual persons in long-term committed relationships in the biblical tradition. Where the Bible is itself silent, the Church may be wise to hesitate to speak.

While Thomas Aquinas regarded all non-reproductive sexual activity as lust, and therefore judged it to be sinful, this is not a position to which the Anglican Church is formally committed. Since the Lambeth Conference of 1958, non-reproductive — or what is commonly referred to today as recreational sexual activity — has been accepted as a normal part of the life of married heterosexual couples. Procreation is frankly and honestly acknowledged not to be the only purpose of marriage or of sexual activity within marriage. The inevitable logic of this modern Anglican assessment of human sexual activity seems to lead in the direction of accepting that some physical expression of the spiritual bond of friendship could be countenanced within same-gender relationships as a degree of recreational sexual activity.

While some physical contact may be seen as innocuous, it may be felt that to specify limits of touch would be as inappropriate for the relationship between couples of the same gender as within heterosexual marriage. Does the Church become involved in this, or is to do so merely an expression of the modern obsession with sex, an example of the voyeurism that is endemic in the modern world imported into the ecclesial environment? The Church might do better to concentrate on what may be positively said about the spiritual quality of such friendships as vehicles for the expression of love, joy, peace, forgiveness, gentleness, mutual respect, care and steadfast loyalty, and leave other matters to individual choice.

The Church might seek to define the limits of certain tolerable physical expressions of friendship, such as hugging, while seeking to uphold the biblical injunction against a man 'lying with' another man. However, this raises the question of the exact meaning of this euphemism. Is it specifically only anal intercourse that is prohibited, or is it to be understood to be inclusive of other tactile but purely manual expressions of a physical kind that might be thought appropriate within a relationship of passionate friendship? It may be noted that the passionate commitment between Ruth and Naomi is described significantly as *davkah bah* (Ruth 'clung to Naomi') which echoes the words of Genesis 2:24: 'Therefore a man leaves his father and his mother and clings (*davak*) to his wife, and they become one flesh'. Likewise, the passionate nature of the relationship between David and Jonathan may be discerned in the NRSV's version of 1 Samuel 20:41: 'He bowed down three times, and they kissed each other, and wept with each other; David wept the more'.[32]

In the moral teaching of the Church, it has been usual to admit a certain degree of physical contact within human relationships as a natural and acceptable way of expressing affection, while prohibiting other forms of behaviour. The precise limits of touch are subject to moral judgment and decision. How we Christians approach this complex and sensitive matter will be the subject of the next chapter. Meanwhile, our first task, before there is any discussion of appropriate physical behaviours, is to pause to reflect and to re-frame the understanding of homosexual relationships themselves within parameters set by the category of friendship. This will help us all, both those within the life of the Church and those in the wider secular society, to come to a deeper appreciation of the rich spiritual value of genuine friendship and of its very great importance to being authentically human.

Certainly, relationships of friendship between heterosexual people and homosexual people seem to be essential for providing an appropriate and supportive context for working out the details of a life of moral goodness. The Church's calling is to foster such friendships.

Endnotes

[1] For example, see Robert Williams, 'Towards a Theology of Gay and Lesbian Marriage' in *Christian Perspectives on Sexuality and Gender*, eds. Adrian Thatcher and Elizabeth Stuart (Eerdmans, 1996).

[2] Stanley Hauerwas, 'Virtue, Description and Friendship' in the *Irish Theological Quarterly*, Vol. 62 (1996-7), 181

[3] This argument runs parallel to that of the Reformers in relation to the perceived need to move in the direction of the relaxation of the requirement of celibacy. As Dr. Muriel Porter has pointed out in her paper in this collection, the Reformers argued that it would be better for clergy to have one wife than to abandon them to a promiscuous life of constant sexual temptation.

[4] As for example, Robert Williams, *Op. cit.*

[5] M. Friedman, *What are Friends For?* (Cornell University Press, 1993), p. 187.

[6] John Inge, 'Friendship and a Christian Understanding of Relationship', *Theology*, (Nov — Dec 1998), 420.

[7] John 15:15. See S. Hauerwas, 'Companions on the Way: The Necessity of Friendship', *The Astbury Theological Journal*, Vol. 45, No. 1, 46.

[8] This is the heresy of Arianism.

[9] Something of the depth of the relationship between David and Jonathan may be discerned in 1 Samuel 18:1: 'When David had finished speaking to Saul, the soul of Jonathan was bound to the soul of David, and Jonathan loved him as his own soul'. See also: 1 Samuel 18:3: 'Then Jonathan made a covenant with David, because he loved him as his own soul', and 1 Samuel 19:1: 'Saul spoke with his son Jonathan and with all his servants about killing David. But Saul's son Jonathan took great delight in David'.

[10] 2 Samuel 1:26: 'I am distressed for you, my brother Jonathan; greatly beloved were you to me; your love to me was wonderful, passing the love of women'.

[11] Ruth 1:16: 'But Ruth said,"Do not press me to leave you or to turn back from following you! Where you go, I will go; where you lodge, I will lodge; your people shall be my people, and your God my God"'.

[12] Luke 7:2: 'A centurion there had a slave whom he valued highly, and who was ill and close to death'.

[13] John 19:26: 'When Jesus saw his mother and the disciple whom he loved standing beside her, he said to his mother, "Woman, here is your son".

John 20:2: 'So she ran and went to Simon Peter and the other disciple, the one whom Jesus loved, and said to them, "They have taken the Lord out of the tomb, and we do not know where they have laid him"'.

John 21:7: 'That disciple whom Jesus loved said to Peter, "It is the Lord!" When Simon Peter heard that it was the Lord, he put on some clothes, for he was naked, and jumped into the sea'.

John 21:20: 'Peter turned and saw the disciple whom Jesus loved following them; he was the one who had reclined next to Jesus at the supper and had said, "Lord, who is it that is going to betray you?"'.

[14] Aristotle, *Nichomachean Ethics*.

[15] *Ibid*., 258.

[16] Stanley Hauerwas, 'Virtue, Description and Friendship', Op. cit., 179.

[17] Graham Little, *Friendship* (The Text Publishing Co., Melbourne, 1993), chapter 6.

[18] Brian Wren, *What Language Shall I Borrow? God-talk in Worship:A Male Response to Feminist Theology* (SCM Press, London, 1989), 211.

[19] Brian Keenan, *An Evil Cradling* (Vintage Press, London, 1992), xvi.

[20] *Ibid*., 124.

[21] C. S. Lewis, *The Four Loves* (Collins, London, 1960), 56.

[22] *Ibid*., 60.

[23] *Ibid*., 67.

[24] Lewis therefore argues that 'the typical expression of opening Friendship would be something like, "What? You too? I thought I was the only one"'. *Ibid*., 62.

[25] *Ibid*., 58. See also 63: 'Hence we picture lovers face to face, but Friends side by side; their eyes look ahead'.

[26] See for example, Mary E. Hunt, *Fierce Tenderness*, (Crossroad, New York, 1991), Chapter 4.

[27] E. M. Forster, *Maurice*, 53.

[28] *Ibid*., 15.

[29] Elizabeth Stuart, *Just Good Friends* (Mowbray, London, 1995), 46.

[30] 1 Samuel 20:17: 'Jonathan made David swear again by his love for him; for he loved him as he loved his own life'.

[31] The emergence of a clear awareness of homosexual as distinct from heterosexual orientation is a phenomenon only of the mid-nineteenth century. It cannot have formed part of the mental makeup of people in the first century in the same way as it does today.

[32] Other versions tell of David weeping until he 'recovered' or 'exceeded' himself. Wayne R. Dynes, *Encyclopedia of Homosexuality* (St James Press, London), Vol. I, 298, argues that this text may refer to sexual excitement. One suspects that this may be somewhat fanciful.

CHAPTER NINE

Anglican Moral Decision-making and the Challenge of Same Sex Unions

Scott Cowdell

Once again history has thrown up an issue that is causing the Anglican Church and its members a lot of soul-searching. It has to do with our acceptance of homosexuality, and whether we can give formal sanction to any expression of it. Homosexuality was once a collection of immoral practices; then, in late Victorian times, it became a named thing, a 'way of being', and subsequently, a medical condition. In recent decades, however, homosexuality has found growing acceptance throughout the Western world. Debate continues as to whether it is a natural state into which one is born, like left-handedness, or else an acquired identity, or perhaps nothing so clearly defined as that, but only a constraining designation 'constructed' by social forces. Not surprisingly, many recognise a continuum of influences, from nature to nurture to some search for self-definition through 'living the lifestyle'.

Certainly, it is important to learn from gay and lesbian people themselves, who tell a range of stories about their orientation — from the gay man who knew he was gay from boyhood to the militant lesbian feminist who has found, at last, a satisfying platform for her assault on patriarchy. But for many men and women, same-sex orientation is simply how they are. And like many of those in the heterosexual mainstream, there is a widespread desire to find a soul mate and life partner, and to settle down.

Gay and lesbian individuals and couples are present in increasing numbers in some of our congregations, where they are often welcomed and treated no differently from heterosexual individuals and couples by the people of God. But while in many places 'house blessings' and other such informal recognition of gay and lesbian commitment are celebrated by communities of faith, there is nothing 'official' in Australian Anglican practice to openly encourage and bless same-sex unions. Indeed, there is significant opposition within our Church toward such accommodation, from the High Church claim met in some quarters that same-sex relationships are 'against nature', through to implacable opposition by Evangelical Anglicans, many of whom are genuinely torn between compassion toward the plight of gay and lesbian fellow Christians, on the one hand, and the literal claims of Scripture on the other. Clearly, this is not a simple issue, but it is a pressing one. A significant part of our constituency looks to us for a wise and discerning response. And, as ever, the world looks on, pressing its proper claim on us: 'Sir, we wish to see Jesus' (John 12:21).

The Anglican tradition is certainly equal to this moment in Church history. Anglicanism offers a holistic vision of the moral life and rich traditions exploring it, which must be addressed as part of our wider search for the mind of Christ on this issue. In what follows, the work of a theologian who is not a specialist in Christian ethics, strands of those traditions will be considered under headings of 'Scripture', 'tradition' and 'reason', as they might impinge on the issue of same-sex unions. But first, the briefest historical comments, to indicate how traditions have varied within Anglican ethical reflection:

The classic Anglican 'threefold cord' was first woven by Richard Hooker as the theological method emerging in *Of the Laws of Ecclesiastical Polity* (1593-7). It served reflection on moral issues in the period of convulsive social and religious change in seventeenth-century England, in the hands of so-called Caroline divines.[1] They were a High Church party, taking up Hooker's challenge to the Puritans, on the one hand, and claims from Rome on the other. They were more open to scriptural authority than was the Roman Church, and more insistent on the preservation of tradition and the role of reason (understood in terms of intuition, rather than yet-to-flourish scientific rationality) than were the Calvinistic Puritans. Their ethical writings guided Anglicans striving to discern the right as members of Christ's body living a holy life in society—a vision of Christian life the English Prayer Book set out to foster.[2]

But this threefold dependence is not uniformly invoked within our communion. Evangelical Anglicans commonly claim that it undermines the primacy of Scripture (though this is not the intention of those who adhere to it). Following upon a developing Puritan tradition, away from the emphasis on informed conscience and appeal to nature which an early Puritan Churchman like William Perkins[3] shared with his High Church contemporary Hooker, in the direction of increased rigorism, the voice of God came to be only reliably discerned in Scripture.[4] By contrast, Anglo-Catholic moral theology until the mid-twentieth century tended to follow Roman Catholic traditions of ethical reflection, driven by needs of the newly reintroduced confessional, favouring 'reason' in theoretical assessments of God's will revealed in nature, and its discernment in structures of human psychology and conscience. This Anglo-Catholic approach shared the pastoral focus and holistic mood of Caroline moral theology, but was less shaped by its threefold source.[5]

'Reason' is also exalted in the main liberal trend of more recent Anglican moral theology. So-called 'situation ethics' arose during the 1960s ferment in America, sharing the increasingly widespread complaints that Roman Catholic appeal to 'nature' is no longer tenable, and that Evangelical appeal to Scripture is insufficiently aware of its context-dependence. What made 'situationism' distinctive, however, was flexibility in dealing with the moral precepts of Church tradition. These were valued as guides and resources for right action, but were not uncritically followed. The single scriptural principle of 'love' was exalted, and love's ends sought in each specific ethical situation. In effect reason, largely in the form of intuition, was what counted in ethical decision-making.[6]

I will now seek to follow the classic Anglican appeal to Scripture, tradition and reason in addressing the issue of same-sex unions, in the light of lessons learned from Puritan, Anglo-Catholic and liberal trends in ethical reflection. I conclude that same-sex unions are in principle compatible with the Anglican vision of holiness. Then, addressing the *real politic* of Anglican life in Australia, I highlight a further moral issue bedevilling our discussion of same-sex unions. It has become a self-definitional imperative for some of us to condemn gay and lesbian sexuality, and I want to argue that this itself is not moral. In closing, I will appeal to the best instincts of Anglican divinity in calling for a tolerant and mutually respectful debate.

Scripture

There can be no doubt that gay and lesbian sexual activity receives no clear warrant in Scripture, and appears to attract blanket condemnation. There is an extensive literature on several 'classic texts' of the Old and New Testaments, and debates over their interpretation are carried on elsewhere in this report of the Doctrine Panel. Suffice it to say that for every Evangelical reading claiming that Scripture disallows homosexual acts, there are alternative readings which insist on the context-dependence of such injunctions—for instance, that Israel's cultural purity is what rigid Levitical codes of the Old Testament foster, with homosexuality condemned only insofar as invasive foreign practices of all sorts are being condemned. In this same vein, culturally licensed Greek pederasty is understood to be the target of Paul's disapproval in the New Testament epistles, in his wider rejection of pagan attitudes and lifestyles as incompatible with the new dynamic of life in Christ. Read in this way, neither set of texts applies to homosexuality as such liberal readers understand it today.

Other passages are occasionally suggested as germinal to the scriptural debate, such as those reporting the love between David and Jonathan in 1 Samuel 20, the love of Ruth and Naomi in the Book of Ruth, and even the healing by Jesus of a Centurion's beloved servant in Luke 7 and Matthew 8, re-establishing a relationship that some would claim to have been of a widely recognised homosexual type. But none of these texts are clear enough in their intent to sway those convinced by more explicit texts condemning homosexual acts.

In passing, I would mention the apparent sexual pragmatism Paul demonstrates in 1 Corinthians 7. There we find none of Christianity's later focus on childbearing as the chief end of marriage, but only the pragmatic need to restrain sexual passion among those who are not, like Paul, blessed with sufficient continence. There is no rhetoric of God granting continence to any who are struggling, but only the concession that those so afflicted ought to marry. If Scripture might be seen to provide a pattern of behaviour, rather than specific rules, then might we not find in such Pauline pragmatism a potential warrant for monogamous gay and lesbian relationships as an antidote to promiscuity, on the pattern of Paul's advice to heterosexual Christians? I want to be clear, however, that if there is at best only the most marginal warrant for homosexuality in Scripture, then there is absolutely no warrant for *porneia*, understood to be sexual activity outside the marriage bond. From the start Christianity has hallowed marriage in its understanding of how Christ's members ought to order their sexual lives, when not along celibate lines.

If today's social norm of significantly deregulated sexual activity among heterosexual people—of what I call 'non-vocational sexuality'—is incompatible with any vision of committed Christian love, and the seriousness with which sexuality ought to be taken; if a lifestyle characterised by sexual self-indulgence is incompatible with the apostolic seriousness God calls forth from all the baptised, as part of the Church's political witness to a hardened and coarsened world, then there can certainly be no warrant for similarly uncommitted gay and lesbian sex either. But what about committed gay and lesbian relationships? Here the possibility of a gay and lesbian parallel to Christian marriage is raised. But more of this in the subsequent discussion of tradition.

Having addressed key Scriptural themes that have emerged in the Doctrine Panel debate, I now wish to shift gear, and consider what I believe to be the most fruitful line of New Testament inquiry on the subject of gay and lesbian relationships. If we are inclined to accept patterns of possible response in Scripture, rather than always demanding clear-cut rules of behaviour, then the New Testament account of a particular episode assumes central importance for our discussion. And it is not explicitly about homosexuality. Acts 10-15 shows us a Jewish Church confronted by an entirely unexpected development. The Spirit of God appeared to be leading the Church to a fundamental rethink of deeply-held defining principles, so that Gentiles could be admitted to baptism and full membership. 'Remember, please, the stakes', insists New Testament scholar Luke Timothy Johnson:

> The Gentiles were 'by nature' unclean, and were 'by practice' polluted by idolatry. We are obsessed by the sexual dimensions of the body. The first-century Mediterranean world was obsessed by the social implications of food and table fellowship. The decision to let the Gentiles in 'as is' and to

> establish a more inclusive form of table fellowship, we should note, came into direct conflict with the accepted interpretation of Torah and what God wanted of humans.[7]

The Scripture here testifies to the way God's Spirit acts to reinterpret past Scripture and shape Scripture for the future. Through the experience and witness of Paul, Peter and Barnabas (Acts 15:4-12), in particular following upon the extraordinary personal experiences of Peter in his dream of clean and unclean animals and his summoning by the Gentile Cornelius (in Acts 10), the Church at Jerusalem began to reinterpret Scripture inclusively, according to these new insights (Acts 15:13-20), whereupon a new mission of the Church was instituted. Is that crucial moment of Church history now matched by another equally crucial moment, in which a whole new group long thought to be 'outside the pale' are being drawn to full acceptance by the Spirit of God?

But such a concession does not authorise every excess of gay and lesbian sex; the Council of Jerusalem did not hesitate to impose conditions on the Gentiles (Acts 15:20), including one against fornication, which would carry over directly in the gay and lesbian parallel. Such an approach does, however, suggest how the Spirit drives a revaluation of scriptural evidence, as is the case in other recent attempts to reinterpret apparent scriptural condemnations of homosexuality. The key to this Acts account is the encounter by apostles of plain holiness among former outsiders, bearing evidence of the Spirit's work. 'Such witness is what the Church now needs from homosexual Christians', concludes Johnson. 'Inclusivity must follow from evidence of holiness', he insists; 'are there narratives of homosexual *holiness* to which we must begin to listen?'[8]

A sophisticated conservative rejoinder to this attempted parallel with Gentile inclusion is offered by Richard Hays who, in order to be convinced, would need a corollary to Paul's thorough theological reconstruction of Old Testament theology, which Paul came to see as 'Gentile-inclusive' all along. But no-one has yet shown how 'this development (i.e., concerning acceptance of homosexuality) can be understood as a fulfilment of God's design for human sexuality as previously revealed in Scripture'.[9] Stephen Fowl responds that 'human sexuality' is a modern idea, and that Scripture will not necessarily manifest the relevant teaching about human relationships unproblematically according to today's categories.[10] One might add that more recent theology is augmenting scriptural witness in this area.

Consider a related example. The successful Christian case against slavery did not rely on specific anti-slavery texts, with which the Bible is anything but replete, in order to make a scriptural case for human emancipation. The theological work was done in the period after the canon was closed, as is the case in any number of other instances where Scripture is called upon to deal with issues that have arisen since the period of Christian origins. Hays demands something here that the Church has not been in the habit of demanding—a fully-scripturally-based theology for new things it wishes to do. Instead, we need to see how Scripture serves the wider mission of the Spirit's work in forming the mind of Christ. One aspect of that is the role of tradition.

Tradition

Muriel Porter, in her contribution to this collection, notes that Christian tradition has not always been as concerned about homosexuality as many in the Church have become more recently. Similarly, other practices once thought to be 'unnatural' and otherwise inappropriate for Christians have now become entirely normal, such as charging interest on loans. The Lambeth Conference of 1930 and, more definitively, that of 1958 , reversed earlier Anglican attitudes toward artificial birth control based on a new appreciation of the relationship dimension of marriage. It is to this change, and the redefinition of what 'natural' means, that I would like to draw attention. We have changed our minds on a major moral issue to do with the primacy of relationship before. Perhaps we will do so again, in another area once thought to be 'unnatural'.

The earliest Anglican marriage rite added 'mutual society, help and comfort' to more traditional emphases, whereby marriage served 'as a remedy against sin, and to avoid fornication', as we have already noted in Paul, and also 'for the procreation of children', to which Roman Catholicism gives top priority as the 'natural' end of marriage (though, to this, Anglicanism adds what amounts to an Evangelistic extra: that children may 'be brought up in the fear and nurture of the Lord, and to the praise of his holy Name'). Here we already see tradition being not only honoured but also developed. Martin Bucer argued in 1551 that 'mutual society, help and comfort' ought to be placed first, rather than third, among the reasons given for marriage, becoming its primary purpose: 'For a true marriage can take place between people who seek neither for children nor for a remedy against fornication'.[13] So, too, for the prominent Caroline moral guide Jeremy Taylor: 'Society was the first designed' — which conclusion he based on Scripture (Genesis 2:18, 'It is not good for man to be alone').[14] The Protestant Churches have tended to emphasise this 'unitive dimension' of marriage above its 'procreative dimension', and Roman Catholic moral theology has more recently sought to bring them into closer balance.

Here is a development in the tradition of marriage that might go further, in the direction of affirming gay and lesbian unions as 'marriagelike'. Some argue for our doctrine of marriage itself to be developed so that it embraces both heterosexual and homosexual forms, thereby cutting the nerve with procreation altogether[15] (although children are raised in an increasing number of gay and lesbian households, and their presentation for baptism in our churches may prompt a further unfolding of this debate). Others, especially lesbian feminists, feel that present notions of marriage are impossibly patriarchal, and that we need to evolve something beyond marriage, which Elizabeth Stuart calls 'covenanted friendship', of which we might recognise both homosexual and heterosexual forms.[16]

Stanley Hauerwas draws attention, in this context, to the heterosexual Christian couple not blessed with children but thereby able to give particular witness to the primacy of relationship in marriage. As a partner in such a marriage myself, I have come to see this as a primary vocation of the childless Christian couple. I am sympathetic to Hauerwas' further suggestion, that there might be a similar vocation for the monogamous union of lesbian and gay Christians,[17] witnessing to the primacy of covenantal love as God's way for human beings.

So here we see possibilities for the doctrinal development of Christian marriage, in keeping with a trend rooted in the Reformation use of Scripture, as well as in the developing Puritan tradition of covenant as the central theme of ethics. But what about the problem of such a solution being 'against nature'? To the role of reason in our decision-making we now turn.

Reason

Here the issue is chiefly whether homosexuality is 'natural'. Nature as God's other book, alongside Scripture, is well established in Hooker and the Caroline Divines. With Bishop Butler and Archdeacon Paley in the eighteenth century, it assumed its more contemporary Anglican shape, appealing to a rapidly developing body of scientific truth. Yet natural law as a guide was seen to be limited from the start of Anglican moral reflection,[18] and this for two reasons. First, Protestant concern about the insufficiency of sinful human minds to know God unaided was a factor, and this for High Church writers as well as Puritans (though not to the same extent, of which more shortly). Second, many issues purporting to be resolvable with reference to natural law turn out not to be as plain as they ought to be, 'whereas', for Jeremy Taylor, 'if the law of nature were such a thing as is supposed generally, these differences would be as strange and impossible as that men should disagree about what is black, or what is yellow'.[19]

The fortunes of natural law have declined since the time of Butler and Paley, especially as we came to appreciate the extent of cultural diversity and the changing history of ideas since the nineteenth century. The 'universal precepts' of natural law are reduced to such things as 'avoid the evil' and 'do the good', and these are platitudinous, concludes Bishop James Pike. Furthermore, the natural law approach is discredited by its chequered history, having been used to 'defend anything and everything—feudalism, capitalism, socialism, fascism, both the "divine right of Kings" and democracy, denial of political and religious liberty ('error has no rights') and affirmation of the same ('conscience is always to be followed')'.[20] Joseph Fletcher concludes that Christian belief stands behind natural law maxims invoked by Anglican theology which, apart from prior Christian conviction, have no useful independent existence. 'The natural law may persist as an ontological affirmation', he concedes, 'but it is dead as an epistemological doctrine'[21] (i.e., we may acknowledge its presence in the background of things, but it is hard to read, and draw conclusions from).

Nevertheless, the possible 'natural' status of homosexuality remains on the agenda, despite these problems that have arisen in our understanding of natural law. It is important to comment on this ongoing discussion of what is natural, for it remains significant, despite its increasingly dubious credentials.

The possibility of a 'homosexuality gene' is widely canvassed, for instance, as are the effects of sex hormones on the foetus, with the possibility that homosexuality might be caused by conditions in the uterine environment. There are some for whom such possibilities are good news, providing ready grounds for approval of homosexuality on the basis that 'those whom God has joined together, let no-one put asunder'. Such supposed compatibility of homosexuality with 'nature' is a key factor in The Church of Sweden's blessing of same-sex unions, though should such scientific support fail, their decision is reversible. What are we to make of such a ready solution to our problem?

To be sure, such a solution is likely to carry the day for some Anglicans. For many of our people, the literal reading of Scripture is not something to which they are committed, but the sense that God has ordered the world in a certain way does carry important moral weight. As homosexuality ceases to be seen as unhealthy (apart from the safe-sex issue, which applies to heterosexuals also), and in any sense pathological, but rather a normal condition for a small percentage of humans, no more problematic than left-handedness, then the fears of many Anglicans will be assuaged. But there are some complications here.

First, an alternative understanding of nature has to be considered. There is a tradition reaching from Augustine in the fifth century to John Calvin in the sixteenth century, to the Puritans in the seventeenth century, to Karl Barth in the twentieth century, and hence to 'radical orthodoxy' in the hands of contemporary Anglican theologians like John Milbank, for whom 'the natural' must be distinguished from 'fallen nature'. This theological tradition, which Evangelical Anglicanism represents, is unconvinced by many conclusions of human reason — because the world and the human mind share in 'the fall', and can provide no guide for us as to how things ought to be, apart from the unmediated confirmation and correction provided by Scripture. So just because something is 'natural' will not convince Evangelical Anglicans that it is allowable — because Scripture suggests to them that it is not part of the world as God intended it. And this scripturally-revealed state of affairs is the true meaning of nature for such readers—nature refers to the world as God intended it, rather than the world as it is.

Second, we do well to ask whether questions of what is natural are adequate to explain a phenomenon (or set of phenomena) as complex as lesbian and gay experience. I point to a widespread sense that homosexual behaviour on the part of some people is learned, and voluntarily entered into, rather than flowing from natural inclination. Simple evidence for this understanding can be found wherever men are thrown together without the company of women for long periods, as in prisons or on long sea voyages. Homosexual behaviour can be a feature of such periods for otherwise heterosexual men. Fathers have long feared the bad influence of gay friends in the formative years of sons' lives. The 'LUG' phenomenon, 'lesbian until graduation', is certainly present among young university women.[22] Indeed, full-blown protest lesbianism is described as a lifestyle of choice in militant feminist circles. And there is bisexual experimentation among many young people today. Is all of this perfectly natural, so that no real choice is involved?

Or is the radical historian of ideas, Michel Foucault, right that human sexuality is essentially fluid, and that ordering and controlling forces of society are what create and police sexual identities, so that: 'The sodomite had been a temporary aberration; the homosexual was now a species'?[23] From this influential thesis of Foucault comes gay and lesbian protest rhetoric. The notion that homosexuality is 'natural' is seen to be a constraining, disempowering definition, insensitive to the cultural reality of gay and lesbian experience. These lifestyles are understood to be subversive, according to such a reading, and attempts by the rational, ordering Western mind to 'normalise' homosexual reality is seen to be politically motivated, and oppressive. Foucault's essentially Marxist thesis resists the definition, control and hence discipline of experience which capitalist society requires of its members, so that they will be good, predictable workers and consumers.

In keeping with her alternative reading of cultural history, cultural historian and literary critic Camille Paglia understands homosexuality as 'a resistance to the grossest of human dependencies, our enslavement by nature',[24] hence it is fundamentally a matter of choice, and 'unnatural' on purpose.

Further bursting the balloon of nature is newly-minted 'queer theory', whereby gay and lesbian studies seek to carve out a transgressive identity in the academy.[25] Following the post-structuralist currents in which Foucault also swims, there is a swelling of gay and lesbian voices rejecting any attempt to 'domesticate' homosexual experience. What are we to make, in terms of neat categories, of Pat Califia's detailing of 'a lifestyle that doesn't fit the homosexual stereotype. I live with my woman lover of five years. I have lots of casual sex with women. Once in a while, I have casual sex with gay men. I have a three-year relationship with a homosexual man who doesn't use the term gay. And I call myself a lesbian'?[26]

Yet, in less politically charged circles, there is a lot of testimony to the normality of gay and lesbian experience from those who find themselves in the midst of it. Regardless of its origins, in nature, genetics, biochemistry or wherever, there is a sense that no choice has been made by many who discover their sexuality naturally, as part of growing up. This is the burden of many poignant testimonies in a recent volume of Australian 'coming-out stories'.[27] Robert Dessaix, a much-loved gay Australian writer, and himself no advocate of a conventional life lived behind the white picket fence, is sceptical when 'contemporary cultural historians, ensconced comfortably inside linguistic models of reality, claim that since the word homosexuality did not exist until the late nineteenth century, homosexuality as such did not exist until then'.[28] So, while there is certainly a cultural politics of gender and sexuality that forms a part of the gay and lesbian issue, there is also the brute fact of homosexual inclination, however you account for it.

I have laboured this point because liberal theology seems committed to a particular theory of homosexuality — that it is natural. Yet many voices dispute such a conclusion. 'Once again', complains lesbian feminist theologian Elizabeth Stuart, 'we have to reclaim our bodies and experiences from medicine, psychology and tolerant liberals who accept us because we "cannot help being the way we are" and claim the freedom to choose to whom we relate sexually'.[29] Such voices have not been heard adequately in our Church's debate. But as I say there are also voices claiming the normalcy and ideological neutrality of homosexual experience, though without necessarily delving into the why of it, nor seeking its scientific clarification.

Where, then, do we stand on these complicated issues? Despite the insufficiency and perhaps even the undesirability of scientific explanations, and despite the complexity of cultural factors involved, many Anglicans will still see same-sex preference as a normal and unproblematic — albeit a minority — orientation, welcoming its acceptance in the Church in the same way they welcomed its decriminalisation by society at large. Yet most will draw the line at condoning sexual practice entered into for motives of self-definition, political assertion and ideological vandalism, just as they will condemn the idle dabbling in same-sex relationships that is a feature of recreational sex on the part of some among today's young. Among those not inclined to accept the normalcy of homosexual orientation, scientifically established or otherwise, because of a prior commitment to Scripture defining what is most truly 'natural', no understanding of homosexuality will suffice to change their mind. Indeed, the presence of insistent voices among the homosexual community and its intellectually sophisticated advocates explaining the whole thing as a lifestyle of choice, essentially of protest, will only serve to confirm for them Paul's unsparing assessment in Romans 1:24, whereby 'God gave them up in the lusts of their hearts to impurity, to the degrading of their bodies amongst themselves, because they exchanged the truth about God for a lie…'. In all, nature will not solve this problem for us.

In Conclusion: How Might We Move Forward?

We do well to ask ourselves just why it is we oppose reform on this issue, if such is our stance. Is it purely because our understanding of the natural law precludes homosexuality? Or is there an element of protest behind our conviction, resisting all the unwelcome change and social upheaval that this issue illustrates? Is it because we find homosexuality personally distasteful, or maybe because affirming the blessing of same-sex unions lets the genie of robust sexuality out of that bottle of bloodless piety where many Christians have preferred to keep it? Do we oppose it purely because Scripture forbids us to budge? Or is there a deeper reason, to do with our self-understanding as Bible-believing Christians, for whom this has become a crucial test case?

Anglican scholar Stephen Barton, in analysing this debate in the English Church, finds much insight in the realm of sociology and anthropology. Following the classic anthropological work of Mary Douglas, *Natural Symbols*, Barton reminds us how the rules and boundaries a society needs to define itself over against other societies are often echoed in the way sexual and other bodily boundaries are established, so that we feel our society's constraints viscerally, as if written onto our own bodies. This is as true of our strong negative reaction to certain experiences of touch and taste, and of our intolerance of pollution at bodily orifices, as it is sexually. Yet Barton points to Jesus as a regular transgressor of social boundaries, in touch with the unclean and defiled, redrawing the map of society along the lines of God's gracious covenant of transforming love.[30] This dimension of the Gospel is frequently uncomfortable yet, equally, the Church regularly demonstrates the acceptance of God for the humanly unacceptable (though often in less politically partisan ways). Think of Mother Teresa and her Christlike witness among the social outcastes of Indian society. Thus the Christian gospel overrides 'nature' — in reality, socially constructed prejudices — in all manner of ways, in the New Testament and also today. Barton suggests that our rejection of homosexual persons needs challenging in the light of this realisation.

But there is an ecclesial version of this rejection that may cut even deeper. Barton is aware that Church party lines are drawn on this issue. This insight is also traced at length by two Australian Church historians. David Hilliard does so directly, referring to homosexuality within Anglicanism. He uncovers the cultural roots of opposition to homosexuality in the English Church, linked to the angry Protestant reaction against Anglo-catholic ritualism in the nineteenth century, which was despised as 'unenglish and unmanly'. Homosexuality and Anglo-catholicism found a natural affinity, according to Hilliard, chiefly because both are minority movements disaffected with the Protestant establishment.[31] That antipathy still exists, as Hilliard is able to chart in his historical analysis of the homosexuality debate in our Anglican Church of Australia. He compares attitudes in the largely Anglo-catholic Diocese of Adelaide, a city where tolerance of homosexuality was pioneered in Australia, with Anglican attitudes in evangelical Sydney, among whom opposition to homosexuality came to be a defining issue of fidelity to Scripture and opposition to worldliness.[31]

The pre-history of this attitude in Sydney is provided by a historian and son of that diocese, Bill Lawton. He identifies, with Hilliard, the self-definition of Sydney Anglicanism against Tractarianism in the nineteenth century. He goes on to trace a developing theological debt to nineteenth-century millenarian thinking (not primarily to Reformation principle) that led to a Kingdom of God theology antagonistic to the world. Conservative evangelicals in this mould rejected social reform currents among their more liberal evangelical brethren, yet fought a number of battles 'on principle' over a range of linked issues: Christian temperance, Sabbath observance and opposition to more liberalising marriage laws, all of which combine 'family values' with the anticipation of heaven and Christian duty to fight off the secularist bogey. Lawton concludes that these attitudes continue among the conservative evangelicals of Sydney Diocese, naming an ongoing militant utopianism that he understands as the perennial obverse of secularism.[33]

This history sheds light on the way more recent issues affecting gender are received in Sydney Diocese, namely women's ordination and the call to bless same-sex unions.

But does this assertion of party spirit disqualify those making it from claiming any moral superiority in this debate? On this point, G.F. Woods was surely right that

> When we reflect upon the grounds of our moral decision, we may come to see quite clearly that we were not at the time fully conscious of all the factors which led to our decision. It is our duty, when we are made aware of these unconscious grounds, not to despair of making well-grounded moral judgements but actively to examine whether we can morally

> approve or disapprove of the factors which have unconsciously influenced our decision. I think it is convenient to distinguish between the causes of our moral judgements and the reasons by which we seek to justify them.[34]

Thus we recognise that there are not one but two moral issues confronting us in this homosexuality debate. One has to do with homosexuality. The other has to do with the sort of debate we are going to have about it. Will it be an exercise in self-definition by Church parties, ideologically driven, or will it be characterised by the sort of vigilant attention to Scripture which frankly acknowledges our biases in reading it, so we might be able to discern any new leading from God's Spirit? There is, after all, the challenge of Jesus to ensure the body sees aright, to 'consider whether the light in you is not darkness' (Luke 11:35).[35] To assist us we need to cultivate an eye for what Bishop Rowan Williams, in a plenary address to the 1998 Lambeth Conference on this issue, called 'the grammar of obedience',[36] so we recognise one another's seriousness and faith commitment and match it with our own.

I conclude that the blessing of same-sex unions can be seen as a valid development in line with Anglican moral sensibility. I have suggested that tradition does not forbid it and, indeed, may point the way to it through our developing doctrine of marriage as relationship. I have suggested in a discussion of reason that nature is a problematic category in Anglican moral reflection, besides which homosexuality is such a complex issue that to assess whether it is natural, assuming one could, is not enough. In a discussion of Scripture I concluded that our decision on this matter is of a familiar form, paralleling the move to Gentile inclusion in the first decades of Christianity. Yet in this process Scripture is not the only key. God's Spirit led the Church in its struggle with Gentile inclusion to rethink the interpretation of Scripture, based on plain evidence of what the Spirit was doing among Gentile Christians. I submitted that in attending to testimonies of faith and holiness among homosexual people today, the Church may again find the will to reinterpret Scripture more inclusively.

In all of this, the decision has to do not simply with a text, nor with an abstract principle, nor again with inviolate tradition. Anglicanism finds its identity in the living conversation between Scripture and life in the context of a deepening incorporation into Christ. In this process, at once spiritual, liturgical and moral, personal, congregational and public, we seek the mind of Christ, at one with each other in a mystical fellowship more fundamental than any difference in 'churchmanship'. This process expresses the vision of a Reformed Catholic Church living integrally in society, of the sort imagined in our earliest Prayer Books. Nothing less than this is worthy of the subtle, if sometimes perplexing, genius of Anglican moral decision-making.

Endnotes

[1] The classic work is still H. R. McAdoo, *The Structure of Caroline Moral Theology* (Longmans, Green & Co., London, 1949), though it is suggested that he overstates the commonality of approach among the Caroline divines; see Timothy F. Sedgwick, 'Revising Anglican Moral Theology' in Paul Elmen, ed., *The Anglican Moral Choice* (Morehouse-Barlow, Wilton, CT, 1983), 121-140. Also helpful on this period is Thomas Wood, *English Casuistical Divinity During the Seventeenth Century: With Special Reference to Jeremy Taylor* (SPCK, London, 1952) and Kevin T. Kelly, *Conscience: Dictator or Guide? A Study in Seventeenth-Century English Protestant Moral Theology* (Geoffrey Chapman, London, 1967).

[2] This holistic moral vision is beautifully evoked in John E. Booty, 'The English Reformation: A Lively Faith and Sacramental Confession' in Paul Elmen, ed., *The Anglican Moral Choice*, 15-32.

[3] See Thomas F. Merrill's 'Introduction' to his *William Perkins* 1558-1602: *English Puritanist* (De Graaf, Nieuwkoop, 1966).

[4] See, e.g., James T. Johnson, 'Puritan Ethics' in John Macquarrie and James Childress, eds., *A New Dictionary of Christian Ethics* (SCM, London, 1986), 519-522.

[5] Three landmark works will serve to chart the emergence of this trend: Kenneth E. Kirk, *Some Principles of Moral Theology and Their Application* (Longmans, Green & Co., London, 1921), R.C. Mortimer, *The Elements of Moral Theology* (Adam & Charles Black, London, 1947), and Herbert Waddams, *A New Introduction to Moral Theology* (SCM, London, 1964).

[6] The classic text, by an Episcopalian seminary professor in ethics, was Joseph Fletcher, *Situation Ethics: The New Morality* (SCM, London, 1966).

[7] Luke Timothy Johnson, *Scripture and Discernment: Decision-Making in the Church* (Abingdon, Nashville, 1983) 147. Other important contributions on this parallel of Gentile and gay/lesbian inclusion are Jeffrey S. Siker, 'Homosexual Christians, the Bible, and Gentile Inclusion: Confessions of a Repenting Heterosexist' reproduced, for example, in Siker, ed., *Homosexuality in the Church: Both Sides of the Debate* (Westminster/John Knox, Louisville, 1994) 178-194, and also Stephen Fowl, *Engaging Scripture: A Model for Theological Interpretation* (Blackwell, Oxford, 1998) 119-127.

[8] Johnson, *Scripture and Discernment*, 148.

[9] Richard Hays, *The Moral Vision of the New Testament* (Harper San Francisco, 1996), 399.

[10] Fowl, *Engaging Scripture*, 124, n. 54.

[11] Report of a Committee on 'The Life and Witness of the Christian Community…Marriage and Sex', especially pp. 89-98 on 'Birth Control' in *Lambeth Conference* 1930: *Encyclical Letter from the Bishops with Resolutions and Reports* (SPCK, London, 1930).

[12] Report of a Committee on 'The Family in Contemporary Society', especially the section on 'Family Planning', pp. 2.146-2.150 in *The Lambeth Conference 1958: The Encyclical Letter from the Bishops Together with the Resolutions and Reports* (SPCK, London, 1958).

[13] Martin Bucer, *Censura*, 'The Order of Service for the Consecration of Matrimony'; 'The First Reason for Matrimony', tr. E.C. Whitaker, *Martin Bucer and the Book of Common Prayer* (Alcuin Club Collections No. 55, 1974), cited in Robert Williams, 'Toward a Theology for Lesbian and Gay Marriage' in Adrian Thatcher and Elizabeth Stuart, eds., *Christian Perspectives on Sexuality and Gender* (Gracewing, Leominster, 1996) 279-300.

[14] Jeremy Taylor, 'The Marriage Ring', Sermon XVII in *A Course of Sermons for All the Sundays in the Year*, Vol IV, in Reginald Heber and Charles Eden, eds., *The Whole Works of the Right Rev. Jeremy Taylor, D.D.*, cited in Robert Williams, 'Toward a Theology of Lesbian and Gay marriage', 284.

[15] Robert Williams, 'Toward a Theology of Lesbian and Gay Marriage' (Williams is an Episcopalian in a 'gay marriage').

[16] Elizabeth Stuart, 'Lesbian and Gay Relationships: A Lesbian Perspective' in Thatcher and Stuart, eds., *Christian Perspectives*, 301-317.

[17] Stanley Hauerwas, 'Virtue, Description and Friendship: A Thought Experiment in Catholic Moral Theology', *The Irish Theological Quarterly* 62 (1996-7), 171-184.

[18] The rise and fall of natural law thinking in Anglican moral theology is traced in a fine essay by Joseph Fletcher entitled, 'The Ethics of Natural Law', reproduced in Fletcher, *Moral Responsibility: Situation Ethics at Work* (SCH, London, 1967) 58-78, 246-249; see also a similarly withering discussion in Harmon L. Smith, 'Contraception and Natural Law: A Half-Century of Anglican Moral Reflection' in Paul Elmen, ed., *The Anglican Moral Choice*, 181-200, 268-271.

[19] Jeremy Taylor, *Ductor Dubitantium*, II.i.1.

[20] James Pike, *A Time For Christian Candor* (Longmans, Green & Co., London, 1964) 41-50, cited in Fletcher, 'The Ethics of Natural Law', 71.

[21] Fletcher, 'The Ethics of Natural Law', 72-3.

[22] Hugh Mackay, *Turning Point: Australians Choosing their Future* (Macmillan, Sydney, 1999) xxiii.

[23] Michel Foucault, *The History of Sexuality*, Vol 1, tr. Robert Hurley, this tr. 1978 (Penguin, London, 1990) 43.

[24] Camille Paglia, *Sexual Personae: Art and Decadence from Nefertiti to Emily Dickinson* (Penguin, London, 1992), 158.

[25] A very helpful overview of this movement is provided by Annamarie Jagose, *Queer Theory* (Melbourne University Press, 1996).

[26] Pat Califia, 'Gay Men, Lesbians and Sex: Doing It Together', *Advocate*, 7 July 1983, 24-7, p. 25, cited in Jagose, *Queer Theory*, 67-8.

[27] Erin Shale, ed., *Inside Out: An Australian Collection of Coming Out Stories* (Bookman, Melbourne, 1999).

[28] Robert Dessaix, 'Through Pink-Coloured Glasses: A Gay Perspective on Australian Literary History', reproduced in (*and so forth*) (Macmillan, Sydney, 1998), 241-272.

[29] Elizabeth Stuart, 'Lesbian Perspectives in Feminist Theology', in Lisa Isherwood and Dorothy McEwan, eds., *An A-Z of Feminist Theology* (Sheffield Academic Press, Sheffield, 1996), 118-121.

[30] Stephen C. Barton 'Homosexuality and the Church of England: Perspectives from the Social Sciences', *Theology 92*(1989), 175-181.

[31] David Hilliard, 'Unenglish and Unmanly: Anglo-Catholicism and Homosexuality', *Victorian Studies* 25 (1982), 181-210.

[32] David Hilliard, 'Australian Anglicans and Homosexuality: A Tale of Two Cities', *St Mark's Review* 163 (Spring 1995), 12-20.

[33] William Lawton, *The Better Time to Be: Utopian Attitudes to Society Among Sydney Anglicans 1885-1914* (The Modern History Series # 11; The New South Wales University Press, Sydney, 1990).

[34] G.F. Woods, 'The Grounds of Christian Moral Judgements' in A. R. Vidler, ed., *Soundings: Essays Concerning Christian Understanding* (Cambridge University Press, 1962) 194-217.

[35] See the searching meditation on this passage in Stephen Fowl, *Engaging Scripture*, 75-83.

[36] Rowan Williams, 'Address at Lambeth Plenary on Making Moral Decisions—July 22, 1998', The Lambeth Conference 1998, Press Release #35 (LC98/GEN/031.1) 7.

CHAPTER TEN

Ordination and the Practice of Homosexuality

Peter Jensen

It is easy enough in investigating a subject like this to omit the human concerns that are behind it. The Doctrine Panel's meeting with homosexual people in November 1999 was a very significant element in the final shaping of all our papers. So, too, is our individual experience of listening to those who have confided in us about themselves. We owe such friends a great debt.

The chapter that follows addresses a particular problem in the usual way of investigation, analysis and argument. But it is written in the powerful and personal recollection of the realities which impact on so many lives.

Ordination

The standard of life for those seeking ordination stems in large part from the teaching given in the Pastoral Epistles. Christ rules his Church by his word, and we read of the minister of the word that:

> the overseer must be above reproach, the husband of but one wife, temperate, self-controlled, respectable, hospitable, able to teach, not given to drunkenness, not violent but gentle, not quarrelsome, not a lover of money. He must manage his own family well and see that his children obey him with proper respect. (If anyone does not know how to manage his own family, how can he take care of God's church?) He must not be a recent convert, or he may become conceited and fall under the same judgment as the devil. He must also have a good reputation with outsiders, so that he will not fall into disgrace and into the devil's trap.

Reflecting these biblical injunctions, the Collect in the Ordering of Priests (*Book of Common Prayer*) asks that God will 'replenish them so with the truth of thy doctrine, and adorn them with innocency of life, that, both by word and good example, they may faithfully serve thee in this office, to the glory of thy Name, and the edification of thy Church'.

As a consequence of this understanding of Christ's will for his people, Church law has never allowed the ordination of those in irregular sexual relationships, heterosexual or homosexual. But new points of view are emerging. Have we reached the point when a bishop may, in good conscience, ordain a practising homosexual? Despite the arguments in favour, I remain unpersuaded, and this chapter explains why. I will begin, however, by briefly outlining the case that is put forward to support such an action.

1. A case for ordaining homosexually active persons

Defining the recipient of such ordinations

The discussion is not about promiscuous persons. All agree that a lifestyle involving multiple sexual partners is sinful and inconsistent with the exercise of Christian ministry.

The discussion is not about wilfully chosen homosexual activity by a person who could equally relate to a member of his or her own sex as to a member of the opposite sex. This would clearly fall under the apostolic condemnation of Romans1:24-27, even if Paul knew nothing of the innate homosexual disposition.

The discussion is not about non-sexually active persons of a homosexual disposition: there has never been a barrier as such to such persons being ordained.

The discussion is only about those persons of an innate homosexual disposition who live in a stable, committed, exclusive but homosexual relationship. The relationship is admittedly not marriage, but it has some of the features of marriage. Provided that a bishop were satisfied that this characterised the lifestyle of a homosexually active person, it is now argued by some Christians that he could ordain him or her.[1]

Explaining the Bible

There is no doubt that both biblical Testaments condemn the practice of intercourse between members of the same sex.

'You shall not lie with a male as with a woman; it is an abomination' (Lev 18:19); 'Their women exchanged natural intercourse for unnatural, and in the same way also the men, giving up natural intercourse with women, were consumed with passion for one another. Men committed shameless acts with men and received in their own persons the due penalty for their error' (Rom 1:26-27; see also Lev 20:13 and 1 Cor 6:9).

But what exactly is condemned here? Several lines of argument are thought to modify or put aside the apparent rigour of the biblical word:

First, the definition of homosexuality. It is argued that until the nineteenth century it was assumed that homosexual behaviour was chosen by people who were basically heterosexual. It was thought to be a chosen deviance or perversion, a matter of the will. The insight of the nineteenth century was that for some at least (and perhaps for many), homosexual behaviour arose from a disposition, not a choice as such. The source of the disposition may be nature or nurture, or a mixture. It was in itself no more condemnable than being left-handed, however, and acting upon it was likewise 'natural'.

Since this insight was not one understood by ancient people, it is said that the biblical condemnations do not take it into account. Texts such as Romans 1:26-27 may still stand as condemning promiscuity and 'unnatural' sexual actions by heterosexual persons. But, it is argued, they do not condemn either the homosexual disposition, or the actions based on it, as long as the latter are undertaken in the context of a loving, committed and exclusive relationship, and may even be reinterpreted as 'natural'.

Second, a better exegesis of biblical narratives and words. Thus the story of Sodom is one of rape and mob violence, not of homosexuality as such. The use of the Sodom story to cover all expressions of homosexuality is a tragic misunderstanding of the Bible. As well, it is argued that the Greek expressions for homosexuality in a passage such as 1 Corinthians 6:9 do not relate to ordinary homosexual practices. Note the NRSV translation of this passage: 'Fornicators, idolaters, adulterers, male prostitutes, sodomites...none of these will inherit the kingdom of God'. At the least, there are doubts about the correct translation of the relevant words.

Third, the standing of the Old Testament in the Church. The menacing law of the Old Testament needs to be put into its context. There are other OT laws (e.g., food regulations) which we freely ignore. The question is raised: why should we insist on observing the Levitical ban on homosexual practice?

In sum, it is said, the Bible is not clear. In such circumstances, liberty of action is called for. There are legitimate differences of opinion that, at the very least, may lead to differences of practice.

Coping with Tradition

Just as the Bible appears to be opposed to homosexual activity, so is the historical verdict of the Church through its traditions and its laws. Once again this seems so clear as to require little justification. Once again, however, various factors are advanced to mitigate or overturn the severity of this judgement.

First, as with the biblical writers, it is said that the theologians of the Church did not possess the modern insight into the homosexual disposition. In the ancient world the form of homosexuality often practised was pederasty, for example, and this was obviously opposed to God's will. But it is not the same thing as an adult, committed, loving and exclusive relationship.

Second, there are phases of history where homosexuality was not so sternly rebuked and may even have existed amongst the ordained in a semi-approved way. In other words, the Christian tradition may not unanimously oppose homosexuality.

Third, the pre-modern understanding of sex, both physiologically and psychologically, was inadequate. In particular, sex was regarded as being primarily or only for the purpose of procreation. This was its only natural use. Thus, even sex within marriage, if it did not have the procreative end in view, was regarded as possibly lustful. Homosexual sex was forbidden precisely because it unnaturally did not allow for the conception of children. Likewise, contraceptive practices were forbidden. But the contemporary Church has changed its mind. It encourages us to think of pleasurable and affectionate sex between committed married heterosexual partners as innocent, and contraception as allowable, or even as a possible duty. Likewise, there is no reason to condemn sex between same-sex partners as unnatural merely because it cannot lead to conception.

Fourth, since we have come to the view that matters thought impossible because forbidden in scripture or in tradition are permissible – we ordain women to the priesthood, for example; we use contraception; we allow for wide latitude in divorce and remarriage – we also have the freedom to change the traditional view of homosexuality. In doing so we should not encourage the sort of sins that would be wrong for either heterosexuals or homosexuals, such as promiscuity. But we should allow for committed, faithful exclusive sexual relationships even between persons of the same sex.

In sum, it is said that our ecclesiastical ancestors were context-bound. We may respect the insights of the past, while not being subject to them.

2. A case against ordaining homosexually active persons

The case for allowing the ordination of actively homosexual persons in loving, exclusive and committed sexual relationships is thus lucid and, in its own terms, cogent. As I have already indicated, however, I do not find it persuasive. Reasons for that position I will now explain.

The case against may be summed up in this way: the Bible is clear, as is evidenced by the way in which it has been read and acted upon until very recently. It commends the restriction of sexual intercourse to marriage. It opposes all fornication, and specifically includes fornication between members of the same sex. It understands dispositions as the spring of behaviour, but does not excuse the behaviour on that ground. Given the authoritative status of Scripture and the standards of behaviour expected of those in ministry, active homosexuality cannot be consistent with ordination. I will now explain this case by looking at the teaching of the Bible and the witness of tradition in order.

The teaching of the Bible

The context for a consideration of the biblical teaching is not homosexual behaviour as such, but the scriptural approach to marriage and so to the ethics of sex. The starting point in every way remains the opening chapters of Genesis, with the creation of male and female and the divine instruction, 'Be fruitful and multiply, and fill the earth and subdue it' (Gen 1:28). In later words, 'a man leaves his father and mother and clings to his wife and they become one flesh' (Gen 1:24). This becomes the basis for Paul's description of Christ and the Church (Eph 5:21-33), in which the singular love of the husband and the faithfulness of the wife to her own husband are wonderfully exemplified. The 'one flesh' of Genesis reminds us of the original oneness of man and woman, that woman came from man.

To this oneness they return, but in a new way. For there to be 'one flesh', the two cannot be two males (or two females), any more than the Church in this metaphor can be masculine.

The relationship of husband and wife is described as a covenant (Mal 2:14) — in other words, an exchange of promises. Such promises involve lifelong, exclusive possession of one another (1 Cor 7:4). It is only in the security of a relationship built on such promises that the intimacy of sexual intercourse is entered into with freedom from guilt. For this reason, the biblical strictures against breach of covenant in adultery are powerful. So despoiling is the sexual act outside of marriage that it is one of the only grounds of divorce. The possibility of divorce is allowed, but hedged with restrictions, since 'I hate divorce, says the LORD, the God of Israel' (Mal 2:16), a word endorsed by Jesus himself: 'what God has joined together, let no one separate' (Mtt 19:6).

Within this bond, created by the exchange of promises, sexual activity is blessed and sanctified. Whatever some strands of the Christian tradition may have made of sex, the biblical perspective is fundamentally positive. 'Let marriage be held in honour by all, and let the marriage bed be undefiled; for God will judge fornicators and adulterers' (Heb 13:4). But, as this citation shows, it is positive about sex within marriage. Paul's advice to those who are unmarried, if they are troubled by lack of self-control, is not that they should fornicate, but that they should marry: 'For it is better to marry than to be aflame with passion' (1 Cor 7:8). His wish that Christians should remain unmarried 'as I myself am' is not through misogyny or asceticism, but because the unmarried have more opportunity for the Lord's work (1 Cor 7:7, 32-35).

The biblical standard is certainly inconsistent with promiscuity; but that is not the real issue. Its standards are higher than that. It is also inconsistent with adultery and fornication, that is, with sexual intercourse between those who are married to someone else, and intercourse between those who are not married at all. It puts sexual intercourse into the context of the covenant of marriage.

In this context the biblical authors could not have sanctioned homosexual intercourse, even between those who may be committed exclusively to each other. Indeed the Bible seems to stand out from Greek moralists by its opposition both to 'active' and 'passive' same-sex practices. This relationship is not marriage – it is not based on prior promises of lifelong and exclusive union, and cannot lead to a one-flesh union, with all its kinship implications, for that is explicitly premised on the male/female duality. And, since it is not marriage, it ought to find no sexual expression, however significant a friendship may be involved. Sexual expression arises from those inner desires that are right when rightly directed, and wrong when wrongly directed (see 1 Cor 7:36-38). The biblical interest is not merely in actions, but in the passions and desires which can lead to actions (see Rom 1:26).

What, however, of the threefold argument which appears to modify this position? It has led some to the view that the Bible is not clear and cannot be directly applied to the situation of faithful same-sex relationships. I will address these three points in turn.

First, the definition of homosexuality. It is said that the biblical writers could not be condemning what they did not know about. It is true that most references to homosexuality are to the activity rather than the inner disposition. This is necessary, since such behaviours in fact may or may not be connected with an inherent 'homosexual' disposition. The concrete condemnation of the activity by the inspired authors covers all cases.

Unlike the tendency of the Greek moralists, the Bible's condemnation included the 'penetrative' act. Its focus on the deed itself makes for universality and clarity – but is it also limited by ignorance of the homosexual orientation? If it is, would the authors not have agreed that same-sex activity in a committed relationship between people who are disposed towards homosexuality, is acceptable? These are unwarranted assumptions for the following reasons.

The original proposition is flawed. Is it in fact the case that 'homosexuality' was invented in the mid-nineteenth century? Of course in one immediate sense it was not. If it exists now, it has always existed, and there must at least have been some people who have recognised themselves to be inherently homosexual, whether they had the words to describe their feelings. Stephen O Murray writes:

> 'It is not only in the modern West that some persons have noticed same-sex sexual desires, either their own or that of others. I consider it incredibly arrogant – specifically chronocentric and ethnocentric – to proclaim that no one recognized homosexual

desires before the late-nineteenth century forensic psychiatrists wrote about it. As examples throughout this book will make abundantly clear, there have been both non-Western and pre-modern patterns of homosexual behaviour. Not only has such conduct been noticed, but many languages have labels for kinds of persons known to engage in it recurrently.'[2]

Indeed, the evidence for a wider recognition of homosexual disposition is also available in the pre-modern period. Popular authors, and even academics have been too quick to draw conclusions about matters of this sort, including the meaning and prevalence of homosexual activity in the ancient world. There is a great deal to be said for the wise opening sentence of Bruce Thornton's recent book on ancient sexuality: 'The little we know about everyday life and behaviour in ancient Greece is dwarfed by how much we don't know.'[3] Thornton himself points to evidence from Aristotle, Plato and Aristophanes for 'the ancient Greek belief that homosexuals are born and not made'.[4]

David F Greenberg is aware of the same phenomenon, albeit as a minority view: 'The most vulnerable claim is that the notion of homosexual as a distinct "species" originated only about a hundred years ago, an invention of the medical profession or a product of capitalist urbanisation'; he adds, 'Physiological explanations for homosexual desire or distinct homosexual roles have a long pedigree, dating back to the world of classical antiquity. Psychological explanations are not exactly new either...'[5] No doubt this explains Greenberg's slight note of caution when dealing with Paul.[6]

More recently, Bernadette J Brooten has added further evidence that homosexual orientation was recognised in some circles at least – and perhaps by Paul. Her study of ancient astrological texts shows that astrologers recognised a variety of sexual preferences, which they linked to the stars. Thus, 'contrary to the view that the idea of sexual orientation did not develop until the nineteenth century, the astrological sources demonstrate the existence in the Roman world of the concept of lifelong erotic orientation'.[7] Furthermore, some at least among the medical profession of the ancient world regarded aspects of homosexual behaviour as an illness: 'Some ancient writers saw particular same-sex acts as symptoms of a chronic disease that affected the entirety of one's identity'.[8]

Brooten's main focus is on lesbianism in the ancient world. Her evidence makes her far more willing than Greenberg to suggest that Paul may have known of homosexual orientation: 'Thus both arguments fall short (that Paul condemns only heterosexuals committing homosexual acts and not homosexuals *per se*, and that the distinction between sexual orientation and sexual acts would have made no sense to him). Paul could have believed that *tribades, kinaidoi,* and other sexually unorthodox persons were born that way and yet still condemn them as unnatural and shameful, this all the more so since he is speaking of groups of people rather than of individuals'.[9]

It is noteworthy that Brooten's rigorous exegesis leads her to this conclusion: 'I hope that churches today, being apprised of the history that I have presented, will no longer teach Rom 1:26f as authoritative'. In short, she is impelled to agree that Paul condemns all same-sex practices, whatever the disposition of those involved. It is the present application of this conclusion that she so strongly disputes.

In fact, however, even if the biblical writers were utterly unaware of sexual orientation, it would not follow that the condemnations of Scripture are irrelevant. The Bible is not a supporter of voluntarism in the sense that we make choices free from our nature as sinful human beings, and that our choices have no impact on us. The Bible regards us all as prey to desires that are both addictive and condemnable (Jn 8:34, Rom 7:7-26). It is a short step to see that for some these desires are or become habitually oriented to those of the same sex (Rom 1:24, 26), just as for many they are habitually oriented promiscuously to those of the opposite sex. But this disordering of the inner life does not justify behaviour that gives expression to our evil desires.

Although the Bible writers may not have been aware of the homosexual orientation as such, on the broader front they were well aware of dispositions and desires that seek to rule our behaviours (Rom 6:12). Mere voluntarism is alien to their thought. The biblical treatment of the inner life may not coincide with modern insights, but it intersects with them and speaks powerfully to them.

Thus, drunkenness is opposed in Scripture; and qualification of the bishop includes the phrase 'not a drunkard' (1 Tim 3:3).

In recent years (rightly or not) we have come to think of some people as 'alcoholics', that is, inherently disposed toward the abuse of alcohol. But understanding of alcoholism does not involve the ordination of those who have a pattern of drunkenness; nor does it forbid the ordination of alcoholics who have this problem under control. Not alcoholism, but drunkenness is the test. Likewise, there may well be people whose disposition is toward bestiality or pederasty. The mere fact of having such a disposition, even if it proved to be physically based, gives no moral ground for expressing it. Such desires are not morally neutral.

The second observation about the Bible is exegetical. When a challenge is made to conventional understandings of Scripture, it is absolutely necessary to return to the text and to test once again the meaning of the relevant passages. The present volume of essays contains work of exactly this nature. The results are available and it is likely that the story of Sodom has been overemphasised (at least) in connection with homosexuality as such (though see the treatment by Thomas E Schmidt in *Straight and Narrow*[11]). On the other hand, it is also obvious that the OT legal material, such as Leviticus 18, forbids the practice of homosexuality, as does the NT. Our problem is not so much with the clarity of Scripture, as with its authority and application, as Bernadette Brooten illustrates.

The third observation is, therefore, hermeneutical: what is the status of OT legal material for Christian ethics? This is, of course, no new question. It faced the earliest Christians almost at once (e.g., Acts 10). Any answer must be based on the principle that the Bible is a unity, and that we ought to interpret the parts in the light of the whole. The decision about whether we eat in accordance with the prescriptions of the Torah is settled for us within the pages of the NT itself (Mark 7, Acts 10, etc), On the other hand, there are principles of the Torah which are repeated, explained, endorsed and even enhanced in the NT (e.g., Mtt 5-7).

Anglicans have enshrined within their Articles a rule of interpretation which has been accepted and employed in the liturgy and in countless books and sermons:

> 'Although the Law given from God by Moses, as touching Ceremonies and Rites, do not bind Christian men, nor the Civil

precepts thereof ought of necessity to be received in any commonwealth; yet notwithstanding, no Christian man whatsoever is free from the obedience of the Commandments which are called Moral' (Article VII).

It is true that this rule still makes for some difficult decisions. Is the law of Leviticus 18:19, 'You shall not approach a woman to uncover her nakedness while she is in her menstrual uncleanness', part of the ceremonial or moral law, for example? But in the case of homosexual practices, there is no doubt, since the NT endorses the OT at this point, that the stipulation is part of the moral law of God.

In short, the testimony of the Bible, both in its theology of sex and marriage and in its details, is clearly negative to the practice of same-gender sex. This includes the desire for it and also the practice of it. The reasons given for modifying this verdict are insufficient to persuade.

The witness of tradition

For the purpose of this discussion, tradition may be defined as the Church's response to the scriptural revelation, discernible in teaching, pronouncements, worship, and law, by which we may compare and correct our own understanding of Scripture, identify ourselves, and appropriate the treasures of the past. Tradition gives a voice to the past in our understanding of the word of God. It must be weighed with great seriousness, but not given the ultimate say in the meaning of Scripture. In the appropriate appeal to the trio of scripture, tradition and reason, priority belongs to the Bible as God's word written.[12]

Tradition and reason may well err. Both tradition and reason help explicate the Scriptures, but they both remain subject to the word of God. Nonetheless, the onus is on those who would vary the tradition to show that the judgement of the past was wrong: '(we should not) lightlie esteeme what hath bene allowed as fitt in the judgement of antiquitie and by the longe continewed practise of the whole Church, from which unnecessarelie to swarve experience hath never found safe'.[13] It is worth noting, for example, that the past, while subject to its own cultural limitations and pressures, is often free of our limitations and pressures, and may, therefore, give a clearer rendition of the meaning of Scripture than we are capable of. Of course, the reverse also applies.

On the subject of homosexual acts, it is usually understood that the tradition of the Church was overwhelmingly negative. Thus, for example, this was the verdict of the early Church according to Professor David Wright: 'All the evidence indicates that the teaching mind of the early church unreservedly condemned homosexual activity. Yet, although clearly viewed as contrary to God's will in scripture and nature, it was not singled out for special execration. Its practitioners were debarred from the catechumenate by the church orders and condemned by councils from the early fourth century (e.g., Elvira, can. 71; Ancyra, can. 17), but conciliar reprobation was not frequent'.[14] However, as indicated above, there are four features that are held by some to modify the impact of the tradition. How may we comment on them?

First there is the question of whether the homosexual disposition was understood. This is the same question as confronted us in connection with the writers of the Bible, and the material adduced there remains relevant. We may, I believe, easily agree that the conceptualisation of homosexuality has changed over the years, not least in our own time. We may accept that the word 'homosexual' is a nineteenth-century invention. But, as we have seen already, there is a real danger of hasty historical generalisations. Even more important, there is no evidence that we may safely move from accepting the reality of a person's sexual orientation to endorsing an act flowing from it.

Indeed, if there is one thing clear, even from a cursory knowledge of this field, it is how little we know of it as yet. It may be, in fact, that the idea of the homosexual couple, committed and exclusive, is itself the result of projection by those who judge homosexuality by their own heterosexual standards. Certainly there are many ways of being gay – 'homosexualities', to use the word from the title of Murray's book. If homosexuality is to be no bar to ordination, will it not be homosexuality on its own terms?

Something of this insight is inherent in the hesitation to call such a relationship 'marriage'. There are those, indeed, who claim that there are very few exclusive long-term commitments among homosexual men and women, that this is not characteristic of modern egalitarian homosexuality. One older study found that, 'The expectation for outside sexual activity was the rule for male couples and the exception for heterosexuals'.[15] This verdict is endorsed in more recent studies cited by Schmidt.[16] Certainly the Doctrine Panel had striking personal testimony to this possibility from one source at least.

Second, there is the contention that the condemnation of homosexuality was less unanimous in the Christian tradition than is generally thought. This thesis is particularly but not exclusively linked to the name of John Boswell, who advanced it in his 1980 book, *Christianity, Social Tolerance and Homosexuality.*[17] David Wright voices the opinion of other scholars when he calls the book, 'influential but highly misleading on the early church'. There is evidence to suggest that homosexuality was not singled out as the worst sin; there is evidence for a certain amount of tolerance in practice; there is evidence for different amounts of condemnation during the two-thousand-year history with which we are dealing; there is evidence of the relatively undisturbed practice of homosexuality at some times in Church communities. But the suggestion that there were in fact homosexual marriages, and the idea that these variations amount to a significant variation to the tradition of the Church is little more than wishful thinking.

Jeffrey Richards sums up the evidence of the Middle Ages thus: 'For all the invaluable illumination that Boswell's book throws on the subject of attitudes to and the practice of homosexuality in the Middle Ages, his two principal theses seem to me to be contrary to the evidence. Christianity was fundamentally hostile to homosexuality ... there was never any question of homosexuals being allowed to carry on with homosexual activity unpunished. They were obliged to give it up or risk damnation.'[18]

No Church Father, no noted theologian, no official liturgical practice, no canon law endorsed the practice of homosexuality. It may be the case that, as legal expert Norman Doe notes, 'The canon law of no church expressly lists a person's engagement in sexually active homophile relationships as a bar to ordination'[19] But, as Doe also points out, even the mild contemporary approach of the English House of Bishops, in which the onus of conscience is ordinarily put upon the candidate for ordination, is accompanied by the warning that a sexually active homophile relationship is 'a pattern of life which the church does not commend'.

The fact is that if the canons of the church do not specifically mention it as one of the bars to ordination, it is because it comes under the general heading of morality of life. Doe also comments that 'the bishop must be satisfied about the candidate's spiritual and moral qualities'.[20] S. J. Grenz is right to conclude that: 'Whenever the church was confronted with sexual practices involving persons of the same sex, Christian teachers spoke out against such behaviours. Despite differences between them, the ecclesiastical sources Boswell and others cite never expressed moral approval of, or even indifference to, same-sex behaviour. On the contrary, explicit moral references to such behaviour in the Christian tradition were consistently negative.'[21] On behalf of Judaism, Dennis Prager makes the same point: 'It is impossible for Judaism to make peace with homosexuality because homosexuality denies many of Judaism's most fundamental values'.[22]

Third, it is argued that the traditional understanding of the purpose of sex is now outmoded, and that this directly impacts on our understanding of homosexuality. It is certainly the case that much of the teaching about sex, its meaning and purpose in the ancient and medieval Church is premised on ideas at odds with contemporary culture. Most obviously, we may refer to the emphasis on procreation being the 'natural' end of intercourse, to the view that marriage was also given to avoid fornication, and to the teaching that, even within marriage, sinful lust may occur, especially when sex is freed from mere procreation. In modern Christian thought, by way of contrast, sex can have chiefly the function of delight in union, apart from the conception of children. If this is so for heterosexuals, some would argue that it must be so for homosexuals. To this line of argument there are several responses.

Our appeal is first to Scripture rather than tradition. Parts of the tradition — compulsory clerical celibacy, for example — are unscriptural. It is important to note, however, that the Reformation, which saw the re-assertion of the principle of scriptural supremacy, also began the task of re-examining what the Bible says about sex and marriage. The emphasis undoubtedly remained on procreation as the first duty of marital sex, and on marriage as a remedy for fornication, but there came to be a recognition of affectionate companionship in marriage evident, for example, in the *Book of*

Common Prayer. From this has emerged a more biblical tradition of interpretation, which had a place for sex as the potentially joyful and fulfilling union of husband and wife.

Thus the great contemporary of Hooker, William Perkins, writes, 'The communion of man and wife is that duty whereby they do mutually and willingly communicate both their persons and goods to each other, for their mutual help, necessity and comfort'.[23] He also teaches, 'And for this cause some schoolmen do err who hold that the secret coming together of man and wife cannot be without sin'.[24] According to Edmund Leites, 'Puritans, in a very central area of life, upheld a life-affirming, life-accepting attitude: within the confines of the marriage bed, sexuality and sexual pleasure were not only permitted, but seen as good things. Sex was not simply for procreation or to avoid fornication, but was good in itself to the degree that it gave pleasure and comfort to both husband and wife.'[25] The renewal and correction of tradition by Scripture still found nothing in Scripture, however, to encourage sex outside the bonds of marriage.

Our appeal is first to Scripture rather than to human reason as such. The hold of Aristotelian philosophy on medieval theology, with its emphasis on the natural and the *telos* of the natural, was challenged by the Reformation. It was no longer necessary to assume nature revealed that the chief end of sex was conception: 'Calvin saw the sexual act as a gift of God, which it was meet to "use joyfully" and which was justified in itself, apart from its final end, which was procreation.'[26] Or, if we are dissatisfied with Calvin, we may note this from Jeremy Taylor on the reasons for marital intercourse: 'a Desire of children, or to avoid fornication, or to lighten and ease the cares and sadnesses of household affairs, or to endear each other'.[27]

Such an attitude at least opens the way for the question of whether contraception is valid. The absence of a directly biblical answer has eventually allowed the churches of the Reformation to give a very different verdict from the Roman Catholic Church. On the other hand, the idea that children are a natural end of marriage is not merely reasonable; it is scriptural, and the long hesitation of the Protestant churches is justifiable. To this extent, the appeal to the nature of things is valid, since God created the nature of things and told us what they are used for. It is by no means certain that all the gains of contraception exhibited in contemporary sexual mores are as great as we may assume.

The Bible certainly knows positively about the pleasures of love and sexual experience. We need only instance the presence of the Song of Songs in the canon. It knows, too, however, of the powerful and destructive sexual liberties of the surrounding cultures of its day. The ancient world may not have been so very different from the world of recreational sex that we inhabit. For this reason, the very practical advice of the Apostle ('it is better to marry than to burn with passion'), together with his exhortation to fulfil the marital duty, may be far more relevant and helpful than the mores of contemporary sex manuals. Thus, too, the idea that it is possible to indulge in the sin of lust within the marriage bond is neither as unscriptural (depending on how we read 1 Thess 4:3-6), nor as unhelpful as many suppose. The problem may be more with us, than with the tradition.

No doubt there were unfortunate cultural influences that distorted the response to the biblical revelation – the treatment of the Song of Songs is evidence of that. But we would do well to be less certain that contemporary insights into sexual behaviour are better than those which emerge from scholars who read the Bible in the early Church, influenced by the experience and thoughts of the great pagan philosophers. Thornton argues that 'we who have abandoned shame and who ridicule tradition, are deaf to the wisdom of the Greeks… Indeed, our cultural ideals and institutions are saturated with Romantic sentimentalism and Enlightenment arrogance, an unholy alliance inciting us to a profound disrespect for and trivialisation of eros, a disrespect whose wages we now see in illegitimacy and its frequent effects – crime, random violence, poverty and social barbarism.'[28]

Instead of assuming, therefore, that the Bible itself forbade homosexual acts for the same reasons as an Aristotelian philosopher, we may at least consider whether the biblical insights are more profound than contemporary ones. Herein lies the peril of confusing the Cultural Spirit with the Holy Spirit. The Holy Spirit's words in Scripture may not explain why we are to abstain from certain patterns of behaviour. But the forbidden acts may have much to do with the impact of sex on our psyches, on the seriousness of the sexual act and the need to channel the power of the sexual drive. Aspects of the sexual revolution of the 1960s have caused great pain, and we would have done better to accept the wisdom of Scripture even though we may not have understood it.

Thus there is evidence that the sexual behaviour which has marked the last three decades – e.g., unmarried cohabitation – has not led to happiness, good health, and fulfilment, but to widespread suffering instead: 'In England in 1992 over half the children born out of wedlock were living with two unmarried parents. But cohabitation, it has been pointed out, is no substitute for marriage, since such arrangements are far less stable than marriages, only 16 percent lasting more than five years'.[29] There are those who judge that the gay movement has also brought about widespread pain and destruction.[30] Are we confident that they are wrong? Confident enough to vary the established reading of Scripture and symbolically endorse homosexuality by being willing to ordain a practising homosexual?

Fourth, it is argued that since matters previously thought forbidden are now accepted as permissible – the ordination of women, contraception, divorce and remarriage – we ought to accept that homosexuality (at least when practised in a secure, committed, exclusive relationship) is also now permissible. Once again, however, this argument hardly bears examination. Let us compare the two issues of contraception and the ordination of women to the priesthood.

With regard to the first, there is no direct biblical material either to support or oppose. There are, of course, relevant biblical considerations about sex and the family, and doubtless they were consulted in the debates of the early twentieth century. But there was no biblical text with a long tradition of interpretation as such to overcome. On the subject of the ordination of women, the problem is quite different – and so, among the Protestant churches, is the result. There are specific texts whose voice must be accounted for in some way, and which remain in some minds at least, to bear witness against the practice. The result has been continuing division and unease.

Conclusion

I began by saying that the arguments for the ordination of practising homosexual persons leave me unpersuaded. The reasons for that conclusion have been advanced. I conclude with two observations.

First, I think that it is important not to confuse the interpretation of Scripture with its application. As can be seen from what I have written (and from both the Jewish and Christian reading of Scripture over the centuries), I believe that the teaching of the Bible in this matter is clear. That is not to say that there are no legitimate questions, or that we should not re-examine it to make sure that we are reading it correctly. But I note that after her research, this is the position, too, of Bernadette Brooten. In her case, she disputes not the interpretation of Scripture, but its authority and application.

Second, I want to observe that holding to the traditional position may be *exactly* what the Church is being called to do in this culture. Whatever we may think of the post-modern world, surely it is sex-obsessed in physically, emotionally and spiritually unhealthy ways. A witness to the value of sex within the conventional bonds of marriage only may be precisely what is needed for the good health of individuals and society. A move towards endorsing same-sex relationships, even deeply affective relationships, confuses this important witness. It also devalues the quiet but heroic commitment of the many, many Christians, both men and women who, for the sake of Christ and in the midst of overwhelming temptation, have remained celibate. This, too, is a powerful witness that must not be compromised.

Endnotes

[1] It is worth noting that in the language of the Kuala Lumpur statement even such an arrangement would be characterised as promiscuity (see section 6).

[2] Stephen O. Murray, *Homosexualities* (University of Chicago Press, Chicago, 2000), 8.

[3] Bruce S. Thornton, *Eros: The Myth of Ancient Greek Sexuality* (Westview Press, Oxford, 1997), xi.

[4] *Ibid.,* 105. It is worth observing that Thornton offers a strong challenge to such conventional views as [i] The Greeks regarded homosexual relationships as normal or good. [ii] The Greeks approved the practice of pederasty. [iii] The Greeks regarded married sex as being for procreation rather than loving union. We should certainly not take such assertions at face value.

[5] David F. Greenberg, *The Construction of Homosexuality* (The university of Chicago Press, Chicago and Lond, 1988), 485.

[6] *Ibid.,* 215.

[7] *Love Between Women* (The University of Chicago Press, Chicago and London, 1996), 140.

[8] *Ibid.,* 144.

[9] *Ibid.,* 233.

[10] *Ibid.,* 302.

[11] (InterVarsity Press, Downers Grove, Illinois, 1995), 86ff.

[12] See Nigel Atkinson, 'Hooker's Theological Method and Modern Anglicanism', *Churchman,* Vol. 114, 1 (2000), 40-70.

[13] Hooker, cited by Atkinson, 58.

[14] E. Ferguson, ed., *Encyclopedia of Early Christianity,* 2nd ed., Vol 1 (Garland Publishers, New York and London, 1997), 542-3.

[15] Quoted by Jeffrey Satinover in *Homosexuality and the Politics of Truth* (Baker Books, Grand Rapids, 1996), 55.

[16] *Straight and Narrow,* 105-8.

[17] University of Chicago Press, Chicago, 1980.

[18] Jeffrey Richards, *Sex, Dissidence and Damnation* (Routledge, London and New York, 1991), 149.

[19] *Canon Law in the Anglican Communion* (Oxford University Press, New York, 1998), 132.

[20] *Ibid.,* 130.

21 S. J. Grenz, *Welcoming But Not Affirming* (Westminster/John Knox Press, Louisville, 1998), 80.

22 'The Public Interest', 112, Summer (1993).

23 *The Work of William Perkinds,* I. Breward, ed. (The Sutton Courtenay Press, Appleford, 1970), 423.

24 *Ibid.*, 420.

25 *The Puritan Conscience and Modern Sexuality* (Yale University Press, New Haven, 1986), 12.

26 André Burguire and François Lebrun, 'Priest, Prince and Family', in A. Burguire et al, *A History of the Family,* Vol. II (Harvard University Press, Cambridge, MA, 1996), 101.

27 *Holy Living,* Ch. 2, section 3,2.

28 *Ibid.,* 218.

29 Gertrude Himmelfarb, *The De-Moralization of Society* (Alfred A. Knopf, New York, 1994), 232; the whole of Himmelfarb's fine book is worth reading, but especially the epilogue, 'A De-Moralized Society'.

30 See the sobering estimate of Thomas Schmidt, *Op cit.*,100-31.

CHAPTER ELEVEN

Starting with the Spirit: A Personal Reflection on Sexuality and Spiritual Gifts

Graeme Garrett

Negative Capability

Writing to his brothers (George and Tom) in 1818, John Keats drew attention to what he regarded as an essential quality required of all true poets. He called it 'negative capability'. Negative capability, Keats wrote, 'is when man [*sic*] is capable of being in uncertainties, Mysteries, doubts, without any irritable reaching after fact & reason …' Given the divided state of the Anglican Communion on matters relating to homosexuality and lesbianism, a division graphically symbolised by the heated debates at the 1998 Lambeth Conference, I want to approach this subject with as much of Keats' quality of negative capability as I can muster. That doesn't mean I have no firm opinions, feelings, or arguments. But it does mean a sense of limitation, an awareness of mystery and conflict, and a good deal of pain are going to be a part of what I can say. If the truth be known, I wish I didn't have to say anything at all, because I don't feel qualified to speak. At least not with the kind of authority that arises from extensive experience.

It seems to me that the positions we adopt in relation to this subject often arise from levels of our being that are, so to speak, 'upstream' from argument, concept and even language. A gut reaction determines our felt *disposition*, which in turn colours our argued *position* on the matter. For example, I find I can watch the depiction of explicit acts of lesbian sex that sometimes appear in movies these days without feeling unduly disturbed. But when similar acts of a homosexual kind are portrayed, I have a strong involuntary negative reaction. Such a reaction seems to indicate that, for me at any rate, some fundamental issue of gender identity comes under threat when boundaries that normally determine my sense of myself as a man are blurred or transgressed. This emotional, pre-linguistic disposition remains despite the fact that my consciously accepted and argued position on the question wants to make no moral, personal, or theological distinction between the two kinds of behaviour. (Of course, people whose orientation is to same-sex relations may well have similar kinds of reaction to the contemplation of heterosexual activity.)

Such dispositions are fuelled with all the energy of a self defending its being against the threat of dissolution. And a threatened self is not interested in argument. It is interested in neutralising danger. Many discussions of these sexual matters that I have been involved with, however apparently rational on the surface, simmer with such unspoken feelings. These feelings shadow debates about what is 'natural' or 'unnatural', what elements of Scripture and tradition are appealed to, what weight is given to 'ontological' versus 'social construction' theories of conscience, and so on. Some sense of negative capability seems essential if we are to negotiate such complex issues. In these waters we navigate with uncertain lights both within and between ourselves.

This means it is imperative to listen before we speak. The Church is being pressured to come to some clear and official stand on questions concerning the moral and spiritual status of gay and lesbian actions and relationships, the matter of eucharistic fellowship with and ordination of those who adopt such orientations, the blessing of homosexual and lesbian 'marriage', and so on. No doubt there are urgent contextual reasons for this pressure. But sometimes, I feel, we do our thinking and arrive at our positions using all the paraphernalia of theological and moral disputation (revelation, Scripture, tradition, reason, philosophy, science) while the voices of those most affected go unheard. Yet in the final analysis, this is not just a matter of the Church responding to criticisms or challenges from an indifferent or hostile society that does not share its creed. The challenge is put most powerfully to us by those of the 'household of faith'. It is fellow disciples, people who have no wish to damage the cause of Christ, who by their lives and words are raising these matters. For that reason alone, we cannot ignore them. But for that reason, too, we have a duty of fellowship to listen with open hearts to what they say before we feel certain that *we* know what they should do. The parallels between this discussion and that concerning women's circumstances in the Church are too obvious to need mention.

And there are other matters, near to home.

For my Grandmother
My ancestors frown on me, they always glare
I disturb their rest with my Western ways
Plus I'm a girl, I'm Nature's dud-card
Springing forth to disappoint and creeping
Meekly about thereafter on three-inch feet
Slave to Father and Husband and Son.
A woman who loves a woman in China
Is lower than a beggar and fears for her life.
Not tied to a man, she's cast adrift
The titles Daughter Wife Mother Widow
Are silhouettes of iron that pass her by
Wandering outside she has no form
No name, no voice, no past, no kin
The only word she knows for her love
Is Wrong.
When we make love I feel their censure
Each kiss uproots the ancestral tables and
When you come in the wetness of my mouth
My father's house trembles and shudders and
Comes crashing down.
The bindings fall from my feet and I
Run to you through the wild green grass.[1]

Those words were written by a young woman who happens to be my niece, my sister's daughter. Asiopean or Eurasian (whatever term), she is child of a Chinese father and Euro/Australian mother. She is a brilliant person, loving, open, gentle. By trade a doctor committed to care of the sick and suffering. A gifted writer. A loyal friend. A staunch defender of a fair go for the underdog. Her quality of life, her moral seriousness, her commitment to truth and justice, are at least the equal of mine, or of my sister (her mother) or of her (Chinese) father. We all recognise that. And our various emotional reactions in the family have had to come to terms with it. Joo-Inn's spiritual quality is what it is. And she is lesbian. She has lived a lot of her life in fear and despair for what we, her own family, might do if we were to know the truth. It took great courage to declare what for her was not choice but discovery of her sexual orientation. Now at 26 she has told her story, or part of it, in the book, *Inside Out*. Because it is in the public domain, and because she has agreed, I feel free to speak about it here. Joo-Inn travels at a distance from the Church. She might well call it a 'safe distance'. The publicity of the Lambeth Conference merely confirms what she already feels: the Church has no real understanding of her humanity, integrity, or personhood. The Church's only, or at least most prominent, word to her is 'no'. She feels (if she thinks about it at all) that the Church judges and condemns before it even deigns to hear her story. It brings God to speak against her —'you are unacceptable'.

This experience close to home has changed me. I find now that I cannot engage in debates on the rights and wrongs, the theologies and moralities, theories of the 'natural' and the 'unnatural', biblical texts of condemnation (some of which call for execution: cf. Lev 20:13), without measuring these things against the real life of a person near and dear to me. Sometimes when I hear myself in these debates, and then try to hear myself as my niece might hear me, I feel confused and angry, as if she had asked for bread, and all I offer is a stone.

I have mentioned one example, a family situation. But I can think immediately of other people, whose families are well known to me and are deeply involved in the Church, to whom similar circumstances apply. For the most part, although not without exception, I am happy to say, these people have experienced the Church in terms of rejection, isolation, condemnation and, sometimes, hostility and vilification in relation to their sexual orientation.

I know that matters of virtue and vice cannot be decided merely from a context of personal sentiment. Wider issues of revelation, reason, tradition and Scripture must be a part of any judgement the Church seeks to make. But I am also aware that I have been deeply affected by personal relationships in this regard. They have changed my mind and heart, and heavily influenced the stand I take in the debate. The long and short of it is that I have a gut-level sense of what is right in the matter. I guess I am looking for ways of reading the truth of God in this light.

A Third Way?

The Archbishop of Canterbury at the recent Lambeth Conference stated that he could see 'no room in Holy Scripture or the entire Christian tradition for any sexual activity outside matrimony of husband and wife'.[2] This leaves the Church with only two options in relation to sex and sexual orientation: Way 1—traditional heterosexual marriage, and Way 2—celibacy. For many Christian people these days, this is an example of the Church adopting the time honoured 'Nelson stance'. It puts the telescope to a blind eye and claims to see nothing. I am not convinced this can work in post-modern Australia. Indeed, my experience is that the Church at the grass-roots level muddles along with much more complex ways of dealing with human relationships than our official sex ethics acknowledges. Rapidly changing social circumstances (again inside and not just outside the Church) mean that the classic 'two-ways theory' just doesn't deal with the realities of life. Contraception, IVF and other bio-technologies of reproduction, issues of over-population, pollution, longevity, extended periods of education for the young, large numbers of single-parent families, divorce, postmodern pluralism and so on — all these put enormous pressure on people to find appropriate ways to live out their sexuality. The gay and lesbian issue is just one of these challenges. Is there a Way 3 open to us?

I hope it goes without saying that, in wanting to explore a third way, I am not recommending or condoning any and every expression of gay sexuality, any more than any and every expression of straight sexuality is acceptable. The kinds of abhorrent behaviours catalogued in, say, Genesis 19:4-11; Deuteronomy 23:17-18; or I Corinthians 6:9 are no part of a faithful life before God. Rape, promiscuity, paedophilia, violence and the like are to be questioned on the same grounds for homosexual as for heterosexual ways of being. I am speaking here of the kind of gay and lesbian relationships that are clearly emerging in our time and in our churches. I mean loving, respectful, just partnerships between two adult, responsible, free persons whose commitment to each other meets the sorts of requirements we hope for in Christian marriage, but who happen to be of the same sex.

What are the broad options that are presently under debate in the Church? (I will confine myself here to the matters of eucharistic fellowship and ordination.)

Option A:
One end of the spectrum presents a hard line against all acceptance within the Christian community of gay and lesbian relations. Any such relations, according to this account of the faith, are sinful in the sight of God. The choice for those who admit to the orientation is repentance and amendment of life before full fellowship can be offered or ordination contemplated. If it is correct that gay orientation is the discovery of a predetermined disposition, not the choice of a lifestyle, celibacy is the only acceptable option.

Option B:
At the other end of the spectrum, the argument runs strongly in favour of the possibility of both full fellowship with and ordination for gay and lesbian persons subject, of course, to certain other criteria that apply to anyone seeking membership or leadership in the Church. This account of Christian life includes the view that gay and lesbian orientations are not *per se* sinful in the sight of God. If this is the case, so the argument goes, the Church has no business excluding such persons on these grounds only, from full participation in the life and leadership of the community of faith.

Option C:
A third option represents an intermediate or 'mixed message' stance. This account of Christian life does not rule out acceptance of gay and lesbian participation in the eucharistic life of the Church. These orientations are not *per se* sinful in the sight of God. But for various practical and political reasons, in the present climate of Church and society, it is deemed pastorally unwise for such persons to take full leadership within the community. The faith, so this position argues, does not reject gay and lesbian lifestyles outright, but neither does it wish to recommend them as of equal appropriateness with the married or celibate state. Moreover, ordination requires vocation to be recognised and accepted by the broad company of the people of God. At the present moment in Australian Church history, such a consensus is not possible. To proceed with ordination in this climate would risk splitting the Church, and that is not a price that can be paid.

I find myself, on the whole, in group B. Although with a good dose of Keatsian 'negative capability', I am acutely aware of the serious and sincere reasons fellow believers in group A have to oppose this, and also of the concerns for good order and unity in the Church which fellow believers in group C put forward. But the parallel circumstances surrounding the Church's struggle with questions of sexism, racism and apartheid press me hard at this point.

Starting with the Spirit

How do we tell what the Spirit is saying to the churches at any point in history? The answer to such a question is never straightforward, of course. The story of the Acts of the Apostles and the Corinthian correspondence are enough to establish that. Revelation, Scripture, reason and tradition are all a part of it. But I want to start with the Spirit and experience, an obvious place to begin, given the above introduction. There are dangers in the approach. Claims to read the winds of the Spirit or to catalogue the gifts of the Spirit are notoriously slippery in the Church. Paul's injunction, 'Now we have received not the spirit of the world, but the Spirit that is from God, so that we may understand the gifts bestowed on us by God' (I Corinthians 2:12) is a great truth. But it is not always easy to apply in particular circumstances. Karl Barth's question to Schleiermacher hangs over any such starting point. 'What Schleiermacher constructed by means of his theology of awareness by planting himself in the centre which for the Reformation had been a subsidiary centre, could be the pure theology of the Holy Spirit; the teaching of man [sic] brought face to face with God by God, of man granted grace by grace.' But is it so in fact? 'Will this [theology] show if it is not only intended to be, but if it is in truth the divinity of the Holy Spirit which forms this actual centre of his?'[3] That is the question!

Any genuine understanding of the living presence of the Spirit of God in the world, in the Church and in individual lives includes an element of creativity, newness and surprise. No doubt the loving kindness of God remains unchanged yesterday, today and forever. But the way that love finds expression in the open-ended (as well as sinful) operation of history is never exhausted, nor can it be completely circumscribed in human word and thought. The wind blows where it wills, not where we will it to blow (John 3:8). Peter's dream in the house of Cornelius came as a complete surprise to him. Where he had thought it quite clear from Scripture and tradition that the Spirit of the Lord was not to be found in 'unclean' places (in this instance, Gentile circles), the vision revealed otherwise. 'You yourself know it is unlawful for a Jew to associate with or visit a Gentile; but God has shown me that I should not call anyone profane or unclean' (Acts 10:28).

There seems to have been a number of times in the history of the Church where such surprising revelation of the presence and action of the Spirit has drawn the Church (often reluctantly) into new and uncharted areas, which have required re-thinking of traditional models of action and traditional interpretations of Scripture. Without going into detail, we could flag the issues of slavery, exclusion of handicapped/injured persons from the sanctuary, apartheid, racism and ethnocentrism, women's secondary status, the prohibition of divorce and remarriage, especially for clergy. All of these issues at one time or another have been defended on the grounds of Scripture and tradition as the 'will of God'. After much heartache, debate, prayer and prophetic action, most of these positions have been undermined and a new vision of where and how the Spirit of God is at work has redefined things. Some are still controversial. But others (e.g., slavery, apartheid) have been re-thought, like Peter's dream, with the force of dogma. These things, once acceptable practices within the Church (or parts of it) are no longer regarded as compatible with a genuine appreciation of the 'grammar of the Gospel' in the world today.

How do we judge the presence of the Spirit of God (and not the spirit of the world) in people who seek fellowship with the Church? How do we discern a genuine vocation of the Spirit to ministry and ordination in the Church? I don't have space to try to answer these questions fully, but we know the drift of things. In general terms, the Spirit is the power by which the redemptive grace of God manifest in the life, death and resurrection of Jesus Christ is made effective in the believer and the community (Romans 15:13,19; I Corinthians 2:4; Ephesians 3:16, 17; I Thessalonians 1:5). But what is this effect, as far as can be humanly judged? Here are some significant indicators (taken only from Paul): Faith in the risen Christ (Romans 10:9);

evidence of the love of God (Romans 5:5; 15:30); knowledge of God and the Gospel (I Corinthians 2:10-16; Ephesians 1:17); life and peace (Romans 7:6; 8:2,6; 2 Corinthians 3:6); righteousness, peace, joy (Romans 14:17); access to God (Ephesians 2:18); adoption as children of God (Galatians 4:5-6; Ephesians 1:5); the gifts of the Spirit (I Corinthians 12:4-11; Ephesians 4:1;-13; Romans 12:3-8); faith, hope, love (I Corinthians 13:13); a willingness to live under the cross and bear the wounds of Christ (2 Corinthains 4:7-12; 6:4-10; 11:23-29; 12:7-8); and so on.[4]

And what are the evidences of vocation of the Spirit to ministry in the Church of God? Again a whole essay could be written. But we all know in general the signs that we look for. In addition to the kinds of spiritual qualities noted above, we expect evidence of a personal sense of vocation, verified and tested capacities of mind and heart that are needed for preaching, pastoral care, leadership in worship and perseverance in service, confirmation of vocation from the people of God with whom the person is in fellowship, and evidence of a fruitful ministry in the name of Christ.

A hypothetical

Suppose a person were to come to us (the Church) seeking eucharistic fellowship with us and even requesting ordination on the basis of a steady sense of vocation of the Spirit. And suppose, with all the usual concern and diligence, we were to examine the person's life in the light of the above manifestations of the Spirit. And suppose, again, that after due consideration, consultation and prayer, we were to conclude, in the councils of the Church, that here is a person on whom the Holy Spirit rests and in whom the Holy Spirit is moving for leadership and ordination in the Church. Would we not proceed in the direction requested?

But, now, after all this has been done, suppose we were to learn that this person was of gay or lesbian orientation, and was living in a stable relationship that, to all intents and purposes, meets the standards set out for traditional marriage, but is a same-sex union. Would this knowledge of itself and without further ado be sufficient to determine the ineligibility of that person for (a) ordination or (b) full Christian fellowship or (c) both? In short, is the matter of gay or lesbian orientation, if once expressed in action, of itself conclusive evidence, despite all other indicators, of the absence of the Spirit in the life in question, or at least the absence of the Spirit in requisite measure to permit an affirmation of genuine discipleship and/or authentic vocation?

The question is not really hypothetical. It confronts us now. There are people who seem to fit, as far as we can judge, the criteria of Spirit-led lives. Some are already in ordained ministry. Yet they are also gay or lesbian. Where, then, is the will of God in the matter? On the experiential level, on the level of the discernment of the living presence of the Spirit in the Church, I want to argue that the weight lies, at very least, with an open mind. A lesbian or gay orientation does not constitute a stand-alone disqualifier of the presence and vocation of the Holy Spirit.

The *filioque*

But Barth's question remains. For all this claim to the presence, the leading and the teaching of the Spirit, can I be sure that the spirit here appealed to is the Holy Spirit of God and not the spirit of the world?

I can't, of course. Not in an absolute way. Though I feel that the burden of proof lies with those who want to discount the signs of the Spirit I have noted. But a reputable Spirit theology is always an integral part of a trinitarian theology. The Holy Spirit proceeds 'from the Father and the Son' (*filioque*). Thus trinitarian theology is, in the words of Pfitzner, 'a preventative against pneumatology degenerating into a vague spiritism that is divorced from the Gospel and the triune God who creates, redeems and sanctifies'[5] (Cf. I Corinthians 12:1-3). This means that the case I have mounted must be tested against the revelation of God as creator (Father) and as redeemer (Christ). I cannot attempt to go into this in detail, but it might include the following matters.

A discussion of the order of creation pertaining to sexuality and relations between the sexes. This would include an examination of the theology of the *imago dei*, and what that implies for an understanding and lived expression of the full meaning of our humanity. The claim that the relationship between man and woman is the fundamental human relation intended by God and upon which human freedom, community and procreation are founded needs to be tested. Do same-sex intimate relationships always violate irredeemably this created order of being? Or, if we locate the *imago dei* not in male and femaleness (Barth), but in differentiation and mutual relatedness, are we able to acknowledge a full and God-honoured humanity of those who do not enter male/female relations, and to respect the genuine humanity of their same-sex relationships?[26]

Examination of the christological issues raised by gay and lesbian relationships is a further requirement confronting any theology of the matter that wants to begin with the Spirit. I don't have an altogether clear picture of where this might lead. But it could include an examination of the attitude of Jesus toward those who were outcasts from the traditional religious rituals and institutions of his day (e.g. Luke 7:36-50; 14:1-24, etc). Is it appropriate to draw parallels between the discrimination experienced by gay and lesbian people in the Church today and that experienced by the maimed, blind, unclean, and socially unacceptable people of Jesus' day? Is there a theology that parallels Paul's christological argument against prostitution in terms of the meaning of the body of Christ in 1 Corinthians 6? And, if so, where does it take us?

Word and Spirit

Last but not least, any approach to the matter of gay and lesbian sexuality that begins with the Spirit is obliged to come to terms with the witness of the Word of Scripture. The well-known texts: Genesis 19; Leviticus 18:22, 20:13; Deuteronomy 23:17-18; Judges 19-21; I Kings 14:21-25, 15:12, 22:46; Romans 1:26-27; I Corinthians 6:9; I Timothy 1:10 all, in one way or another, condemn homosexuality. In some cases, they do so with the severity of capital punishment.

Are such texts enough to settle the matter? My conviction is that they are not. But I haven't the expertise or space to argue the case in detail. We would need to consider if in many of these instances it is violent, lustful, promiscuous activity and cult prostitution that is condemned, not the kind of loving and faithful relationships about which I have been talking. I think there is a case to be made that such same-sex loving relationships were not in the mind of the biblical authors at all.

But if, in the end, some of these texts do uncompromisingly condemn any and every same-sex orientation and same-sex intimate relationship, it still remains to be demonstrated that this, by itself, is strong enough to stand against the case developed on the grounds of contemporary science, experience and a broad trinitarian theology. After all, as I have mentioned, there are any number of particular issues which can find textual support here and there in Scripture—slavery, usury, divorce, ethnocentrism, subordination of women, exclusion of handicapped people from the temple of God, and, not least, the summary execution of homosexuals—concerning which, in the course of long experience with the biblical witness as a whole, and the leading of the Spirit in new circumstances, the Church now acts and thinks contrary to the letter of the text, because it believes itself to be holding true to the Spirit of the Gospel.

Let us proceed with caution, to be sure. But let us also not close our hearts to compassion, understanding, and the possibility of a new creation in the Spirit of God.

Endnotes

[1] Joo-Inn Chew, in *Inside Out*, ed. Erin Shale (Bookman Press, Melbourne, 1999), 51-52.

[2] Report on Lambeth Conference, www.mcjonline.com/news/news2575.htm, p 1.

[3] Karl Barth, *Protestant Theology in the Nineteenth Century: Its Background and History* (SCM, London, 1972), 460.

[4] Cf Victor C. Pfitzner, 'The Spirit of the Lord: The Christological Focus of Pauline Pneumatology,' *St Mark's Review*, Winter (1999), 11-12.

[5] *Ibid.*, p 3.

[6] Cf Geoff Scott, 'When Relationality Takes Centre Stage: Sexuality, Homosexuality and Self-Transcendence,' in *Occasional Papers No 1*, Uniting Church of Australia, 1996, 7. It is worth noting that Barth in his old age expressed serious doubts about his negative attitude to homosexuality as expressed in C.D. III/4, 166, on the grounds of new developments in medical and psychological investigation of the phenomenon. See *Karl Barth: Offene Briefe 1945-1968*, ed. Diether Koch (Theologischer Verlag, Zürich, 1984), 543.

CHAPTER TWELVE

Conclusion

The voice of the psalmist often reflects the truth to us in a flash of light: quick and precise, unmistakably expressing what we know in our hearts but cannot frame ourselves.

> For you created my inmost parts;
> you knit me together in my mother's womb.
>
> I will thank you because I am marvelously made;
> Your works are wonderful and I know it well. Ps.139:12-13

If there is any reason for the Church to inquire about homosexuality, it is this: that as creatures of God's own hand, we are marvelously made. But we are as easily perplexed by the workings of God's creation as we are moved to awe by them. In the realm of human sexuality, this perplexity is an intimate one, as each of us knows something of the realm of sexual desire: its thrill and anxiety, that it smolders but also explodes, it delights and confounds, it brings pleasure and pain, it expresses joy and shame. Once in the life of the Church, it seemed sex was simple; it is no more.

The original brief for this Panel, from General Synod Resolution 70/98, called on us to 'prepare a statement on human sexuality with particular reference to discipline in this Church'. It is interesting to note that, in the climate of the past few years, the phrase 'human sexuality' has become a euphemism for homosexuality. In the context of the General Synod Resolution, this is manifestly clear since it stems from the synod's discussion of the Kuala Lumpur Statement, which was primarily concerned with homosexuality. It might be pointed out that there are many other aspects of human sexuality on which the Church could comment and which affect a larger segment of society, such as pre-marital and extra-marital sex. The Doctrine

Panel acknowledges that these and other important dimensions should be included in a responsible discussion of human sexuality. We believe, however, that we are rightly responding to the concerns of General Synod by confining our inquiry to one aspect of human sexuality.

Over the course of two years, the members of the Doctrine Panel have tried to look carefully at the discussion about homosexuality in the Church and the world. There can be no question that secular attitudes toward sexuality in general, and particularly homosexuality, are rapidly changing — so much so that many of us can recognise hardly any congruence between the sexual mores of our younger days and those of today.

As people of Christian faith, who acknowledge ourselves as marvellously made, we have a responsibility to use our bodies in godly ways and to engage in relationships that reflect the substance of the covenant of love and mutual respect into which we enter at our baptism. At the heart of the current discussion are the questions of whether and how a homosexual person can fulfil this responsibility.

We have considered the biblical material, we have looked at the history of the Church's attitudes, we have queried the moral tradition, we have reflected theologically, we have consulted the scientific data, we have spoken with people of various backgrounds and convictions and, through it all, we have prayed that God might guide us by the Holy Spirit to discern more clearly the mind of Christ.

As a panel, we represent different experiences and viewpoints; this is as it should be in a Church that also represents a diversity of experience and perspective. We have certainly found areas in which we differ – sometimes strongly. But there are also points of agreement on which to build, and in drawing conclusions from the work we have done. It is perhaps best to begin with these points of agreement.

We are compelled to speak with one voice on the following points:

- We believe that all people, made in God's own image, are image-bearers of God and therefore deserving of respect and dignity. On this basis alone – if no other – the arms of the Church must be open to welcome all who seek to know God in communion with those who have been called together in the name of Jesus Christ.

- We are convinced that the issues of human sexuality in general and homosexuality in particular are important ones for the Church to engage and that the extraordinary complexity of the topics demands that they are approached with seriousness of purpose, discerning minds, and pastoral sensitivity.
- We affirm the witness and authority of Scripture, which must be acknowledged. It is clear, however, that while specific texts do settle the questions for some, they do not settle the questions for the whole Church, since opinions on the clarity of Scripture vary. Texts must be considered in light of the whole message of the Gospel and, like all texts, need to be interpreted. The Church may need to acknowledge and wrestle with an increasing diversity of viewpoints.
- We recognise that our own cultural contexts and personal experiences condition the way we approach the complex web of questions around homosexuality and therefore qualify our ability to come to a common resolution as to the mind of God.
- We affirm unequivocally that promiscuity is contrary to the Christian ideal of committed, monogamous relationships that reflect the faithfulness of God.
- The irrational fear of homosexuality and homosexual persons and the persecution which has so often stemmed from that fear are not faithful expressions of Christian witness and are, in fact, an affront to the example of love which Christ set for us.
- The scientific, medical and psychiatric communities have much to contribute to the discussion but by no means do they provide widely accepted answers to very difficult questions.
- We believe that the Church will benefit from further exploration, discussion, listening and careful study undertaken in a prayerful, compassionate and generous spirit in order to discern more clearly God's will for God's people.

The contemporary question of discipline for this Church has two immediately clear elements to it: the blessing of same-sex unions and the ordination of gay and lesbian people. Each of these topics deserves some comment.

With regard to the blessing of same-sex unions, support for a range of possibilities is represented on the Panel. There are those of us who believe the Church should develop rites for such blessings and authorise them; others would tolerate such unions being blessed in the Church, but would not be willing to preside at such celebrations; still others feel strongly that such rites are and should remain prohibited in the Church.

We believe the diversity of opinion on this issue amongst members of the Panel very likely reflects the diversity of opinion in the Church at large. The matter is further complicated by a lack of understanding of what exactly we believe the Church would be doing in such a rite. The institution of Christian marriage is not what it once was. More and more in Australia, people choose not to be married in Church. Divorce rates continue to climb. And the relationship between marriage and sex is not so clear and dependent as it was a generation or so ago. What would the Church be doing by introducing the blessing of same-sex unions to this context? Furthermore, we do not note in the life of the Anglican Church of Australia a groundswell of demand for such rites, such as may exist in other parts of the Anglican Communion.

On the other hand, some see this as an opportunity for the Church to lead rather than follow. Might the current debate be an opportunity to provide a context for committed, exclusive relationships for same-sex couples where until now no such context has been available? In this way, some would say, the Church could appropriate the traditional ideals of loving, committed, monogamous Christian relationships, now confined to marriage, in response to a pressing contemporary issue. Or, as a means of helping people avoid a life of promiscuity, it might at least be considered the lesser of two evils.

In the absence of any kind of consensus in the Church, however, we do not feel it is appropriate to make a recommendation for the life of the Church at this time. What is clear is that the question of blessing same-sex unions will be a part of the continuing discussion about the Church and homosexuality.

The matter of the ordination of gay and lesbian people is rather different. Most dioceses will have confronted the question of the appropriateness of such ordinations if not explicitly, then tacitly. The Church has — both wittingly and unwittingly — ordained gay and lesbian people to Holy Orders. Sexual orientation has not historically been cited as a barrier to ordination. The need for such a barrier has not been recognised, since the Church's understanding and teaching has been that sexual relationships are appropriate only within the bonds of Holy Matrimony. Character of life has traditionally been the relevant criterion for fitness to ordination and continuing in ministry. The Church has expected ordinands to conduct themselves in a chaste and godly manner and this expectation has included an appropriate management of sexual activity and expression, in accordance with the Church's traditional teaching.

The question that faces the Church now is whether or not a gay or lesbian person who is engaged in a committed and exclusive relationship with a person of the same sex displays the appropriate character of life for entry into Holy Orders. At its heart, this question is about sin. Is same-sex sexual activity, by its nature, sinful? If so, no matter what the parameters of the relationship, any same-sex relationship that includes sexual activity defines the partners as something like notorious and unrepentant sinners, and identifies them as unfit for ordination.

As a Panel, we have not reached one mind on this matter. We are agreed that resolute faithfulness in human relationships reflects something of the character of God. Our convictions stemming from the implications of that observation vary widely. Some believe that same-sex relationships can provide the context for faithful witnesses of Christian life. Others believe that such relationships can only ever be sullied by the sinfulness of sexual activity between persons of the same sex. And some of us are simply uncertain.

It will be obvious by now that the single greatest point of divergence of opinion in addressing these questions is the use and interpretation of Scripture. None of us wishes to undermine the authority of Scripture for the Church or for individual Christians. All of us believe that the Scriptures have a crucial role to play in the way we make our moral and ethical decisions. It is plain to us that the fundamentally different ways in which we approach the texts, and the way we assign degrees of importance to particular passages are what generally control the different conclusions we reach. We have not yet discovered a way to draw our different approaches together in a unified understanding. At times we have had to agree to disagree. And we have been forced to wonder how much diversity the Church can tolerate in this regard.

We have been encouraged, however, that a group as varied as we are has been able to engage this discussion in an atmosphere of seriousness and mutual respect. We cannot provide final answers to these complex questions for the Church. But we know from our experience that productive and enlightening discussion is both possible and rewarding.

In recent years, many of us have been familiar with work on the theology of the human person. This enterprise has focused on how God's creative power and divine will are expressed in the marvel and mystery of the human being. The insights of this reflection have shown us that there is an intrinsic value in being and that, in some sense, it is our vocation simply to be that which God created us to be. Regardless of the conclusions we have drawn from the body of work collected here, we are of the strong conviction that all Christians do in fact share this vocation to be.

Literature abounds that recounts the struggle of gay and lesbian people – adolescents and adults alike – to acknowledge and accept who and what it is that God has made them to be. We do not believe that God calls us to lives of shame, self-hatred and deceit: qualities that have so often characterised the response of homosexual people to this struggle. We believe that we are called to a life of love made possible by the grace of Jesus Christ, who calls every Christian to turn from sin to be reconciled with God and with one another. This reconciling love of Christ is the essence of Christian hope and the promise of it is available to every human being.

Whatever word the Church speaks on this issue must finally be a word of hope and promise.

We believe that as a Church we can only reach that stage after a great deal more study, discussion and prayer that includes a broad segment of the Church and of society. We realise that it has become a cliché throughout the Anglican Communion to defer decisions and definitive statements on homosexuality in favour of study and dialogue. But we believe this pattern has emerged with good cause. Differences on the nature of biblical interpretation go to the very heart of our faith. Questions about the nature of human relationships are unavoidable in a Church that believes in the incarnate God. Because we take seriously the communion we share as people of faith called together in the name of Jesus Christ, we do not take lightly any issue that threatens to unsettle our fellowship.

We believe the Church must commit to further study of the many, varied and complex issues raised in this publication. And we hope that by making our work broadly available, we can widen the discussion to include Anglicans and non-Anglicans all over the country.

Above all, we call for the thoughtful prayers of the whole Church. In doing so, we call on the Church and on all Christians to strive to live into the vocation of being: honestly to plumb the depths of our hearts and minds and souls to discern God's true will for us as individuals and as a community called together in Christ's name. We believe that such inquiry leads us along the path of faithfulness, wherein God's desire for us is to be found.

And we join with the psalmist in thanking God, because we are marvellously and mysteriously made.

BIOGRAPHIES

The Doctrine Panel

The Most Reverend Dr Peter F Carnley AO, Chairman, has been Archbishop of Perth since 1981. Prior to his consecration he served as Warden of St John's College at the University of Queensland. He is an honorary fellow of St John's College, Cambridge University, where he was awarded his PhD in 1969. In 2000 he was elected Primate of the Anglican Church of Australia.

The Reverend Dr Scott Cowdell is the Principal of St Barnabas' Theological College, Adelaide, and Senior Lecturer in Theology at Flinders University. He also currently serves as president of the Adelaide College of Divinity, and as a member of the Strategic Issues Advisory Panel of General Synod. He has taught at Trinity College Theological School, Melbourne, and at both university and theological college in Brisbane during nine years of parish ministry there. He earned his PhD at the University of Queensland in 1994.

The Reverend Dr Glenn Davies is the Rector of St Luke's, Miranda, in the Diocese of Sydney. He was Lecturer in Biblical Studies at Moore Theological College from 1983 to 1995. He earned his PhD at the University of Sheffield in 1988. He serves as a member of General Synod, and was recently appointed Canon Theologian of the Diocese of Ballarat.

The Reverend Dr John Dunnill is Director of Biblical and Theological Studies at the Anglican Institute of Theology and Religious Education in Perth and Lecturer in New Testament at Murdoch University, where he has also been chair of the Theology Programme. He was awarded his PhD by the University of Birmingham in 1988. He is a canon of St George's Cathedral in Perth, and a member of General Synod.

The Reverend Dr Don Edwards is Coordinator of Theological Education at St Francis' College, Brisbane. He teaches theology and spirituality in the Brisbane College of Theology and is a visiting fellow of Griffith University. He is a member of the International Commission for Anglican/Orthodox Theological Dialogue. In 1984 he was awarded a PhD from the University of Queensland. He is Canon Theologian of St John's Cathedral, Brisbane.

The Reverend Dr Graeme Garrett is a Senior Lecturer at St Mark's National Theological Centre in Canberra. He was awarded his ThD from the Graduate Theological Union at Berkeley, California in 1971. He is Canon Theologian of the Diocese of Canberra/Goulburn.

The Reverend Dr Peter Jensen is Principal of Moore Theological College in Sydney. In addition to many years of teaching at Moore College, he has taught at the University of Sydney. He was awarded his DPhil from Oxford University in 1980. He is a canon of St Andrew's Cathedral, Sydney.

Dr Muriel Porter has been a Senior Lecturer in Journalism at the RMIT University, Melbourne since 1995. She holds a PhD in Church History from the University of Melbourne. She is the author of several books, including Sex, Marriage and the Church: Patterns of Change. She writes regularly for The Melbourne Age and The Church Times. She is a member of the General Synod.

The Reverend Cathy Thomson provides parish ministry to the parishes of Mallala and Two Wells in the Diocese of Adelaide and serves as Chaplain to Trinity College. She is a candidate for a PhD at Flinders University. She is a member of General Synod. Prior to her current ministries, she held appointments in several parishes and chaplaincies.

Contributor

The Reverend Sean Mullen is Chaplain to the Archbishop of Perth. He received his theological training at The General Theological Seminary in New York City. He served in parish ministry in the United States before coming to Australia. Since 1998 he has served as secretary to the Doctrine Panel.

APPENDIX ONE

The Kuala Lumpur Statement on Human Sexuality

1. God's glory and loving purposes have been revealed in the creation of humankind. (Rom 1:18; Gen1:26, 27). Among the multiplicity of his gifts we are blessed with our sexuality.

2. Since the Fall (Gen. 3), life has been impaired and God's purposes spoilt. Our fallen state has affected every sphere of our being, which includes our sexuality. Sexual deviation has existed in every time and in most cultures. Jesus' teaching about lust in the Sermon on the Mount (Matt 5:27-30) makes it clear that sexual sin is a real danger and temptation to us all.

3. It is, therefore, with an awareness of our own vulnerability to sexual sin that we express our profound concern about recent developments relating to Church discipline and moral teaching in some provinces in the North — specifically, the ordination of practicing homosexuals and the blessing of same-sex unions.

4. While acknowledging the complexities of our sexual nature and the strong drives it places within us, we are quite clear about God's will in this area which is expressed in the Bible.

5. The Scripture bears witness to God's will regarding human sexuality which is to be expressed only within the life long union of a man and a woman in (holy) matrimony.

6. The Holy Scriptures are clear in teaching that all sexual promiscuity is sin. We are convinced that this includes homosexual practices between men or women, as well as heterosexual relationships outside marriage.

7. We believe that the clear and unambiguous teaching of the Holy Scriptures about human sexuality is of great help to Christians as it provides clear boundaries.

8. We find no conflict between clear biblical teaching and sensitive pastoral care. Repentance precedes forgiveness and is part of the

healing process. To heal spiritual wounds in God's name we need his wisdom and truth. We see this in the ministry of Jesus, for example his response to the adulterous woman, "...neither do I condemn you. Go and sin no more." (John 8:11)

9. We encourage the Church to care for all those who are trapped in their sexual brokenness and to become the channel of Christ's compassion and love towards them. We wish to stand alongside and welcome them into a process of being whole and restored within our communities of faith. We would also affirm and resource those who exercise a pastoral ministry in this area.

10. We are deeply concerned that the setting aside of biblical teaching in such actions as the ordination of practicing homosexuals and the blessing of same-sex unions calls into question the authority of the Holy Scriptures. This is totally unacceptable to us.

11. This leads us to express concern about mutual accountability and interdependence within our Anglican Communion. As provinces and dioceses, we need to learn how to seek each other's counsel and wisdom in a spirit of true unity, and to reach a common mind before embarking on radical changes to Church discipline and moral teaching.

12. We live in a global village and must be more aware that the way we act in one part of the world can radically affect the mission and witness of the Church in another.

APPENDIX TWO

General Synod Resolution 70/98

That this General Synod

(a) notes the Kuala Lumpur Statement issued by Anglican delegates from Provinces in the Developing World who met at the Second Anglican Encounter held in Kuala Lumpur, Malaysia in 1997, and

(b) takes seriously the concerns of Anglicans from developing nations in affirming a faithful assertion of Biblical and the long held traditional Anglican teaching on human sexuality, and

(c) calls on the members of this Synod who will attend Lambeth 1998 to study and respond sympathetically to the Kuala Lumpur statement.

(d) requests the standing Committee to appoint a task force to prepare an Australian Anglican statement on human sexuality, with particular reference to discipline in this Church, for consideration by the next General Synod.

APPENDIX THREE

Lambeth Conference 1998 Resolution 1.10 - Human Sexuality

This Conference:
(a) commends to the Church the subsection report on human sexuality;
(b) in view of the teaching of Scripture, upholds faithfulness in marriage between a man and a woman in lifelong union, and believes that abstinence is right for those who are not called to marriage;
(c) recognises that there are among us persons who experience themselves as having a homosexual orientation. Many of these are members of the Church and are seeking the pastoral care, moral direction of the Church, and God's transforming power for the living of their lives and the ordering of relationships. We commit ourselves to listen to the experience of homosexual persons and we wish to assure them that they are loved by God and that all baptised, believing and faithful persons, regardless of sexual orientation, are full members of the Body of Christ;
(d) while rejecting homosexual practice as incompatible with Scripture, calls on all our people to minister pastorally and sensitively to all irrespective of sexual orientation and to condemn irrational fear of homosexuals, violence within marriage and any trivialisation and commercialisation of sex;
(e) cannot advise the legitimising or blessing of same sex unions nor ordaining those involved in same gender unions;
(f) requests the Primates and the ACC to establish a means of monitoring the work done on the subject of human sexuality in the Communion and to share statements and resources among us;
(g) notes the significance of the Kuala Lumpur Statement on Human Sexuality and the concerns expressed in resolutions IV.26, V.1, V.10, V.23 and V.35 on the authority of Scripture in matters of marriage and sexuality and asks the Primates and the ACC to include them in their monitoring process.